LONGMAN LINGUISTICS LIBRARY
Title no 14
PHILOSOPHY AND THE NATURE OF LANGUAGE

LONGMAN LINGUISTICS LIBRARY

Title no:

Philosophy
and the
Nature of Language

David E. Cooper
Lecturer in Philosophy
University of London Institute of Education

LONGMAN

B
808.5
C57
1973

LONGMAN GROUP LIMITED LONDON
Associated companies, branches and representatives throughout the world

© Longman Group Ltd 1973

First published 1973
Cased ISBN 0 582 55051 3
Paper ISBN 0 582 55052 1

Printed in Great Britain by
Lowe & Brydone (Printers) Ltd., Thetford, Norfolk

To my parents

Preface

I should like to thank Professors Gilbert Ryle and Howard Pospesel, and Miss Deirdre Wilson for commenting upon material which is included in this book. I should also like to thank countless students who, by saying what I told them could not be said, and by refusing to say what I told them could be said, have saved me from peppering this book with more of the erroneous intuitions about language, to which philosophers are prone, than it actually contains.

University of London Institute of Education   DEC
March 1973

Contents

Acknowledgments

We are indebted to the following for permission to reproduce copyright material:

The Clarendon Press, Oxford, for extracts from 'Other Minds' from *Philosophical Papers*, 2nd edn, 1970, *pp* 87, 98 & 99–100 by J. L. Austin; The M.I.T. Press for extracts from *Language, Thought and Reality* by B. L. Whorf, and Prentice-Hall, Inc, for extracts from *Philosophy of Language* by William P. Alston, ©1964, reprinted by permission of Prentice-Hall, Inc, Englewood Cliffs, New Jersey.

Chapter 1

Introduction

To become interested in questions about language, one has to stop taking it for granted. Virtually all of us are pretty fluent employers of language; we grow up with it as we grow up with the ability to walk or run; we do not have to ponder over it to use it. Language can seem too easy, as it were, to require deep explanation – no deeper, anyway, than that of walking or running. To see how truly remarkable language is, we must, as Wolfgang Köhler put it, retreat to a 'psychic distance' from the subject. If some astronauts were to find a community of Martians who could, apparently, communicate without a whisper, and without the flicker of an eyelid, through no physical medium, this would be strange enough to require explanation. Our ability to communicate by making certain noises from our throats, or by making little scratches on paper, must appear equally startling to less sophisticated beings who could communicate only by pushing, pulling, clubbing, or kissing.

Language, it would seem, is the most complex and sophisticated of our possessions. Only very recently, for instance, have grammarians begun to uncover the enormously complicated rules of grammar which underly our languages. Computers can be marvellous mathematicians, and amazing chess-players. Yet no computer in the offing is at all close to the reproduction of human verbal abilities. Computers are, at best, second-rate users of language; *animals* are not users of language at all, except in the most strained sense of the term. It may be that we should take the advice of Saul Bellow's hero, Herzog, and put a moratorium upon definitions of human nature. If we ignore this advice, though, as good a definition as any of man might be *homo loquens*, man-the-talker. No doubt men are the only creatures who laugh, and have two legs and no feathers – but that is not too interesting. Man may be the only creature who uses tools (*homo faber*), and the only creature who organizes politically (*zoon politikon*) – and this is more interesting. Still, amongst many peoples the

use of tools, and political organization, are extremely rudimentary, whereas all known communities have possessed sophisticated languages.
Further, it is probably easier to find analogues in the animal world to tools
and politics than it is to language. Many animals, of course, are capable
of producing noises which cause their friends or enemies to respond in
certain ways, but these noises are so different in kind from human speech
that it is, at best, a misleading analogy to speak of such noises being part
of a language. First, animals are incapable of organizing their noises into
sequences, beyond the most primitive level; whereas the most salient
characteristic of human talkers is their ability to form an infinite number
of sequences from a limited stock of noises. As Herbert Read once remarked, 'no difference between man and beast is more important than
syntax'. Second, animals produce their noises in direct response to
stimuli in their environment, as when the bird squawks at the approach of
the cat. Such noises are analogous to human cries of pain or alarm, not to
the sentences we produce. Nothing in my environment 'stimulated' me
to write down the sentence I just wrote down. Our production of speech
is independent of stimulus-control in a way in which animal noises are
not.[1] In the light of this it is easier to understand those followers of René
Descartes who found it impossible to suppose that animals could be
capable of any mental activity. 'If beasts reasoned,' said one of them,
'they would be capable of true speech with its infinite variety.' We might
not want to go as far as that, but at least we must admit that speech is
one, if not *the*, salient feature of human nature which distinguishes it
from any other sort of nature.

Not only is language our most sophisticated possession, and our most
important unique possession, it is also, remarkably enough, an almost
universal human possession. As already mentioned, all known human
societies have possessed a language, whatever else each of them may have
lacked. Not only that, but whereas there are mathematical geniuses and
chess-playing geniuses, when it comes to language most men, if not equal,
are at least in the same league. Of course, some men – poets, orators,
impersonators, and polyglots – have special skills in the field of language.
But nearly all of us are capable of producing, and understanding, an infinite number of sentences. If we had the same trouble with language
that most of us have with algebra, the world would be in a sorry state
indeed. No doubt, in our attempts at school to learn new languages we en-
counter as many difficulties as we do in algebra, but our absorption as
young children of our native language is not something that some find
radically easier than others, with a few exceptions. The differences in
linguistic competence pale in comparison with the similarities.

Not only is language remarkable in its complexity, species-specificity,
and ubiquity, it is also remarkable in its versatility. By uttering the
appropriate noises, in the right circumstances, a single man in a single

day can easily do each of the following: inform others of what is happening, beseech them to do something, command them, excite them, promise them, insult them, soliloquize, let off steam, and get married. As some of these examples show, we do not in general utter noises as an activity separate from other activities; rather, talking is usually part and parcel of some wider activity. We do not talk as we knit: as some more-or-less self-contained performance isolated from others. Rather we perform actions with words, actions which it would be difficult, inconvenient, or even impossible to perform without words. The number of such possible actions is indefinitely large.

I have made these points to show, if it needs to be shown, that language is an extraordinary institution. It stands in as much need of explanation as any other aspect of human life, possibly more.

This book deals with two different disciplines which, whilst closely related, need to be distinguished. On the one hand is the philosophy of language: on the other is linguistic philosophy. The philosophy of language is a branch of philosophy in which philosophers attempt to analyse, elucidate, and investigate certain crucial linguistic concepts; for example, meaning, reference, and truth. It may be regarded as part of the philosophy of science; the attempt to analyse concepts employed by scientists. Just as the philosopher of science is concerned to analyse concepts such as that of the electron, or the gene, which are employed by physicists or biologists, so the philosopher of language is concerned to analyse concepts employed by professional linguists.

It is not, in fact, easy to distinguish sharply between the interests of a scientist and a philosopher of science. Both in their ways study genes, electrons, causes, motives, laws, meanings, or substances. At least this can be said: any scientist employs certain crucial terms which play a large part in his thinking, and in the formulation of his hypotheses. Often he is unable to give a clear, precise account of these terms. Usually and fortunately, this does not impede his scientific work. A chemist may be unable to define 'cause' accurately, and not interested in doing so; but that does not prevent him from telling us what causes what in the laboratory. A psychologist may be hard put to provide a clear account of what a drive is; but that does not prevent him from telling us interesting things about the effects of hunger and thirst upon animal behaviour. The philosopher of science, though, is distinguished precisely by his attempts to clarify these concepts as employed by scientists, as well as by his examination of the methodology employed by them. Partly he is interested in doing this for its own sake. It really would be intellectually satisfying to know exactly what is involved in the concept of an electron, or of causality. However, there may be a more practical interest, too. I mentioned that inability to define concepts accurately does not usually impede scientific work. Sometimes, though, it does. For example, there is a great deal of disagreement amongst psychologists of motivation as to the value of various experiments, which is due to differing conceptions of what a motive is.[2] Certainly it is hard to devise informative tests measuring motivation unless we know what we are supposed to be measuring.

The need for clarifying concepts is especially acute during the infancy of a science when, as it were, the concepts have not yet matured to clear, adult identity. For this reason, one finds that natural scientists get into less semantic, conceptual fracas than social scientists. Now linguistics is in its infancy. For centuries, of course, men like Jacob Grimm had been doing scholarly work in etymology, and the comparison and classification of languages. But the systematic attempt to examine the structure of language is a recent endeavour. Sometimes it is only dated during the early years of this century, with the works of the French pioneer, Ferdinand de Saussure. At any rate, it is particularly clear that linguists, like sociologists, are often plagued by having to employ concepts of which they find it hard to give clear, adequate, theoretical accounts. As we shall see, concepts like those of meaning, reference, truth, speech act, subject, predicate, and even concept itself, are in great need of clarification. Again, this is not to say that linguists cannot do their job without help from philosophers of language, or from their more conceptually-minded colleagues. The linguist can still compare the meanings of French and English words; or work out what the rules of grammar and phonetics are. But it is possible that he could do his work better with such help. At the very least it would enable him to formulate his hypotheses more clearly, to distinguish between conceptual problems on the one hand and substantive, empirical problems on the other, and to feel pleasantly satisfied that the foundations of his science can be given logical clearance.

There is another way we might try to distinguish the philosopher of language's interest from the linguist's. While many philosophers now study language for its own sake, this interest was originally motivated by other considerations. Basically, philosophers became interested in language for what they could get out of it for philosophy. Consequently, philosophers of language tend to ask questions about language, the answers to which are likely to help them, or other philosophers, tackle the traditional questions of ethics, epistemology, metaphysics, or whatever. For example, there are numerous questions that can be asked about the uses of words, but many of these will not be of interest in relation to the questions philosophers have been asking throughout the centuries. It may be interesting to know that the most commonly used words in English are five-letter ones, but this could have no bearing upon any philosophical problem. On the other hand, the discovery that certain words are essentially used to commend or to grade will certainly interest the moral philosopher concerned with understanding the nature of our moral concepts.

At this point, I must say something about the other discipline this book will concern itself with – linguistic philosophy. Philosophers have always been dimly aware, and their practice shows it, that philosophical investigation must give a special place to linguistic phenomena. When philosophers in the past have claimed to be laying bare the nature of X-ness or Y-ness, we can often describe what they were doing as analysing the meanings of the words 'X' and 'Y'. Hume and Kant said they were investigating the nature of our *ideas* or *experience*. So they were, in a way; but we can often describe this way as the attempt to understand certain words.

In this century, beginning with the work of Bertrand Russell and G. E. Moore, this dim awareness of the importance of language has been replaced by very bright awareness – too bright, according to continental critics of Anglo-Saxon philosophy. While this self-conscious awareness took a long time to come – more than 2,000 years, apart from the occasional anachronistic insight – it was largely inevitable. After all, once it is insisted, as it has been for a long time, that philosophers, unlike scientists, are not concerned to establish empirical facts about the world, it is difficult to see what philosophers can be doing except analysing concepts. And it is difficult to see how we can analyse concepts without analysing the language in which concepts are expressed. We might, then, give the title 'linguistic philosopher' to anyone, in whatever field of the subject, who insists that philosophical problems can only be solved, or even properly formulated, after due concern with aspects of language. Of course there are many styles of linguistic philosophy – thus the plethora of names such as logical atomism, logical positivism, ordinary language philosophy, formal analysis, informal analysis, linguistic phenomenology, etc.[3] All such 'schools', however, share a common concern with language, whether it be a natural language like English, or an artificial language like Russell's logical calculi. Further, they are largely distinguished from one another, not by doctrinal differences in their conclusions, but by their different views of language, and the relevance of language to philosophy.

One of the most influential philosophers of the century, Ludwig Wittgenstein, said that 'philosophy is a battle against the bewitchment of our intelligence by means of language'.[4] According to him, the job of the contemporary philosopher is to show how past thinkers have gone astray as a result of having failed to understand a bit of language – whether it be the meaning of some important word like 'know', or some more pervasive feature of language, such as the way in which terms serve to refer. This, he said, can only be achieved by the minute analyses of how words are employed in ordinary language. Other philosophers, whilst doubting the value of minute analyses of ordinary language, have still insisted upon the linguistic nature of philosophy. One of these, Rudolf Carnap, described his philosophy as 'construction theory'. Here is what he says about it:

> It is the main thesis of construction theory that all concepts can . . . be derived from a few fundamental concepts. . . . An object (or concept) is said to be reducible to one or more other objects if all statements made about it can be transformed into statements about these other objects.[5]

He tries to show, for instance, that statements about material objects can be transformed into statements about mental sense-impressions, so giving a linguistic form to the traditional claim that material objects are just 'collections of ideas'. At any rate, whatever the brand of linguistic philosophy, one finds time and time again in the contemporary literature the reformulation of traditional questions in a linguistic vein. Instead of 'What exists?' we ask 'What are the referring expressions in a language?' Instead of 'What is truth?' we ask 'What is being done when we use the words ". . . is true"?'

For some years, linguistic philosophy got along without any systematic attempts to explicate some of the concepts, like meaning and reference, to which appeal was constantly being made, in an optimistically intuitive manner, in the course of various philosophical investigations. It was quickly realized, however, that for these analyses to be adequate, philosophers could not play fast and loose with these crucial concepts. And so we get back to the philosophy of language. Philosophers had to get clear about various linguistic concepts if they were to employ them in their discussion of other problems. When philosophers did try to understand these concepts, this began to strongly influence their approach to problems in philosophy. To take one example, which will be discussed fully in Chapter 3, according to some philosophers, a sentence only has meaning if it is empirically verifiable. Obviously this doctrine about meaning was going to have vast implications throughout philosophy. For if unverifiable sentences were nonsense, then much past philosophical speculation about unobservable substances, or transcendent deities, becomes nonsense. Philosophers who wanted to rebut this somewhat suicidal view of the subject could do so only by taking a close look at meaning.

I regard it as one of the major tasks of this book to show, in each chapter, how some view about an aspect of language has influenced, or even determined, approaches or answers to traditional philosophical problems - whether they be about knowledge, innate ideas, reality, perception, good and bad, time, space, or whatever. I want to show how the claims of men, *qua* philosophers of language, have affected the claims of the same, or other men, *qua* linguistic philosophers in ethics, metaphysics, epistemology, or some other branch of philosophy. The influence that views about language have had upon philosophy is matched, to some extent, by the influence commitment to certain philosophical positions has had upon views about language. For example, behaviourist philosophers who attempt to analyse mental phenomena in terms of overt behaviour seem to be committed to a behaviourist account of meaning. They must explain, that is, what it is to understand meanings in terms, say, of behavioural responses to utterances of words. Again, I shall try to show, in various chapters, how such prior philosophical commitments have influenced, or determined, doctrines about language.

So, then, there is the philosophy of language, and there is linguistic philosophy – and these are intimately related through mutual interactions of the sorts mentioned.

What questions do philosophers of language ask? Most of them can, at a pinch, be subsumed under the umbrella question: How is it that a certain group of noises and scratches can be employed to do the fantastically complicated job we call 'communication', and so deserve the title of 'language'?

[1] The first, and most immediate, question that arises under this heading is the question 'What is meaning?' For what most obviously distinguishes those noises and scratches which belong to language from the innumerable ones that do not is that the former have meaning. How is this? What gives this special type of life to a noise or scratch? These questions will be tackled at various points in the book – especially throughout Chapter 2, and in the very last section of the book. Meaning is probably the linguistic concept that philosophers have discussed most, mainly because of the implications that theories of meaning will have upon philosophy at large. Some of these views about meaning, and their influence upon philosophy, will be treated in Chapter 3.

[2] A second question concerns reference and predication. One of the most central purposes to which we can put our noises and scratches is to refer to things, and to describe what we have referred to. What, quite, is it to refer and to predicate? In Chapter 4, we shall see that the answer is by no means easy, and that the most paradoxical answers can gain a certain plausibility.

[3] A further set of questions concerns the relation between language on the one hand, and our mental and social life on the other. Clearly the relation is close; we normally, and perhaps always, think with words. Some thinkers, for example Benjamin Lee Whorf, have insisted that language almost wholly determines our thinking, and is an extremely influential factor in the formation of our social life. I shall try to assess, and make sense of, such claims in Chapter 5.

[4] Another question arises in the following way: for words to play the roles they do, we must have acquired the ability to organize them into

grammatical sequences in accordance with certain rules and principles. Now what must the human mind be like for us to have acquired the ability to operate with such rules and principles? The most influential of contemporary linguists, Noam Chomsky, has argued that we must ascribe to young children a rich, unlearned, innate knowledge in order to account for their linguistic competence. This apparently startling argument will be examined in Chapter 6.

[5] A fifth question concerns truth. One of the most essential aspects of language is that certain bits of it can be true or false. Obviously the communication of truths is one of its greatest uses. What is it for a sentence to be true? How must such a sentence relate to the world? Further, there are some truths, so-called 'analytic' ones, which, it seems to some, guarantee their own truth, in virtue of the very words composing them. How is this so? And how does it relate to the traditional philosophical quest for the nature of necessary or *a priori* truth? These questions will be tackled in Chapter 7.

[6] A final question is this: is it possible to lend any order and system into the multiplicity of functions that language can perform? It may turn out that the study of so-called 'speech acts', and the attempt to classify their types along the lines suggested by the Oxford philosopher J. L. Austin, will be of immense philosophical value. Further, we might be able to tackle the problem of meaning in the light of speech act theory. These questions are discussed in Chapter 8.

I do not say that these are all the questions in which philosophers of language take an interest, but I feel that they are the major ones. I shall, to repeat, be stressing in each chapter the ways in which answers to the above questions have influenced, or determined, the answers which philosophers have given to any number of other questions in whatever area of philosophy. I would hope, then, that we may end with a better understanding of language; and, in the light of that, a better understanding of how to approach a variety of philosophical problems.

A final note: while I am not interested in the pretty fruitless task of giving a formal definition of 'language', I should say a few words about the scope of my use of the term. One of Shakespeare's lines runs 'there's a language in her eye, her cheeks, her lip'. And Lawrence Durrell rather charmingly describes love as being a 'skin-language'. No doubt we can speak of silent, gestural, or bodily languages, as well as of spoken or written ones. But I shall only be dealing with the latter. After all this is the central sense of 'language', and other symbolic systems are described as languages only by analogy with it. Many of the points I shall make, though, could be carried over to these other types of language. So I am not using 'language' as widely as it can be used. However, I am not using it as narrowly as many linguists do. For various purposes, it is useful in several areas of linguistics to treat language as a self-contained set of structures and rules in isolation from context and environment. For example, it is convenient in trying to establish what is grammatically acceptable to ignore cases where a sentence is found unintelligible because of the context in which it is used. The unintelligibility of 'Thank you very much', said by a man to his shoes, is not a matter of grammar. We, however, will often be concerned with language as used in context and in ways of life. Language, for our purposes, is a social activity, not an isolated system of symbols. The reason we look at language in this way is that looking at it in this way is likely to pay off some big philosophical dividends. One writer, summarizing Wittgenstein's views on the matter, says:

> Philosophical perplexity arises when philosophers treat words as if they had no essential relationship to any modes of activity, to any kinds of situation in which they are normally used – when they treat them, in short, abstractly.[6]

So, as philosophers rather than linguists, we shall be interested in the modes of activity to which words are related.

Notes

1 There is controversy over the possibility of animal languages. I am told there is a remarkable chimpanzee, named Washo, with a 'vocabulary' of over one hundred 'signs', some of which it is able to organize into rudimentary sequences. So perhaps linguists will have to revise their pessimism over animal linguistic ability. Still, if humans were just the naked apes of popular vogue at present, one would expect the hairy apes to do better than they do. One thing that is remarkable about our chimp is precisely that it is a remarkable chimp. Some of the points concerning linguistic competence made in Chapter 6 will bear on this question.
2 See R. S. Peters, *The Concept of Motivation*. Routledge & Kegan Paul, 1958.
3 For good accounts of the development of linguistic philosophy during the century, see J. O. Urmson, *Philosophical Analysis*. Oxford University Press, 1956, and J. Passmore, *A Hundred Years of Philosophy*. Pelican Books, 1968.
4 L. Wittgenstein, *Philosophical Investigations*. 3rd edn. Macmillan, 1969. Section 109.
5 R. Carnap, *The Logical Syntax of the World*. 2nd edn. Routledge & Kegan Paul, 1967. pp 5–6.
6 G Pitcher, *The Philosophy of Wittgenstein*. Prentice-Hall, 1964. p 245.

Chapter 2

Meaning

1 Some preliminaries

In this chapter I limit myself to formulating the problems about meaning which will concern us, and to the critical examination of three theories about meaning. Since this examination is critical, I will be returning to the problems of meaning at later stages – in section 2 of Chapter 7, and section 3 of Chapter 8. This geographical dissection of the discussion is necessitated by the fact that some of the things I want to say about meaning cannot be said until other topics have been discussed. I hope that the reader, eager in the field of semantics, will not be too frustrated by this dissection.

It is appropriate that a book on the philosophy of language should begin with a chapter on meaning; for of all linguistic concepts, this is probably the one that has been most studied and argued over by philosophers. The topic is of no less interest to linguists, and is scarcely of less interest to certain psychologists and anthropologists. Nor are poets, propagandists, advertisers, and men-in-the-street without their interest in it too. Why is meaning of such concern to philosophers and linguists? Both study language, and if one was forced to pick upon that characteristic of those noises and scratches which most essentially makes them part of language, their meaningfulness would perhaps be the best candidate. Language is, by definition, composed of signs and symbols; and signs and symbols are, by definition, what have meaning. So, to the extent that linguists and philosophers of language are unclear about meaning, they are unclear as to what constitutes their field of study. The problem of meaning, indeed, is the problem of understanding how that small and important set of noises and scratches which we label 'language', acquires that peculiar characteristic of meaning which entitles them to that label.

It is not only those linguists, semanticists, and those philosophers, namely philosophers of language, who are directly concerned with meaning, that have a stake in finding out what meaning is. Other linguists, phoneticians and grammarians, must also wait upon an adequate account of meaning in order to formulate some of their points adequately. This is because many of the most basic concepts in linguistics – those of the *phoneme* or the *morpheme*, for instance – are extremely hard to define except in terms of meaning. As the great pioneer in linguistics, Leonard Bloomfield, said:

> Practical phonetics and phonology presuppose a knowledge of meanings: without this knowledge we could not ascertain the phonemic features.[1]

Or again:

> Only in this way will a proper analysis (that is, one which takes account of the meanings) lead to the ultimately constituent morphemes.[2]

Bloomfield's point is that we can only define the phoneme and the morpheme as, respectively, the minimum meaningful unit of sound, and the minimum meaningful grammatical element. It follows, then, that unless we can give an account of meaning, we are not clear what constitutes the subject-matter of phonetics and grammar, let alone semantics itself.

Philosophers in all areas have an interest in meaning, too; I said in the introduction that philosophy in this century is very much conceived of as an enquiry into language, and meaning is perhaps the most interesting area for them. The Austrian positivist philosopher, Schlick, went as far as to say 'philosophy is an activity through which the meanings of statements is asserted or explained'.[3] Nor is this special interest in meaning surprising. In the first place, many philosophical theses take the form of asserting that one type of statement is equivalent in meaning to some other type. For example, some recent phenomenalists have argued that statements about material objects are equivalent in meaning to statements about the sense-experiences people have.[4] Some utilitarians have argued that statements as to the rightness and wrongness of actions are equivalent to statements about the happiness or unhappiness actions produce. Obviously it is impossible to judge such theses until we have some idea what sameness of meaning is. Second, even where philosophers are not concerned with general theses as to the equivalence of types of statements, they are always interested in the meanings of particular words or sentences. It is impossible, for instance, to discover what knowledge is unless we can get pretty clear on the meanings of such words as 'doubt', 'know', 'believe', 'certain', etc.

Meaning, as I said, is not the prerogative of academics alone. Each of us knows only too well how arguments between men, which seem to be substantial and which certainly arouse passions, turn out to be no more than arguments as to what certain important words, 'liberty' or 'democracy' for instance, mean. Again, one knows how glib and skilful talkers or writers can, by using words with the appropriate meanings, make what is harmless sound startling, and what is startling sound harmless. We do not alter what is happening by speaking of 'equipment delivery teams' instead of 'soldiers' – but we do alter how men regard what is happening. Few would want to go to the somewhat bizarre lengths of Count Korzybski, according to whom we can radically improve our health by improving our semantics, since

... heart, digestive, respiratory, and 'sex' disorders, some chronic joint diseases, arthritis, ... migraines, skin-diseases, alcoholism, etc, to mention a few, have a semantogenic, and therefore neuro-semantic and neuro-linguistic origin.[5]

Still, one can readily see that clarity about meaning might help each of us in our everyday discourse and understanding.

When I speak of a need for knowing what meaning is, I am not denying that, in a sense, most of us have a pretty good, workaday grasp of meaning. Most of us know that 'lioness' means 'female lion', that 'bachelor' does not mean the same as 'dog', that 'bank' has several meanings, that 'hot' is, and 'toh' is not, meaningful in English – and so on. It is equally true that linguists and philosophers can get along doing their jobs despite lacking an adequate theoretical account of meaning, just as mathematicians and engineers can get along without an adequate definition of 'number'. Still, it would be intellectually satisfying if our practical grasp of meaning could be supplemented by an adequate theory. It would be more than simply satisfying, for while our practical grasp is fine for practical matters, it lets us down on crucial issues. Thus, while our everyday grasp of meaning tells us that 'lioness' means 'female lion', it does not tell us if statements about material objects mean the same as statements about sense-experiences. While this everyday grasp tells us that 'I am happy' is meaningful, and 'happy three John of' is not, it does not allow us to pronounce with any confidence on such sentences as 'Nothing is a special sort of something', 'There exists an infinite necessary being', or 'Thoughts occur without anyone to have them'. It is at the point where our everyday intuitions about meaning let us down that interesting questions arrive and become the concern of the philosopher. It is at this point that we require a theory of meaning to help us out.

Interest in meaning is not only widespread, it is many-sided. That is, there are many diverse questions which can be asked about meaning. Here are some of them:

[1] Are meanings of expressions – words, morphemes, sentences, or whatever – abstract entities of some sort? If so, what sort?

[2] What conditions must an expression meet to be meaningful?
[3] What is it for two expressions to mean the same?
[4] What factors cause words to alter meaning?
[5] What are the minimal linguistic units which possess meaning?

I shall not be dealing with each of these questions; I shall deal only with [2] and [3]. My reason is that these are the questions which are of common interest to philosopher and linguist. Question [4], which is no doubt fascinating, is of primary interest to those linguists or sociologists interested in the history of language. It is difficult to see how the answer to this question could help philosophers in their enquiries. Question [5] is also of concern only to the linguist, since the philosopher can usually get along with the assumption that it is words and sentences that are the units of meaning. He does not have to bother himself, except on very rare occasions, with the meanings of morphemic units such as the prefix 're-', or the suffix '-ing'. Question [1], on the other hand, is of purely philosophical interest, and pretty esoteric interest at that. I cannot see that the linguist is going to be concerned one way or the other by the decision that meanings are abstract entities of this or that sort.[6] What he wants to know is what conditions an expression must meet to be meaningful, and what it is for expressions to mean the same. Further, it is not clear how an answer to this question is going to be of value to philosophers other than those asking just that question. If I want to distinguish between knowledge and belief, for instance, it would hardly help me to be told that 'know' and 'believe' refer to, or express, abstract entities which can be called their 'meanings'.

It is worth pursuing this point more closely. It may well be that the question 'what sort of thing or entity is a meaning?' is a spurious question anyway. In the first place, it should not be assumed that just because we employ the noun 'meaning', there is some thing to which the noun refers. We should fight against the 'temptation, perhaps partly due to peculiarities of the Indo-European languages, to suppose that nouns . . . must stand for things. This is what writers sometimes have in mind when they deplore the "reification" or "hypostatization" of entities'.[7] Certainly this temptation to seek things for nouns to refer to is not always justified. When I say 'I did it in *the nick* of time', I am not saying that there is something, a nick, which belongs to time, and in which I did whatever it was I did: I am saying, simply, that I did it just fast enough. Again, if I say 'I did it for *the sake* of John', I am not saying that there is some entity, a sake, which belongs to John, and for which I did something: I am saying, simply, that I did something to help John. Similarly, when we speak of *the meaning* of a word, there is no great reason to suppose that there exists some entity which is that meaning. Second, it seems that all the questions we want to ask about meaning can be asked without employing the noun 'meaning' at all. Instead of asking 'Is "X" a word with meaning?' we can ask 'Is "X" meaningful?' Instead of 'Do "X" and "Y" have the same meaning?' we can ask 'Are "X" and "Y" synonymous?' Instead of 'Does "X" have more than one meaning?' we can ask 'Is "X" ambiguous?' And so on. This ability to paraphrase questions about meaning into questions which do not contain the noun 'meaning' should remove the temptation to ask a question like 'what sort of entity is a meaning?' A meaning may be no more of an entity than a nick of time, or the sake of John. I shall not say any more, directly, about this sort of question – though some of what I shall say later in this chapter indirectly militates against the view that meanings are entities.

I am agreeing with what the philosopher, W. V. Quine, says when he points out:

> What had been the problem of meaning boils down now to a pair of problems in which meaning is best not mentioned: one is the problem of the notion of significant [*ie* meaningful, D.E.C.] sequence, and the other is the problem of making sense of the notion of synonymy.[8]

That is, any adequate theory of meaning, given the limitations of our interest in meaning, will have to answer the questions [1] How, and in what ways, is an expression meaningful, and [2] What is it for two expressions to mean the same? It seems to me that these are the crucial questions which interest philosopher and linguist alike. For both, plainly, are interested in how it is that certain expressions are meaningful; and, equally plainly, one of the best ways of saying how an expression is meaningful is by saying with what other expressions it is synonymous or roughly synonymous.

In this chapter I shall discuss three theories of meaning which attempt to answer the above questions. Let me briefly mention what these theories are:

[1] *The 'mentalistic theory'*. This theory, of which there are many versions, holds that an expression is meaningful if and only if it is associated, in some manner, with a certain mental item – an image, say, or a thought, or an idea. Correspondingly, the theory holds that two expressions are synonymous if and only if they are associated with the same mental item. So, for example, it might be held that 'puppy' is meaningful because it is connected with a certain mental image; and that 'puppy' is synonymous with 'young dog' because both are connected with the same image. On this view to examine meaning is essentially to examine people's mental states or processes.

[2] *The 'behaviourist theory'*. This theory, of which there are also several versions, holds that an expression is meaningful if and only if utterances of it produce certain behavioural responses in people and/or are pro-

duced in response to certain stimuli. Two expressions will be synonymous, correspondingly, if and only if utterances of them produce the
same responses and/or are produced in response to the same stimuli. On
this view, examining meaning is essentially a matter of examining the
behaviour connected with utterances of expressions.

[3] *The 'use theory'*. This theory, of which also there are several versions,
holds that an expression is meaningful if and only if people can use it for
certain purposes, and in certain ways. Two expressions, correspondingly,
will be synonymous if and only if they can be used in the same ways, for
the same purposes. On this view, examining meaning is essentially a
matter of examining the role that expressions have in human activities.

No doubt it is the case that the average meaningful expression will
have interesting links with mental processes, behaviour, and human
activities. The three theories are incompatible, however, to the extent
that each claims that just one feature is the essential, defining characteristic of meaningfulness and synonymy. Thus a mentalist would insist
that a word is meaningful, provided it was associated with some relevant
mental item, even if it had no behavioural connections, and played no
role in public use. Similarly, a behaviourist would insist that a word is
meaningful if it does cause the relevant behaviour, even if nothing is
going on in the mind in association with the word.

As far as I can see, most of the interesting theories of meaning can be
subsumed under one of the three headings I have given. It might seem,
though, that I am ignoring some approaches to meaning which can be
found in books on semantics by linguists, as opposed to philosophers –
for example, the Field theory of meaning, according to which the meaning of a term is a function of its relative place within a semantic field (*ie* a
set of related terms); or collocational analysis, according to which the
meaning of a term is to be investigated by seeing how it collocates with
other terms (*ie* pairs off with them in a range of sentences).[9] These, however, are approaches to meaning at a different level from our three
theories. Collocational analysis, for instance, is best regarded as a
method for studying the semantic properties of particular words – their
synonymy and antinomy relations for example. It tells us, for instance,
that seeing how 'night' pairs with adjectives like 'dark' and 'black',
rather than 'light', is relevant to understanding its meaning. Now such
a method, it seems, is perfectly compatible with each of the three theories
I mentioned. A mentalist would insist that, underlying collocations of
words, are the interrelations between various mental items. A use theorist
would insist that studying collocations of words is studying a network of
interrelated uses. The point is that collocational analysis, and Field
analysis, are not attempts to answer the theoretical questions 'What is
meaningfulness?' or 'What is synonymy?' but rather methods for

analysing the meanings of particular words. Collocational analysis, etc, stand to our three theories of meaning somewhat as a methodological approach in sociology, say functionalism, stands to theoretical accounts of central sociological concepts, like *society* or *group*. This is not to say that the theory of meaning a linguist accepts, if he is interested in accepting any, will not affect his methodology. A linguist who accepts a mentalistic account of meaning is more likely to rely upon introspectional analyses of meanings than one who accepts a behaviourist picture.

Whatever the connection between the three theories and linguistics may be, it is certainly the case that they are intimately connected with various, more general philosophical outlooks. Let me give an example: a favourite philosophical position has been solipsism. A solipsist is one who sees no good reason to suppose that any other persons besides himself exist. It would seem that a solipsist is committed to a mentalistic account of meaning. For if it could be shown that meaning is necessarily a function of how person*s* behave, or of words being put to *public* uses, it would follow that the solipsist's ability to employ language meaningfully presupposes the existence of other people – for it would only be through their activities that his words take on meaning. One of the most powerful attacks upon solipsism of recent years tries to show precisely that a language whose words derive meaning in terms of 'inner' private experiences is an impossibility.[10] To take an even more obvious example, it would seem that a philosophical behaviourist, according to whom talk about minds is simply disguised talk about behaviour, is committed to some corresponding, behaviourist account of meaning.

There is no lack of connection, then, between our three theories of meaning, and philosophy at large – which is one reason for concentrating upon them.

Before we can discuss these theories, however, there is a matter we must try to clear up. So far I have been using 'meaning' as if it was clear in which of the many senses of the word it was to be taken. I hope, in a way, that this assumption has been justified, and that the reader has a fair idea, from my examples, of what senses of meaning we are concerned with. Nevertheless, it must be stressed that the meanings of 'meaning' are numerous. The word 'meaning', says Max Black, is 'a Casanova of a word in its appetite for associations'.[11] Ogden and Richards, in their exploratory work *The Meaning of Meaning* suggest that there are twenty-three distinct senses of 'meaning'. A later author, even more bountiful, reckoned up no less than fifty-one. I am not going to join this race for discovering new senses of 'meaning'; but it is important to give a rough breakdown of some of these, and to justify my concentration upon only one or two of them.

First we can begin by ignoring those uses of 'meaning' and its cognates, in which it is not expressions which are said to have meaning, but people, facts, events, or things. For example, we are not interested in those senses in which we can say 'he means to go to the cinema' (*ie* intends); nor that sense in which we can say 'spots mean measles' (*ie* provide a sound basis for prediction); nor in that sense in which we can say 'Schweitzer's life was full of meaning' (*ie* purpose). This is not to suggest that such senses are unrelated to the sense we are concerned with. There may well, for instance, be an intimate connection between 'mean' in the sense of 'intend', and linguistic meaning. It has been suggested that the meaning of a word is a function of what people intend when they use it.[12] We shall discuss this point in Chapter 7. For the moment, though, we can make a preliminary isolation of any senses of 'mean' in which it is something other than linguistic expressions which mean.

However, even when we have restricted the field to linguistic meaning, the field is still much too wide for our purposes. That is, there are various senses of 'mean' in which it is expressions that mean and these will not, at least for a while, concern us. Let us try to isolate some of these senses:

[1] There are cases where meaning is apparently ascribed to linguistic expressions, but where this is an illusion. Suppose a headmaster called Smith sees the words 'Smith is a fool' written on the blackboard. He asks his class 'What is the meaning of these words?' Assuming that he is not ignorant of the English language, his question concerns not what the words mean, but what the *action* of writing them means (*ie* what its purpose was, or what its explanation is). In this context, it is not the words, but the writing of them that has meaning. Again, take the slogan 'Beanz meanz Heinz'. Here it may look as if it is the word 'beanz' which means something, but that is not so. If you look up 'bean' in the dictionary, you will find no reference to Messrs Heinz & Co. What is being claimed in the slogan is that if you see a tin with 'Heinz' written on it, that means (*ie* allows one to predict) that the contents will be good beans. At any rate, we are not concerned then with those senses of 'mean' in which it is only *apparent* that it is words which mean. These cases are like those discussed in the last paragraph but one.

[2] In this chapter we will not be concerned with that sense of 'mean', in which it could be replaced by 'refer'. Some writers say that it is a mistake to confuse meaning and reference.[13] This is a misleading way of putting it, for there is a perfectly good sense of 'mean' in which it can be replaced by 'refer'. What is true, though, is that there is a perfectly good central sense of 'meaning' which is distinct from that of 'reference'; and it is with this sense that we are concerned. A person discussing the remark 'The President went to India' might say 'That means Harry Truman, not F.D.R.'. Clearly, though, there is a sense of 'meaning' in which Harry Truman is no part of the meaning of the words 'the President'. A French translation of that sentence will make

no mention of Henri Truman; nor will you find Truman mentioned in any dictionary definitions of 'president'. 'Means' in the sentence has the same sense as 'refers to'.

[3] There is a third sense of 'meaning', frequently employed by psychologists, that will not, for the moment, concern us. This is the sense in which just about any psychological association a word has for a person is said to be part of its meaning for him. I have heard it said, for example, that the word 'Cossack' *meant* something terrible for the Russian peasants of the last century. Again, a person might say 'The name "Melissa" *means* a great deal to me; I used to be in love with a girl by that name'. Only if some linguists and psychologists are using 'meaning' in this sort of sense, is it possible to understand some of the things they say about meaning. One linguist, for example, claims that the more psychological associations a word has, the more meaningful it is.[14] Clearly there are senses of 'meaning' which would make such a claim absurd. In one sense both 'cat' and 'dog' are *perfectly* meaningful, so one cannot be more meaningful than the other. Again, in one sense of 'meaning' the fact that I think of pineapples whenever I hear the word 'X', and you do not, does not imply that 'X' has a different meaning for each of us. If we return to the Cossack example, it is plain that in some sense of 'meaning', 'Cossack' does *not* mean something terrible. You will not find mention of how terrible the Cossacks are in the dictionary definition of 'Cossack'; nor could a French translation of 'Cossack' contain any French word for 'terrible'. It would probably be useful if we did not employ the term 'meaning' to refer to psychological associations of the above sorts at all. We might, instead, use the traditional term 'connotation', and say that the terribleness of the Cossacks, or the beauty of a girl's face, are connoted by 'Cossack' or 'Melissa'.[15] At any rate, I shall not be concerned with 'meaning' in this sense, although in Chapter 3 I will be dealing with the related question as to whether certain emotive powers of words can properly be said to form part of their meaning, in the most central sense of 'meaning'.

If we are not interested in meaning in the senses of intention, reference, or connotation, what are we interested in? Well, no obvious, useful synonym for this sense of 'meaning' comes to mind. Instead I shall say this: we are interested in that sense of 'meaning' and its cognates, as the words appear in the following contexts:

[1] 'Hot' is a meaningful word in English; and 'toh' is not.
[2] 'Puppy' means the same as 'young dog'.
[3] 'Lioness' means *female lion*.
[4] 'Electron' has one meaning, whereas 'bank' has several.

It is the task of our three theories of meaning to explain what meaning is as it appears in contexts like these. It is not their task to explain what meaning as it appears in the following contexts is:

[5] 'Beanz meanz Heinz'.
[6] 'By "the President" I mean Truman'.
[7] '"Melissa" means a great deal to me'.

It might be asked why I shall be concentrating upon the sense of meaning that I am. There are at least three reasons. First, the other senses, if they are discussed at all, can be conveniently discussed under some other headings – such as reference, connotation, or intention. If the use of 'meaning' is to be restricted to one feature of words, let it be the feature we are restricting it to – since there is no obvious word we can replace 'meaning' by here. Second, and much more important, the sense of 'meaning' with which we are concerned is the one that has been of most interest to philosophers. That is, philosophers require a certain concept in terms of which to approach and discuss various issues, and they have usually given the title 'meaning' to this concept. For example, philosophers are very much concerned to decide which properties are entailed by the use of a word as opposed to those which just happen to belong to whatever it is the word refers to. The former properties, they have usually said, belong to the meaning of the word in question. So 'meaning' in the sense of 'connotation' is not what interests them here. [Though see n. 15.] Next, they often find it important to decide when one word can be used interchangeably with another, so that the truth or falsity of what is being said does not alter. Philosophers have usually spoken of any two such words as being alike in meaning. Finally, they are always concerned to distinguish between disputes over matters of fact, and merely verbal disputes. They have usually called these latter disputes, disputes over meaning. So it should be clear philosophers' use of 'meaning' corresponds to the sense I said we should be concerned with, and not with the other senses.

Finally, it is quite arguable that the sense of 'meaning' with which we are concerned is the most central one. This might be so in various ways. First, if one talks of the meaning of a word, and does not qualify this by saying, for example, 'meaning *for him*', one is usually taken to be talking of meaning in our sense. If you tell me that the French word 'jaune' means *yellow*, I shall take it that the words 'jaune' and 'yellow' are approximately synonymous. I shall not take you as saying that 'jaune' is associated in the minds of some Frenchmen with thoughts of marigolds or jaundice. I shall not, that is, take it that you mean 'connotation' by 'mean'. Again, if you tell me that 'bank' has several meanings, I shall not take it that you are simply saying that 'bank' refers to lots of different things, as does just about every word. I shall take it that you are saying that 'bank', unlike 'electron', can be used to talk about quite distinct *kinds* of things – river banks, commercial banks, and so on. I shall, that is, take it that you do not mean 'refers' by 'means'. Second, and more important, it is generally the case that a word can only mean, in the senses of 'refer' and 'connote', if it already means in our sense. For example, unless I know what 'president' means in our sense, I shall not be able to employ it to refer to Truman or anyone else. Again, unless I know that 'Cossack' means, in some central sense, a certain type of Russian, there is no reason why I should have terrible fears when I hear the word. It is in general a precondition of words having a referring role, or the ability to call up certain psychological associations, that their meanings be understood in some more fundamental sense of 'meaning'.

For these various reasons, then, it is meaning of the type roughly indicated with which we shall be concerned in this chapter. Let us now see how our three theories fare in the attempt to explicate this type of meaning.

2 The mentalistic theory of meaning

The following, representative quotations will give the reader a fair idea of the sorts of views I have in mind under the title 'mentalistic':

> The meaning of a word is 'a recurrent set of mental events peculiarly related to one another so as to recur, as regards their main features with partial uniformity'.   [*Ogden and Richards*][16]

> Two words are different in meaning if 'different psychological contexts are involved in the two cases'.   [*Ogden and Richards*][17]

> The ... use of words is to be sensible marks of ideas; and the ideas they stand for are their proper and immediate signification.   [*John Locke*][18]

> In talking *about* things we have conceptions of them, not the things themselves, and it is the conceptions, not the things, that symbols directly 'mean'.   [*S. Langer*][19]

> Propositions ... are to be defined as psychological occurrences of certain sorts – complex images, expectations, etc, ... Where two sentences have the same meaning, this is because they express the same proposition.   [*Bertrand Russell*][20]

What is common to all such views is the claim that words or sentences are meaningful in virtue of associated mental items, and that synonymy is to be explained in terms of the identity of such mental items. Versions of mentalism differ from one another, though, in two main ways. First they may differ as to the nature of the associated mental items – are they images, thoughts, ideas, conceptions, expectations, or what? Second they may differ as to the nature of the association between word and mental item – is it causal, conventional, or what? These differences will not concern us too much, for I shall argue that mentalism of any variety is radically misconceived.

Before examining the deficiencies in mentalism, it is worth glancing at some of the reasons that have made such a theory seem plausible to so many people. First, it is natural to move towards a mentalistic account once the inadequacies in a very simple, popular view of meaning are revealed. On this popular view – sometimes called the 'Fido'–Fido theory[21] – the meaning of a word is the thing, or set of things, which that word refers to or names. Thus 'lion', it might be said, just means those animals, lions, to which it can refer. Such an account fails for any number of reasons. Most obviously it fails because there are many meaningful words which do not refer to anything in the world at all – 'unicorn' or 'three-eyed man' for instance. Now if one still assumes that all meaningful words must refer, it is tempting to conclude that words like 'unicorn' refer, not to things in the world of course, but to things in the mind – say an image of a unicorn. For simplicity's sake, it is then concluded that all words have meaning through this connection with a mental item. The relation between words and the world then becomes indirect. Words first have meaning by being associated with mental items; and these mental items, in turn, can be used to represent things in the world.

Second, it has seemed self-evident to many that it is only their role in human mental life that distinguishes meaningful words from meaningless noises. We cannot think with the latter as we can with the former. And so it is concluded that we should explain meanings in terms of the very mental processes in which the words play a role.

Finally, there are certain things we often say about meaning which suggest that meaning must be some form of inner, mental phenomenon. For example 'I didn't mean what I said'. It is easy to interpret this as implying that some inner, non-verbal process was going on with which, on this occasion, our words did not properly connect. Or again, 'I couldn't find the words to express my meaning'. It is easy to interpret this as implying that there is some inner process of meaning with which we then try, but on occasions fail, to link the appropriate verbal dressing.

I shall return to the plausibility, or rather lack of it, that these three reasons lend to a mentalistic account of meaning.

I mentioned that there have been several candidates – images, ideas, thoughts, etc – for the role of being the mental items which confer meaning. I shall, at first, concentrate upon the view that meaning is to be explained in terms of *images*, since that has tended to be the clearest of the forms of mentalism. My main objections, though, will carry over to other versions, and I shall later mention some extra objections that can be levelled against these other versions. In discussing the imagist account, we need not be concerned with just what an image is. For whatever it could reasonably be supposed to be, the account fails anyway.

The first point to be made is this: it is surely not the case when I utter a sentence or understand one I am hearing, that I have to associate an image with each word. If you read my last sentence aloud to yourselves, you will not find that, in order to understand it, you have to provide a separate image for each word. Now, as it stands, this point will not worry the imagist unduly. For he will reply that words are meaningful provided there are images which we have at some time associated with them, and which we *could* associate with them on any occasion if need be. Whether we actually call them up is irrelevant; all that is required is that we could. But this reply of the imagist will not do. Apart from the fact that he is misrepresenting the relation between talking and thinking, to which we will return later, the following objection can be made: there are many meaningful words to which there do not correspond any relevant images that we *could* call up. If we concentrate on words like 'horse' or 'red', it may be tempting to suppose that all words have corresponding images. But what about words like 'if', 'so', 'all', 'or', 'then', 'for', 'may', 'it', 'at', and so on. What on earth are the images corresponding to these? Even if, by some slim chance, I do associate some image with each of these words, it is hardly likely that I could explain the meanings of them in terms of the nature of these images. I may associate the image of some awful, prehistoric monster with the word 'it' because I once saw a film called 'IT' which was about dinosaurs – but I would not be tempted to explain the meaning of 'it' in terms of the image of my monster. Even if we stick to ordinary noun-phrases, the idea that each word has its corresponding image seems absurd. What about 'four-dimensional space', 'mathematical point', or 'superego'? It is clear that one cannot form images of these theoretical entities in the way one can form images of tables or chairs. If we say that 'table' is meaningful because it refers to an image which corresponds with actual tables, it is impossible to see what analogous account could be given of our theoretical terms. Locke thought that we understood a word when we had an image of the properties which were common to all the things the word referred to. This view will obviously not do for theoretical terms; and I know of no plausible imagist one which will.

A second point is this: some people, it is well known, are much better at imaging than others. If knowing the meaning of a word was a matter of having the right images, it would seem to follow that a person who is very poor at imaging is correspondingly poor in his understanding of meanings. But this is an absurd conclusion. If Shakespeare turned out to be rotten at imaging, we would not revise our opinion about his grasp of English. And if a foreigner continually talks the most bizarre English, we will not say he is a master of the language just because he is a virtuoso at imaging. It is clear, that is, that we do not treat the ability to call up images as a criterion of people's grasp of meanings.

The above points, however, are minor by comparison with the major objection to be levelled against imagism. We are being told, remember, that an expression is meaningful only if it is associated with an image. But what image? Clearly it has to be the right one. If we are to explain the meaning of 'table' in terms of an image, it must be the image of a table rather than a cat or a kidney. Now, though, we face the problem of deciding what makes a given image the image of one sort of thing, rather than of another. A tempting answer, which many have given, Locke for example, is this: an image X is an image of something Y if X and Y are observably similar – if, say, the shape of the image resembles the shape of whatever it is an image of. But this answer, while tempting, is radically mistaken. Consider, by way of analogy, the question: what makes a painting a painting of the Eiffel Tower? Obviously it need not be observable similarity between the two. An avant-garde, surrealist picture, full of swirls and squiggles, might still be a painting of the Eiffel Tower, though no one but the artist could recognize this. Further, even if the painting and the Eiffel Tower were observably similar, it cannot be this fact alone which make it a painting of the Eiffel Tower. Any painting of the Eiffel Tower, if it resembled it, would also resemble the Blackpool Tower in England, since the two towers are themselves alike. Clearly, though, the similarity between the painting and the Blackpool Tower does not make it a painting of that, rather than of the Eiffel. It follows that observable similarity between painting and subject is neither a necessary nor a sufficient condition of the painting's being *of* that subject.

Analogous considerations apply in the case of mental images. First, there is no intrinsic reason why the image I employ of square things should itself be square. Certainly I may use an image of something that is quite unlike that something in observable respects. (It is said that some blind people associate auditory images with colour words.) So similarity between image and thing is not a necessary condition for that image to be an image of that thing. Nor is it a sufficient condition. It may well be that my image of a dog closely resembles a beaver – but that does not make it the image of a beaver instead of a dog.

What is the significance of this point for the imagist account of meaning? It is this: once we realize that the relation between image and thing is not one of observable similarity, we are forced to realize that images are themselves *signs* or *symbols*, are themselves objects which have *meaning*, and must therefore be *interpreted* as being images of one sort rather than another. Just as a painting is only of the Eiffel Tower if that is what the artist means it to be, or how he interprets it, so an image is only an image of a dog, rather than of a cat, if that is how the person means it or interprets it. Once this is realized, it can be seen that appealing to images in explanation of meanings, has got us nowhere – for we are still left with the problem of meaning; namely, how do images mean? As Wittgenstein, the main critic of mentalistic theories, points out:

> If we keep in mind the possibility of a picture which, though correct, has no similarity with its object, the interpolation of a shadow between the sentence and reality loses all point.[22]

It loses point because we are still left with the problem of how images can have meaning or significance.

If we can give an account of that, why cannot the account we give be applied directly to words and sentences? For example, if we explain the meaning of an image in terms of the *use* to which images are put, why should we not by-pass this talk of images, and explain the meanings of words in terms of the *use* to which *they* are put? Clearly it is not the intrinsic nature of an image, any more than it is the intrinsic shape of a word, that gives it meaning and makes it the image it is. 'If God had looked into our minds he would not have been able to see there whom we were speaking of'.[23]

This same point comes out clearly when we examine the inadequacy of an imagist account of synonymy. According to the imagist, two words are synonymous if and only if they are associated with the same mental image. But what is meant by '*same* image'? If it is suggested that two images are the same if they are observably very similar, the account of synonymy fails. First, there is no great reason to suppose that the image I employ whenever I use the word 'puppy' is particularly similar to the image I employ each time I use the expression 'young dog'. However, these expressions may be synonymous, and they do not cease to be merely because different images might be associated with them. Indeed, if one insisted that words mean the same only if similar images are connected, it would follow that a word is not even synonymous with itself; since there is no reason to suppose that I have the same image each time I use a given word 'X'. So observable similarity between images is not a necessary condition of synonymy. Second, I may well employ very similar images in association with words which are plainly not synonymous. To use Wittgenstein's example, I might employ the following

image to represent either a duck or a rabbit; but this hardly

makes 'duck' and 'rabbit' synonymous. So similarity between images cannot be a sufficient condition of synonymy.

No doubt there is a sense in which the various images I associate with the word 'dog' are similar. But this is the trivial sense in which they are similar because they are all images of dogs; or, if you like, because they are all connected with the word 'dog'. However, in this sense, one cannot explain the synonymy of words in terms of the similarity of images, since one can only know that they are similar, in the relevant sense, if one already knows how the images are to be interpreted, or if one already knows that the words connected with them mean the same. Equally, there is a sense in which when I employ  as an image of a duck, I am not using the same image as when I employ  as an image of a rabbit. But again, we can only say that the images are different because we know they are meant differently, or because we already know that the words connected with them are non-synonymous. Either way, we are left with the problem of explaining sameness of meaning; so that appeal to images has got us nowhere. If we knew how to explain sameness of images, we could presumably apply the explanation directly to words themselves. If, for example, we say that two images are the same if they are used in identical ways, we could just as well say that two words mean the same if *they* are used in identical ways.

For the above reasons, then, we must reject an imagist account of meaning. But what about those mentalistic theories which appeal, not to images, but to thoughts, ideas, conceptions, or whatever? Part of the problem with these accounts is their extreme vagueness. What is an idea? What is a conception? Because these questions are not usually answered, I am not sure if the first two criticisms I levelled against imagism could be made to carry over against these other accounts or not. The major objection, though, would surely carry over. For whatever the mental items might be, it will always be the case that they must be interpreted properly. A thought, for example, must be interpreted as being a thought of this rather than of that. But to this extent, any such mental items will themselves represent, signify, mean, or stand for. As such we cannot explain meaning or signification in terms of these items. Again, it will always be the case that what makes any two such items the same will be a matter of how they are interpreted; so that synonymy cannot be explained in terms of them.

There is an important thing to note about these alternatives to imagism. Whatever the defects in imagism, it seems to have one advantage over alternatives. Images are things which, in a sense, we can identify separately from the words used to describe them. We can, after all, have an image, an after-image say, without applying words to it at all. The trouble with ideas, conceptions, thoughts etc, is that there seems no way of identifying or recognizing them except in terms of the words used to express them. Such mental items appear to be *essentially* verbal. We saw that, in the case of images even, we could ultimately only make the relevant identifications in terms of how they are interpreted or described. But in the case of these other mental items it seems immediately obvious that we cannot identify them except via language. If this is so there is no chance of explaining meaning by reference to them, since we must already understand the meanings of words in order to recognize what the mental items are. I must understand the meanings of words to know what makes a particular thought or idea the one it is. As William Alston says about ideas:

> There is, to be sure, a sense of 'idea' in which it is not completely implausible to say that ideas are involved in any intelligible bit of speech. This is the sense 'idea' has in such expressions as 'He isn't getting his ideas across'. In that sense of the term, I don't understand what someone is saying unless I get the idea. But that is because the phrase 'get the idea' would have to be explained as equivalent to 'see what the speaker meant by his utterance'. 'Idea' in this sense is derivative from such notions as 'meaning' and 'understanding', and so can provide no basis for an explication of meaning. If we are to have an explication of meaning in terms of ideas, we must be using 'idea' so that the presence or absence of an idea is decidable independent of determining in what senses words are being used . . . Locke was trying to satisfy this requirement when he took 'idea' to mean something like 'sensation or mental image'.[24]

The same would go for thoughts, conceptions, or whatever. We may put it like this: is it possible to know what thought, idea, etc, took place without knowing the meanings of the words which were employed, perhaps tacitly, in expressing it? If not then we clearly cannot explain meaning in terms of such mental items. Indeed, it seems rather that we should want to explain what it is to have a certain thought or idea in terms of the meanings of various words. What, after all, is it to believe that something is the case except to believe that a sentence is true?

Underlying any attempt to explain meaning in terms of mental items is, no doubt, a false picture of the relationship between words and mental processes. In this false picture, mental processes, like thinking or conceiving, are regarded as inner, non-verbal processes which may or may not receive clothing in the form of words. It is only on this view that we could hope for a non-circular appeal to mental processes in explication of meaning. But the picture is mistaken. If thinking, etc, were inner non-verbal processes, it should be quite possible to go about thinking and meaning things in total isolation from any verbalization, tacit or aloud. Yet this isolation appears to be impossible. Wittgenstein lays down the following challenge for the mentalist:

> Make the following experiment: say and mean a sentence, *eg* 'It will probably rain tomorrow'. Now think the same thought again, mean what you just meant, but without saying anything (either aloud or to

yourself). If thinking that it will rain tomorrow accompanied saying that it will rain tomorrow, then just do the first activity and leave out the second. If thinking and speaking stood in the relation of the words and melody of a song, we could leave out the speaking and do the thinking just as we can sing the tune without the words.[25]

Of course, one does not know how to meet this challenge. Wittgenstein's point, put crudely, is that various mental processes just *are* the processes of using words meaningfully – in which case, as we have seen, it would be hopeless to explicate meaning in terms of these processes in a non-circular manner. We saw that appealing to mental images would get us nowhere; it is even more obvious that we shall get nowhere by appealing to such essentially verbal processes as thinking and conceiving.

We might briefly glance back at some of the reasons which, as I mentioned, have made mentalism attractive to some people. First we noted that mentalism was a natural outgrowth of the view that words have meaning through referring. According to the mentalist, words refer, in the first instance, not to things in the world but to items in the mind. The problem with this reasoning is the assumption that meaning is a form of reference at all. I noted in section 1 that there is a sense of 'meaning' in which meaning equals reference, but that there is another sense, and this is the one that concerns us, in which meaning is quite distinct from reference. There should be no presumption that a word must refer to have meaning in this sense, whether to things in the world or to things in the mind.

Second, it seemed self-evident to many that, since meaningful words play an essential role in mental life, their meaning must be explained in terms of that mental life. I am in no way denying the obvious fact that meaningful words do have an intimate association with mental life. But it is one thing to admit this, and quite another to suppose that the meanings of words can be explained by reference to this mental life. Indeed, the trouble is that meaningful discourse is *too* intimately associated with mental life for us to explain the former in terms of the latter. 'Using words meaningfully is a mental activity': of course it is. But we might do better to explain what mental activity is in terms of using words meaningfully than vice versa.

Finally, there were certain locutions like 'I didn't mean what I said' or 'I couldn't find the words to express my meaning' which, at first sight, suggest a picture of meaning as an inner activity which may or may not receive a suit of verbal clothes. But in these cases, we can make sense of the locutions in better ways, ways which carry no such implication. 'I didn't mean what I said': this may mean no more than that I lied, and that is to say no more than that the sentence I actually produced was not the sentence I believed to be true – not that there was some non-verbal thought in the recesses of my mind which did not receive an appropriate verbal coat. 'I couldn't find the words to express my meaning': this may mean no more than that, until I was furnished with certain words, I did not know exactly what I meant – not that I had non-verbally formulated a precise meaning in my mind but had failed to find the appropriate verbal labels for it.

So while it is not false to regard meaning as intimately associated with mental activity, this gets us nowhere in trying to explain meaning. Any such attempt is circular. If you like we can call the process of meaning things by our words a 'mental activity'. But, as Wittgenstein remarked, we *could* call a rise in the price of butter an 'activity' of the butter. That will hardly explain the rise in price.

3 The behaviourist theory of meaning

Leonard Bloomfield defined the meaning of an expression as 'the situation in which the speaker utters it and the responses which it calls forth in the hearer'.[26] Since his time, any number of attempts have been made by linguists, philosophers, and especially psychologists, to give a comprehensive account of meaning in terms of stimuli and responses.[27] Why has this seemed such an attractive project?

First, it is plain, meaningful talk does have a crucial, intimate connection with behaviour. Meaningful talk is itself a type of behaviour; and such talk affects behaviour in a way that mere gibberish does not, so one might expect that we can distinguish meaningful talk from gibberish in terms of the ways they affect behaviour. The most important factor, though, is the behaviourist's article of faith that explanations of human abilities can be given which make no appeal to mental concepts, like thoughts, desires, ideas, or whatever. This article of faith was given some justification in some areas of psychology, particularly in the realm of animal behaviour. So it was assumed that the same techniques of explanation which had been successful elsewhere could be applied to linguistic phenomena. Bloomfield said:

> It is the belief of the present writer that the scientific description of the universe . . . requires none of the mentalistic terms.[28]

Behaviouristic accounts of meaning are in the spirit of this remark. It is not so much that a behaviourist need deny the existence of thoughts, images, and anything 'inner', as that he regards mention of such things as being superfluous and lacking any place in rigorous scientific definitions and explanations, which must appeal only to the public and the physical.

It is clear, from the first quotation of this section, that Bloomfield thought that both the stimuli prompting utterances, and the responses prompted by them, must be taken into account in explaining the meaning of the utterances. Most writers, though, have tended to concentrate upon one of these factors to the exclusion of the other. I shall begin by looking at an account of meaning in terms of the behavioural responses which are elicited by utterances of words. Later I shall look at an account which aims to explain synonymy in terms of the stimuli which prompt utterances of words.

The crudest possible behaviourist account of meaning is the one which tells us that the meaning of an expression *is* the responses it elicits when uttered. This is too crude to take seriously. In the first place, a word like 'dog' might produce very different responses on different occasions of its utterance – yet clearly it does not alter meaning on each occasion. Second, the utterance of 'dog' might produce no responses on some occasions – yet it is absurd to suppose that it becomes meaningless on those occasions.

In the face of these obvious objections, a more sophisticated account of meaning in terms of responses has been suggested, which is typical of several others. Charles Morris introduces the notion of a *preparatory stimulus*. This is a stimulus which does not itself elicit any responses, but which sets up the disposition in somebody to respond to future stimuli. The food a rat sees is a stimulus which causes it to respond in certain ways. Now suppose the rat has been trained to expect food whenever it hears a buzzer. The buzzer will then act as a preparatory stimulus, since it sets up the disposition in the rat to respond when the actual stimulus of the food arrives. According to Morris, all meaningful symbols or 'signs' as he calls them, including words, are preparatory stimuli. The buzzer can be regarded as a sign of food for the rat. Similarly the words 'Turn right at the corner' will act as a preparatory stimulus, setting up in the hearer the disposition to turn right once the corner is reached. Thus the sentence is a sign.

> If anything, A, is a preparatory stimulus which in the absence of stimulus objects initiating response-sequences of a certain behaviour-family, causes a disposition in some organism to respond under certain conditions by response-sequences of this behaviour-family, then A is a sign.[29]

On the basis of this view, Morris erects a theory of meaning and synonymy. The meaning of a sign, whether it be a buzzer or a word, has two components. First there is the *denotatum* of the sign, which is defined as 'that which would complete the response-sequences to which the interpreter is disposed'. Thus food, or perhaps the eating of it, would be the denotatum of the buzzer – since the food satisfies that sequence of goal-directed responses to which the rat is disposed by the buzzer. Equally food is the denotatum of the word 'food', since that word disposes people to behave in a manner whose goal is the obtaining of food. It is probably best not to regard the denotatum of a sign as part of its meaning, but as what the sign *refers* to. The other component is the *significatum* of the sign. In order for something to serve as the goal of some goal-directed responses, *ie* in order for it to serve as a denotatum, it must have certain properties; and these essential properties are the significatum of the sign. Thus, for something to be food, and serve as the goal we are disposed to achieve by the buzzer or by the word 'food', it must be edible. So edibility is part of the significatum of the buzzer or the word 'food'. A definition of synonymy follows fairly smoothly from this. 'A sign is synonymous with another sign if the two signs . . . have the same significatum'.[30] Suppose, that is, that two expressions 'X' and 'Y' dispose us to certain responses which in both cases would be satisfied by things having the same properties – in that case 'X' and 'Y' would be synonymous. For example, whatever would satisfy the goal-directed behaviour we are disposed towards by 'Get a young dog' would also satisfy the behaviour we are disposed towards by 'Get a puppy'. So 'young dog' and 'puppy' mean the same.

This account of meaning avoids the obvious objections we levelled against the crudest form of behaviourism. For we are no longer committed to saying that a word alters meaning each time we respond differently to it – since the disposition to respond to it may be the same on each occasion. Nor will it make the word meaningless if there is no response on some occasion; for the disposition might still be there, though it has failed to materialize into action for some reason. Nevertheless, this more sophisticated version fails for a large number of reasons, some of which I shall now mention.

First, it is assumed by Morris that, associated with each word having a distinct meaning, there is some distinctive goal-directed response-sequence towards which it disposes us. This does not sound too implausible when we deal with words like 'food' and 'drink' with which, no doubt, there are connected characteristic kinds of goal-directed behaviour. But if we turn to words like 'if', 'at', 'or', 'each', 'for', 'so', etc, it does not sound faintly plausible to suppose that every word in the language has its connection with some distinctive type of goal-directed behaviour. Even assuming that words like those listed can somehow be taken care of, the suggestion fares badly. Take the word 'black'. What on earth are the goal-objects which people hearing this word are disposed to seek out?[31] Black things do not, like food and drink, satisfy any characteristic need, or serve as the objects of any distinctive type of goal-directed behaviour. Most people seek food, or drink, for the same reasons. But people do not seek S.S. uniforms, ravens, liquorice, ink, and black puddings for the same reason. We might say that 'black' at least disposes us towards black things: but that is as helpful as explaining the significance of the buzzer by saying that the buzzer disposes the rat to seek whatever the buzzer disposes the rat to seek. It follows from all this that we shall be unable to explain the meaningfulness of more than a few words in terms of characteristic response-sequences associated with them.

A second objection arises in the following way: we saw that some of the actual responses to words are irrelevant to their meanings. If we did not say this we should be in the absurd position of having to say that the meaning of a word alters each time utterances of it elicit different responses. Appealing to dispositions, instead of actual responses, was meant to help us out of this difficulty. But it does not. Many sentences set up dispositions which, whether or not they materialize into actual responses, are irrelevant to the meanings of the sentences. For example, any sentence which asserts some remarkable fact – like 'I met Attila the Hun at the top of the Empire State building' – no doubt disposes people to react with shock or amazement. Clearly this tendency to amaze or shock is not part of the meaning of such sentences. A translation of the sentence about Attila will make no mention of goggling eyes, or open mouths. It would seem, too, that any account such as Morris's is going to find it hard to distinguish between meaning and connotation (see *p* 18 for this distinction). As we saw, 'Cossack' may dispose Russians to tremble and flee; but reference to such behaviour, while it may explain what 'Cossack' connotes for them, is irrelevant to the meaning of the word. The onus is therefore upon the behaviourist to distinguish between those dispositions which are, and those which are not, relevant to meaning. It is difficult to see how this can be done; and if it cannot, we shall have to bring in some non-behaviourist criterion for making the distinction.

A third criticism concerns Morris's use of the term 'preparatory stimulus'. Signs, including meaningful words, remember, are defined by him in terms of such stimuli. The trouble is, though, that there are many preparatory stimuli which are not signs. As Max Black points out, a shot of morphine will affect one's disposition to respond; but a shot of morphine is not a sign or meaningful symbol.[32] It is no use, either, suggesting that only those preparatory stimuli which are spoken or written are signs. Those who have read or seen *The Manchurian Candidate* will recall that Sgt Shaw has been brainwashed in such a way that the sight of the Queen of Diamonds disposes him to kill whomever he is then told to kill. The Queen is not a sign for Sgt Shaw in the way that this printed symbol is a sign for a man who is playing cards. The player has to interpret and understand the marks on the card in order to act appropriately with it, but Sgt Shaw has to do nothing of the sort. Brainwashed, he simply reacts at the sight of the card with no intervening stage of interpretation. This creates a serious problem for Morris's account. For if not all preparatory stimuli are signs, the onus is upon him to distinguish those which are signs from those which are not. Nothing in his account permits this distinction to be made – so once again it seems that we must bring in some non-behaviourist criterion to show what is distinctive about those preparatory stimuli which are meaningful symbols.

A fourth problem, which will also concern us in section 3 of Chapter 5, arises in the following manner: one can give a non-circular explanation of meaning in terms of behaviour only if it is possible to identify what the behaviour is independently of already knowing the meanings of the words associated with it. Now by 'behaviour', presumably, we mean not just movements of muscles, contractions of ligaments, etc, but human *actions*, like kicking, praying, or building. However, once we include actions under the heading of 'behaviour', it is difficult to see that we are always in a position to identify what the behaviour is without already knowing the meanings of the words we are supposed to explain by reference to this behaviour. For example, suppose an anthropologist visits a strange tribe, and observes that the natives are disposed to certain behaviour by certain words. Can he then explain what the words mean in terms of the behaviour? Hardly. He may observe that they kneel, and wave their arms around; but how is he to decide that this behaviour is to be described as praying, rather than giving thanks, or frightening spirits away? The point is that one and the same set of bodily movements may be involved in the performance of radically different types of actions. I may make the same muscular movements in signing a cheque, making my will, practising my handwriting, and so on – and all of these are different actions. The difficulty is then of deciding what actions are being performed without having some prior understanding of the meanings of the words the natives use to describe their behaviour. If this cannot be done, it seems we must call in some non-behaviourist account of meaning; for unless we do so, we shall be unable to determine what the behaviour is. No doubt studying their behaviour can be used to confirm or disconfirm hypotheses about how they mean their words; but it is difficult to see that we can explain the meaning of their words in terms of their behaviour.

Many of the points I have made will apply if we turn to criticize Morris's account of synonymy. First, recall, Morris's account of synonymy depends upon the assumption that corresponding to each *non*-synonymous word there is some distinctive type of goal-directed behaviour. That assumption we have seen to be false. Consequently we are left in the dark as to how to explain the synonymy of those words which are not connected with distinctive types of goal-directed behaviour. For example, 'black' and 'noir' may be synonymous – yet, as we have seen, they are not connected with distinctive types of goal-directed behaviour. Morris, therefore, has said nothing that could explicate their synonymy. Second, we saw that it might be impossible to decide what behaviour is being performed independently of already understanding the words used to describe it by the agents. Equally, it will be impossible to decide if two bits of behaviour are the *same* unless we already know that the descriptions of them mean the same. Certainly, we cannot say that two actions are the same just because similar bodily movements are involved in the two cases. Getting married and entering into marital union are no doubt the same action – but how can this be decided except in terms of the antecedently understood synonymy of 'marry' and 'enter into marital union'? So it would seem that explaining sameness of meaning in terms of sameness of behaviour would be a circular enterprise.

There is a final, and damning, criticism that we can make of accounts of synonymy in terms of behavioural responses. It might well be the case, as a matter of statistical fact, that most people respond to the command 'Get a puppy' by turning to the right, and to the command 'Get a young dog' by turning to the left. Again, people respond differently, no doubt, to the commands 'Draw a round square' and 'Draw an equilateral, rectilinear figure, all of whose points are equidistant from the centre'. The second command will, at the least, produce more hesitation than the first. Clearly, however, these differences in responses do not affect the synonymy of 'puppy' and 'young dog', or of 'round square' and 'equilateral, rectilinear figure, all . . . etc'. What one wants to say, of course, is that such differences in responses are irrelevant to the synonymy or otherwise of expressions. Certainly they are. The trouble is, how is a behaviourist in a position to regard such differences in responses as irrelevant? If, after all, 'puppy' meant the same as 'dog approached from the left', then the different responses to 'puppy' and 'young dog' would be related to their meanings. The point is that, unless we already have criteria for synonymy, we are in no position to say which differences in behaviour are relevant to meanings. It is because I already know that 'puppy' and 'young dog' are synonymous on some independent ground, that I can discount as irrelevant some of the differences in responses to the two expressions. If this is so, it follows once more that any appeal to responses in explication of synonymy will be circular – since we do not know which responses to look for unless we already know something about what the words mean.

So, then, attempts to explain meaning and synonymy in terms of behavioural responses look pretty unpromising, to say the least. But what about attempts by other behaviourists to explain meaning in terms of the stimuli which elicit utterances – the second of the factors mentioned by Bloomfield? A suggestion might be, for instance, that if a certain type of situation regularly disposes people to make a certain utterance, that utterance is meaningful, and its meaningfulness is to be explained by reference to that situation. Such a suggestion, however, immediately comes up against the difficulties faced by the other brand of behaviourism. For example, it is apparent that not every aspect of a situation which elicits an utterance is relevant to its meaning. I doubt if anyone would utter the sentence 'It is a red book' unless he had been asked a question. Yet reference to the question which 'stimulated' the utterance would not appear in an explanation of its meaning. Second, it is obviously not the case that everything I am disposed to utter, in regular connection with certain stimuli, are meaningful words. I utter a yell each time a pin is stuck in me; but my yell is not a meaningful word in the way that 'Stop' is. One could not, for example, ask for a paraphrase or translation of my yell. So, for reasons like these, and many others, it is doubtful if the attempt to explain meaningfulness in terms of stimuli can even get off the ground.

However, it has been argued that an account of synonymy can be given in terms of the identity of stimuli.[33] Suppose that we have explained, in one way or another, what it is for an expression to be meaningful. Suppose it is then discovered that two meaningful utterances are always elicited by one and the same set of stimuli. In that case, it might be suggested, the words in the two utterances mean the same. The greatest problem for this sort of suggestion concerns the notion of a *stimulus*, and the notion of *sameness* of stimuli. In the animal laboratory, it is possible to treat objects in the immediate environment of the animal as stimuli – a buzzer, say, or a coloured patch. This is possible and convenient because a good deal of the animal's behaviour can be explained and predicted on the basis of his encountering such objects in his environment. Can we, then, regard things in the external, immediate environment of the speaker as being the stimuli which elicit his utterances? If we do, then it seems we can explain and predict very little of his verbal behaviour in terms of stimuli. Suppose, to use an example of Chomsky's, we put a man in front of a painting, which we call the stimulus. Now think of the innumerable different things the man may say – 'Beautiful', 'Hideous', 'Clashes with the wallpaper', 'I didn't know you liked landscapes', 'Eighteenth century isn't it?', and so on. Obviously it would be quite impossible to predict which utterance he makes, or explain why he makes it, simply by reference to the painting's being before him. It seems that we must also take into account such factors as the man's interests, his tastes, his concentration, his memory, his politeness, and so on. Should we, then, include such factors as these, as well as the external things, amongst the stimuli? We could; but if we do, the whole behaviourist approach falls to pieces. For the whole point of behaviourism is to avoid appeal to 'mentalistic' terminology. But if we start including concentration, tastes, interests, etc, amongst the stimuli, we are knee-deep in mentalistic terminology. It then follows that an explanation in terms of stimuli is not even approximately behaviourist in form.

There is a worse difficulty, even, than this one. For if we include amongst the stimuli such 'mental' factors, it turns out that we are quite unable to identify what the stimuli are independently of identifying the responses. Suppose the person responds to the painting by saying 'Beautiful'. He has, we might say, been 'stimulated' by his appreciation of its beauty. But how do we know this apart from the fact that he responds by saying 'Beautiful'? We cannot possibly predict what responses will be elicited by the stimuli, since we have no idea what the stimuli are – *ie* what the man notices, appreciates, takes an interest in, remembers, thinks worth saying, etc – until the responses take place.

Such implications as these make it entirely pointless to employ terms like 'stimulus' and 'response', for they have lost all explanatory function. In criticizing just such a behaviourist account of meaning in terms of stimuli, Noam Chomsky says:

> The word 'stimulus' has lost all objectivity in this usage. Stimuli are no longer part of the outside world; they are driven back into the organism. We identify the stimulus when we hear the response . . . the talk of stimulus control simply disguises a complete retreat to mentalistic psychology. We cannot predict verbal behaviour in terms of the stimuli in the speaker's environment, since we do not know what the current stimuli are until he responds.[34]

Let us see the relevance of this for the attempt to explain synonymy in terms of stimuli. Two expressions, we are told, are synonymous if and only if they are elicited by the same stimuli. But what is meant by 'same stimuli' here? Suppose we say that the stimuli are the same if the things in the speaker's external environment are the same. In that case it will follow that whatever words he utters in this environment will be synonymous. But that is crazy. Obviously 'Beautiful' and 'Eighteenth century isn't it?' do not mean the same, though both may be elicited by the same external stimuli. Suppose, then, we include mental factors in the stimuli. In that case, it will be claimed, two expressions are synonymous if they are elicited by the same stimuli, including such mental factors as interests, tastes etc. But, as we have seen, it now becomes impossible to identify the stimuli independently of the meanings of the verbal responses. Equally, therefore, it is impossible to know that two sets of stimuli are the same unless we already know that the verbal responses are synonymous. If I respond to certain stimuli by saying 'puppy', and to other stimuli by saying 'young dog', then, no doubt, we can infer that the stimuli are in some way the same. But we can infer this only because we already know that 'puppy' and 'young dog' are synonymous. Or put it like this: we may not be able to explain the responses except by reference to the speaker's beliefs. So we might say that two responses mean the same if, *inter alia*, they are 'stimulated' by the same beliefs. The trouble is we can only say that the beliefs are the same because we already know that the words which express these beliefs mean the same. When I believe that something is a puppy, I believe the same as when I believe that it is a young dog. But this fact, far from explaining the synonymy of the words, is explained by that synonymy.

I conclude, then, that any attempt to explain synonymy in terms of identity of stimuli will either be absurd – if we restrict 'stimulus' to external things – or circular, if we include mental factors, such as beliefs, amongst the stimuli.

Any behaviourist accounts of meaning, as far as I can see, must fail – and largely for the same crucial reason; their circularity. We have seen, in various ways, how it is impossible to identify the various behavioural responses or stimuli except in terms of the very meanings which were supposed to be explained in terms of those responses and stimuli. So appeal to such behavioural factors can get us nowhere in defining meaning and synonymy. Before we leave behaviourism, let me guard the reader against two possible misconceptions. First, my criticism of behaviourism should not be taken as denying the importance of observing behaviour for linguists. But, as Sir Karl Popper points out,[35] observation is only of use to the scientist if he has already formulated hypotheses which enable him to tell what the relevant observations would be. Hypotheses are not derived from observations; rather, observations serve to confirm or disconfirm hypotheses which alone tell us what to look for. It is the same with the relationship between observing behaviour and hypotheses about meaning. Once we have theoretically adequate accounts of such concepts as meaningfulness and synonymy, and can formulate hypotheses in terms of these concepts, we can then start observing behaviour to confirm or disconfirm particular hypotheses about what words mean. However, we cannot derive these hypotheses and concepts from observations of behaviour. Until we have the hypotheses, we do not know what behaviour to take note of, and what to ignore. And, as we have also seen, any attempt to define our semantic concepts in terms of behaviour is viciously circular.

Finally, part of my criticism is that the behaviourist must fail in his attempt to avoid 'mentalistic' terminology. This may make it look as if what we need is a return to the mentalistic theory of meaning already discussed. But this is not so. In the last section we saw that many mental terms, like 'thought', 'idea', 'conception', etc, themselves require explanation in terms of meaning. Consequently, to say that behaviourism fails because it cannot avoid bringing in mental concepts is simply to say that it fails to give an account of meaning. For the very mental concepts which the behaviourist is eventually forced to admit are the very concepts which require explanation in terms of verbal meaning. So, it is not mentalism we must return to, but some proper account of meaning that we must progress to.

4 The use theory of meaning

The flavour of the use theory can be got from the following quotations taken from leading proponents of this approach to meaning:

> For a large class of cases – though not for all – in which we employ the word 'meaning' it can be defined thus: the meaning of a word is its use in the language.   [*Wittgenstein*][36]

> ... doesn't the fact that sentences have the same sense consist in their having the same use?   [*Wittgenstein*][37]

> Understanding a word or phrase is knowing how to use it, *ie*, make it perform its role in a wide range of sentences.   [*Gilbert Ryle*][38]

Some philosophers, incidentally, have argued that it is only the meanings of words or phrases, and not whole sentences, which can be explained in terms of use. This is because, according to them, sentences cannot be said to have uses at all; rather, they are what we use words or phrases to make.[39] Frankly, I fail to understand this restriction. Surely it is perfectly sensible to speak of a sentence being used to make a command, say, or a promise. Perhaps the ways in which single words can be used are importantly different from the ways in which sentences can be used, but that both have uses seems to me indubitable.

This view of meaning has been part and parcel of an important philosophical approach in this century. Wittgenstein, the father-figure of this approach, claimed that past philosophers had gone badly astray by failing to understand how certain crucial words were used in everyday life. 'A main source of our failure to understand is that we do not command a clear view of the use of our words'.[40] It was such remarks as this that were the spur to a whole style of philosophy, so-called 'ordinary language' philosophy, which is characterized by the painstaking analysis of how words are used in their everyday, natural habitat. Understanding concepts, many would say, is to understand meanings. So if it is true that we can only understand concepts by understanding uses, it is a small step to equating the study of meanings with the study of uses.

Apart from the insistence that analysing concepts, and so meanings, was a matter of analysing uses, the slogan 'Meaning is use' was important for philosophers in what it implicitly denied. As employed by Wittgenstein, the slogan implied the denial of the view that meaning was to be explained in terms of 'inner', private, mental processes. Rightly enough, as we saw in section 2 of this chapter, it was insisted that it is how a man applies and otherwise uses his words that is the test of whether he knows their meanings, and not what may or may not be going on in the recesses of his mind. Second, the slogan implied the denial of the view that meanings are abstract entities named or expressed by words. Quite rightly it was insisted that we explain nothing about the meaning of 'lion' if we say that it names the abstract entity of 'lionity', or whatever. We only explain meanings to people by showing them how words are employed in life. If meaning is use, meaning is no more an abstract entity than the use of a spade is.

Certainly the theory seemed correct in what it denied. Beyond this, the claim that meaning is use seemed to have two initial advantages over rival claims. First, we have seen that both mentalists and behaviourists had trouble with such 'syncategorematic' words as 'if', 'at', 'for', 'to' etc, since it was implausible to suggest that specific mental items or bits of behaviour corresponded to these words. Presumably, though, each such word has a distinctive use in language; and one might reasonably expect its meaning to be explained in terms of this use. Second, the use theory seems to fit in happily with the facts about how we learn the meanings of words. When I am taught, as a child, what 'lion' means, I am not told to match it up with some mental image; nor am I taught it by seeing how people respond to it. But I am shown how to apply it, and when to use it.

I believe that the slogan 'Meaning is use', if correctly expanded and formulated, is substantially correct. Let me add at once, however, that the problem of expanding it and formulating it adequately is forbidding. If it can be made adequate, this can only be as the result of developing a sophisticated theory of the uses of language. In Chapter 8 I shall describe just such a theory, the theory of speech acts; and I will suggest that meaning can be understood within the terms of that theory. What I wish to point out in the present chapter is precisely the need for such a sophisticated theory. For there are strong objections that are successful against the claim that meaning is use, unless that claim is backed by a theory of speech acts. What follows in this section can be regarded as criticism of less developed use theories of meaning – in the hope, though, of paving the way for a more developed and adequate one.

The basic problem confronting a use theory is that of finding a sense of the word 'use' in terms of which meaning can be explicated. For it should be immediately clear that there are many types of linguistic use which are not relevant to questions about meaning. Here are some such cases:

[1] It might be the case that 'if' was used seven hundred times yesterday in the village of Red Rock – but this fact about the use of 'if' has nothing to do with its meaning.

[2] I can use the words 'Good evening' to terrify the life out of some-

one if, say, I utter them in a Boris Karloff voice on a lonely forest path at midnight. But this use of 'Good evening' is unconnected with its meaning.

[3] Most people know how to use 'Amen' – namely, to put it at the end of their prayers – but do not know what it means.

[4] There are some expressions which obviously have a use, but which do not so obviously have a meaning; proper names, for example. It is at least peculiar to ask 'What does the name "John" mean?' (unless this is just a question about etymology), or 'What is "John" synonymous with?' (For more on proper names, see section 3 of Chapter 4.)

[5] Quite meaningless words can have a use. If I want to convince you that I am insane, it might be a good idea to answer your questions with gibberish. This use of gibberish does not make it meaningful, except in that sense of 'meaning' where meaning equals purpose.

[6] One might explain the use of a given word in a poem by pointing out that it rhymes with another word. This use is no part of its meaning.

Once we realize that many aspects of use are, in ways like those above, irrelevant to meaning, it is certainly tempting to conclude with Paul Ziff that

It is wrong to say 'the meaning of a word is its use in the language', for the use of a word depends upon many factors many of which have nothing to do with questions of meaning.[41]

No doubt it is easy enough to isolate some types of use, and eliminate them as irrelevant to meaning, and as being unintended by the use theory. Professor Ryle, for example, points out that it is not use in the senses of 'usage' or 'utility' in terms of which meaning is to be explicated. That is, in enquiring about meanings we are not [1] enquiring into the utility of words (eg whether 'balderdash' is a good word to shock people with), or [2] enquiring into facts about the usage of words (eg whether 'sidewalk' has more common usage in New York than in London). Rather we are enquiring into the standard or stock uses to which words may be put. Whether a word is a good one to shock people with, or whether it is more commonly uttered in one city than another, has nothing to do with what its standard, non-deviant, proper use is. And it is this sort of use in terms of which meaning is to be explained. In order to discover what these stock uses are, it is helpful to look at deviations from these uses; and this shows that we are not interested in utility or usage. According to Ryle,

Usage is a custom, practice, fashion, or vogue ... There cannot be a misusage any more than there can be a miscustom or a misvogue.[42]

However, even when we have made these distinctions, the theory is still not out of trouble. In the first place, it is often the case that the standard or stock use of an expression is unconnected with its meaning. For example, the sentence 'How now brown cow?' has, as its standard use, its use in elocution classes. Yet this aspect of its use tells us nothing about its meaning. Again, the standard use of 'There's a bull behind you', if it has one, is presumably to warn people. But this warning function is not part of its meaning. We will be told, no doubt, that this sort of standard use is not the type intended by the theory. But we have not yet been presented with a criterion by which to distinguish between those types of standard use which are and those which are not relevant to meaning. It is surely the case, too, that we can speak of misuses of sentences which tell us nothing about their meanings. We could say, for example, that Professor Higgins was misusing 'How now brown cow?' if he kept repeating it long after Eliza Doolittle could say it perfectly. Again, we might call it a misuse, if we uttered 'There's a bull behind you' when it is too late, and you are about to be impaled on the bull's horns. Again we shall be told that these are not the relevant sorts of misuse. And again we must reply that we do not yet have a criterion to distinguish between semantically relevant, and semantically irrelevant misuses.

A second, but related, point is this: it is characteristic of those who claim that meaning is use to say that the study of peculiar, deviant, odd utterances will reveal much to us about the meanings of words as a result of discovering why the utterances are peculiar or odd. Yet, as Fodor and Katz point out, each of the following sentences is odd; but in no case is the oddity one that involves semantic error:

I just swallowed my nose.
I will show you fear in a handful of dust.
This lovely red rose is a red rose.
Physical objects do not exist.
I have just been decapitated.
Pain is the stimulation of C-fibres.[43]

The first, for example, is odd because the fact it reports is so odd. The third is odd since it is too obvious to be worth saying. No doubt there are odd sentences which, if we reflect on what makes them odd, inform us about meanings. For example, 'If it's raining, then it's not raining', or 'I do not exist', or 'I met nobody on the road – he was a nice chap'. The trouble is that, in the absence of some criterion for deciding which types of odd uses are semantically relevant, we cannot appeal to oddity in a non-circular explanation of meaning. All we can say for the moment is that *semantic* oddity is semantically revealing – but then, what is semantic oddity?

Third, it is surely the case that there are many sentences which have no standard use at all, yet whose meanings we can understand. Take the sentence 'My wife is an orange, hairy, medievalist'. I have no idea what this sentence might be used for – would it be an insult, a compliment, a straight report of fact, a metaphor, or what? Yet I know what it means, in that I am quite capable of paraphrasing it and translating it. Again, take one of the above sentences, 'Pain is the stimulation of C-fibres'. At present this has no use in scientific theory; but it might well come to have one. It would be highly implausible to suggest that it only acquires a meaning when it gains this use. On the contrary, we would want to say that it is precisely because it means what it has always meant that it can be given a use within scientific theory.

Most of the difficulties I have mentioned also appear as difficulties for a use theory of synonymy. It is clear, for example, that the uses of 'puppy' and 'young dog' are not identical. The problem is to decide which differences in uses are relevant to the synonymy or otherwise of expressions. For example, the two sentences 'This is a good clock' and 'This clock does the job it was designed to do with great precision' would no doubt be used differently – the first, mainly, to commend, and the second, mainly, to report. Does this difference show up a difference in meaning? Lacking any account of what constitutes relevant differences in use, we are in no position to answer. Again, the mere fact that two expressions *can* be used in very similar ways does not show they are synonymous. An axe and a chopper can be used in very similar ways, but that does not make an axe a chopper. We would also have to decide what are the more central, typical, or paradigmatic uses. We have not yet been told how to decide this.

As I said earlier, I believe these difficulties in the use theory can be dealt with by a sufficiently rich theory of linguistic uses. However, we must conclude for the moment that the use theory suffers from the same crippling debilitation as the other theories so far discussed – namely, circularity. Since not all aspects of use are relevant to meaning, the use theory is reduced to claiming that meaning can be explained in terms of those uses which are relevant to meaning – which is patently circular. So far we have no way of describing what these relevant uses are beyond describing them as the relevant ones. As one critic puts it:

> The notion of use, as it ordinarily exists and is understood, presupposes the notion of meaning (in its central and paradigmatic sense), and . . . it cannot therefore be used to elucidate the latter.[44]

At present, we are in no position to reply to this point. Or we may put it like this: no doubt our intuitions often tell us which uses and misuses are semantically relevant, but as yet we cannot support these intuitions by an adequate theoretical account. Further, as we saw in the 'good clock' example, our intuitions cannot always be relied upon to give us clear-cut answers. I titled this section 'The use theory of meaning'; but, in a sense, that was a misnomer, for what we have been presented with by the scattered remarks of Wittgenstein and Ryle is not a systematic account of meaning which can be called a 'theory'. Rather, as Fodor and Katz point out, it is little more than 'a recommendation that questions about meaning are to be handled as questions about the uses of words or expressions'.[45]

One final point about meaning and use: the failure of philosophers, so far, to justify the slogan 'Meaning is use' has not entirely vitiated the work of philosophers influenced by that slogan. For even if we decided that use was something distinct from meaning it may still be of immense value for philosophers to examine uses. Some philosophers, indeed, realizing the problems involved in equating meaning with use have preferred the slogan 'Don't ask for the meaning, ask for the use'.[46] They are suggesting that whatever 'meaning' might mean, the philosopher can best do his job by studying use. If meaning turns out to be use, all well and good. If it does not, that in no way impugns the value of studying use for philosophers.

This chapter has been a negative one. I hope, however, that it has done a job of clarification. We may not know what meaning is, but at least we know some of the things it is not. We have seen, too, what requirements an adequate account must meet – in particular it must avoid the circularity which has daunted each of the theories discussed in this chapter. I pointed out earlier that most of us have a fair, working grasp of meaning. It must be admitted that so far we have not improved upon that. At later stages in the book, however, I hope to show how we can arrive at something better.

Notes

1 L. Bloomfield, *Language*. Allen & Unwin, 1967. *pp* 137–38.
2 *ibid, p* 161.
3 Quoted in A. Schaff, *Introduction to Semantics*. Pergamon, 1964. *p* 59.
4 See, for example, A. J. Ayer, *Language, Truth, and Logic*. 2nd edn. Dover Books.
5 *Science and Sanity*. Lancaster, 1941. *p* vii.
6 The linguist J. J. Katz has recently urged that meanings are abstract entities (see Chapter 4 of his *The Philosophy of Language*. Harper & Row, 1966). However, I would agree with J. Lyons (*Introduction to Theoretical Linguistics*. Cambridge University Press, 1968. *p* 474) that the value of Katz's theory for linguists is independent of this aspect of the theory.
7 M. Black, *The Labyrinth of Language*. Mentor Books, 1968. *p* 203.
8 'Meaning in linguistics', in his *From a Logical Point of View*. 2nd edn. Harper & Row, 1961. *p* 49.

9 Useful accounts of some linguists' views on meaning can be found in S. Ullmann, *Semantics*. Blackwell, 1962, and J. Lyons, *Introduction to Theoretical Linguistics*. Cambridge University Press, 1968.

10 L. Wittgenstein, *Philosophical Investigations*. 3rd edn. Macmillan, 1969, on 'private languages' in Sections 256 *ff.*

11 *The Labyrinth of Language*. Mentor Books, 1968. *p* 204.

12 See H. P. Grice, 'Meaning', *Philosophical Review*, 66, 1957, 377–88. Reprinted in *Philosophical Logic*, ed P. F. Strawson. Oxford University Press, 1967.

13 See, for example, G. Ryle, 'The Theory of Meaning', in *British Philosophy in the Mid-Century*, ed C. Mace. Allen & Unwin, 1957.

14 C. Noble, 'An analysis of meaning', in *Readings in the Psychology of Language*. ed L. Jakobovits and M. Miron. Prentice-Hall, 1967. *p* 450. Originally published in *Psychological Review*, 59, 1952, 421–30.

15 'Connotation' and its twin 'denotation' have, unfortunately, been used in two quite different ways. As employed by most people, including linguists, the denotation of a word is those central, invariable characteristics expressed by it; while the connotation will include less central, more idiosyncratic characteristics. Thus, being male will be part of the denotation of 'man', while having a hairy chest will be part of the connotation. Philosophers however, following the terminology of J. S. Mill, have counted as the denotation of a word what that word may refer to; while the connotation is those properties which must be possessed by whatever is so referred to. Thus John Smith will be part of the denotation of 'man', and being male will be part of its connotation.

16 *The Meaning of Meaning*. Routledge & Kegan Paul, 1930. *p* 57.

17 *ibid, p* 92.

18 *An Essay Concerning Human Understanding*. Everyman, 1961. *p* 12. Vol 2.

19 *Philosophy in a New Key*. Harvard University Press, 1942. *pp* 60–1.

20 *An Inquiry into Meaning and Truth*. Pelican Books, 1965. *p* 180.

21 See G. Ryle, 'The theory of meaning', in *British Philosophy in the Mid-Century*, ed C. Mace. Allen & Unwin, 1957.

22 *The Blue and Brown Books*. Blackwell, 1964. *p* 37.

23 L. Wittgenstein, *Philosophical Investigations*. 3rd edn. Macmillan, 1969. *p* 217.

24 *Philosophy of Language*. Prentice-Hall, 1964. *pp* 24–5.

25 *The Blue and Brown Books*. Blackwell, 1964. *p* 37.

26 *Language*. Allen & Unwin, 1967. *p* 139.

27 Such attempts can be found in the following works, among many others: B. F. Skinner, *Verbal Behavior*. Appleton-Century-Crofts, 1957; C. Osgood, *Method and Theory in Experimental Psychology*. Oxford University Press, 1953; C. Morris, *Signs, Language, and Behavior*. Prentice-Hall, 1946, and W. V. Quine, *Word and Object*. M.I.T. Press, 1960.

28 *Linguistic Aspects of Science*. Chicago University Press, 1944. *p* 12.

29 *Signs, Language, and Behavior*. Prentice-Hall, 1946. *p* 10.

30 *ibid, p* 22.

31 I owe the example, and the argument, to M. Black, *Language and Philosophy*. Cornell University Press, 1949. *p* 174.

32 *ibid.*

33 See, for example, W. V. Quine, *Word and Object*. M.I.T. Press, 1960. He makes it clear, though, that synonymy so defined only *approximates* to the ordinary, intuitive notion.

34 'Review of B. F. Skinner's *Verbal Behavior*', in *The Structure of Language*,

ed J. Fodor and J. J. Katz. Prentice-Hall, 1964. *p* 553. Originally published in *Language*, *35*, 1959, 26–58.

35 See *The Logic of Scientific Discovery*. Hutchinson, 1959. Especially Part 1.

36 *Philosophical Investigations*. 3rd edn. Macmillan, 1969. Section 43. He does not tell us what the exceptions to the rule 'Meaning is Use' are. He may have been thinking of words like 'Peter' or 'Stalin', whose 'meanings' (*ie: rock or man of steel*) are clearly unconnected with how they are used. Imagine the short shrift a Russian would have received had he refused to use 'Stalin' to refer to the Vozhd on the grounds that he was made of flesh and not steel!

37 *ibid*, Section 20.

38 'Ordinary language', in *Philosophy and Ordinary Language*, ed C. Caton. Illinois University Press, 1963. *p* 120. Originally published in the *Philosophical Review*, *62*, 1953, 167–86.

39 See, for example, G. Ryle, 'Use, usage, and meaning', *Proceedings of the Aristotelian Society (Supplementary Volume)*, *35*, 1961, 223–29. Reprinted in *The Theory of Meaning*, ed G. Parkinson. Oxford University Press, 1968.

40 *Philosophical Investigations*. 3rd edn. Macmillan, 1969. Section 122.

41 *Semantic Analysis*. Cornell University Press, 1967. *p* 158.

42 'Ordinary language', in *Philosophy and Ordinary Language*, ed C. Caton. Illinois University Press, 1963. *pp* 115–16.

43 *The Structure of Language*, ed J. Fodor and J. J. Katz. Prentice-Hall, 1964. *p* 15.

44 J. Findlay, 'Use, usage, and meaning', in *The Theory of Meaning*, ed G. Parkinson. Oxford University Press, 1968. *p* 118. Originally published in *Proceedings of the Aristotelian Society (Supplementary Volume)*, *35*, 1961, 229–42.

45 *The Structure of Language*, ed J. Fodor and J. J. Katz. Prentice-Hall, 1964. *p* 13.

46 J. Wisdom, 'Ludwig Wittgenstein: 1934–37'. *Mind*, *61*, 1952, *p* 258.

Chapter 3

Meaning in philosophy

Views about meaning, especially in this century, have greatly influenced philosophy. Solutions to age-old problems have been encouraged, or even dictated, by views about meaning. In this chapter, I want to consider how three such views have influenced approaches to philosophical problems. I call them 'views' rather than 'theories', since none of them attempts to provide comprehensive answers to the questions about meaning which we formulated earlier. No doubt there are many other views about meaning which have been influential; here I shall consider only the three which are, perhaps, the most important.

1 Verificationism

There does exist a verificationist *theory* of meaning. It is the theory according to which giving the meaning of a sentence *is* simply describing the ways in which it would be verified. According to Moritz Schlick, a proponent of the theory:

> Whenever we ask about a sentence 'What does it mean?' . . . we want a description of the conditions under which the sentence will form a true proposition, and of those which will make it false . . . The meaning of a proposition is the method of its verification.[1]

I did not discuss this theory in the last chapter, since I think it too implausible to take seriously. One example will suffice to demonstrate its implausibility. Until fairly recently the only ways to verify that a man was in pain was to listen to what he said or screamed, or to observe his behaviour. Now, however, we can employ the extra test of observing what happens in his brain, or to the tissues of his body. If the meaning of a sentence, like 'He is in pain', was identical with its method of verification, it would follow that this sentence altered meaning with the advancement of neurology. Moreover it would continue to change meaning each time we discover some new type of verificatory test. But these implications are absurd; so we can reject the theory which has them.

Distinct from this verificationist theory of meaning, there is the *principle* of verification. This is a principle which lays down a criterion which sentences must meet if they are to be meaningful; but it does not attempt to state what the meanings of sentences are, nor what constitutes synonymy. The principle states (with qualifications to be added in a moment): for any sentence to be meaningful, it must be empirically verifiable. According to Schlick, once more, 'No sentence has meaning unless we are able to indicate a way of testing its truth or falsity'.[2] This principle is compatible with any of the three theories of meaning discussed in the last chapter. Thus, it might be that the meaning of a sentence is some complex mental item. However, according to a verificationist, in order to have this meaning, the sentence must be verifiable. It is this principle of verification that I want to discuss, and assess, in this section.

Before we can proceed, a couple of qualifications have to be made to the way I stated the principle. First, it is only *indicative* sentences which must be verifiable in order to have meaning. Commands and questions, since they are neither true nor false, cannot be verified, despite being perfectly meaningful. No doubt it would be argued that for commands, questions, etc, to be meaningful, they must be related in some systematic way to verifiable indicative sentences. Second, it is not claimed that *all* indicative sentences must be empirically verifiable. An exception is usually made for so-called 'analytic' sentences. These are sentences which we do not have to verify empirically, since we can know them to be true or false, supposedly, simply in virtue of the definitions of the component words. Examples would be 'All bachelors are unmarried', or 'Triangles have three sides'.[3] Also exceptions would have to be made for sentences like 'I promise to marry you' which do not serve to state truths, but to perform some other speech act. Let us call them 'performative' sentences.[4] The principle of verification now runs: any non-analytic, non-performative sentence must be empirically verifiable in order to be meaningful. (It might be added that 'verifiable' is being used in a wide way, so as to include 'falsifiable'.)

The implications of this principle, if acceptable, are enormous. The principle was the basic ingredient in a philosophical movement of the 1920s and 1930s known as logical positivism. It was the aim of the positivists to show that a great deal of talk which usually passes as meaningful is, in fact, meaningless. They were particularly concerned to show that many of the utterances of metaphysically orientated philosophers, and of scientists of dubious standing, were nonsense. Consider the following claims that writers have made:

[1] The nothing nothings itself.   [*M. Heidegger*]

[2] The Idea reveals itself in history.   [*G. Hegel*]

[3] All physical objects strive towards perfection.

[4] All physical events are caused by the activities of occult, mystic forces.

Let us assume that there is indeed something unacceptable about such claims. Why are they unacceptable? Not because, with the possible exception of the first, they are ungrammatical. Nor because they are self-contradictory in the way that 'All puppies are feline' is. Nor because they are straightforwardly false descriptions of the facts, like 'Most men have three legs' is. According to the positivists, such claims are, in a special way, senseless or meaningless. And they are meaningless because there is no way in which any of them can be verified or falsified by empirical observation. Genuine science, supposedly, is distinguished by the fact that its claims are capable of empirical verification. It is all the more important to spell out the senselessness of the above claims, since, not being patent nonsense, people have overlooked it. Thus it is insidious nonsense which, just because it is insidious, needs all the more to be unveiled.

It will not only be claims like these which are rendered senseless by the principle of verification. A great deal of *apparently* sensible, past philosophical debate will also be rendered senseless. Consider, for example, the debate between dualists and materialists; the first insisting that there are two quite distinct types of substance, mental and physical, and the latter insisting that there is only physical substance. Both philosophers might be in perfect agreement as to the empirical facts. Both agree that men have thoughts, feelings, etc, and that these occur at the same time as certain bodily events. There is no experiment or observation that could settle the issue between them, for their difference is over how to describe or interpret the observable facts they both admit. But if there is no empirical manner of settling the issue, then according to the positivists there is no genuine issue. Both the dualist and the materialist, since they go beyond stating what is empirically knowable, are talking nonsense.

It was not only academic philosophers who were shocked by the implications of the principle of verification. For what about religious beliefs? Many believers would admit that there can be no empirical evidence for the existence of God; and many atheists would admit that there can be none against His existence. But if so, it follows by the principle that the controversy is a nonsense one. According to one positivist, Sir Alfred Ayer, it is wrong to say that 'God exists' is true; wrong to say that it is false; and wrong to say with the agnostic that one does not know if it is true or false. What one should say is that it is meaningless.[5]

If, then, we accept the principle of verification, it follows that we must reject as senseless a vast amount of past philosophizing, and the mass of theology, as well as the patently unacceptable claims listed on *p* 47 for which, no doubt, less tears would be shed. A principle having such far-reaching implications requires careful assessment.

Before we assess the principle, it is worth glancing at some of the reasons that might be thought to justify it. There are at least three of these. First, as we have seen, there are some claims which are fairly definitely nonsense, and which are unverifiable. It is tempting to generalize from these cases, and conclude that any claim which is unverifiable will also be nonsense in this way. Second, for language to be meaningful, it must in some way relate to the observable world. A language which was incapable of telling us anything about the observable world would indeed be a hard one to imagine. Now how is it that language is able to inform us about the world? The principle of verification offers a temptingly simple answer. It is a condition of a sentence being a meaningful unit of language that it is verifiable in terms of what we observe about the world. That is, it is part of the very concept of meaningful language that it should tell us about the world. Finally, suppose a political scientist were to introduce a new term, 'glutocracy', but was quite incapable of describing the empirical characteristics of a society, which that society would have to have, to be counted as a glutocracy. One would conclude that he does not know what he is talking about. In other words, it appears as a condition that must be met by new words, and old ones used in new ways, that the users of these words can describe the empirical circumstances under which they are applicable. It is tempting to generalize from this and conclude that any sentence, to be meaningful, must be such that we can describe the empirical circumstances under which it would be true.

Let us now turn to assessment of the principle of verification. The great difficulty the positivists faced was that of stating the principle in a precise and acceptable manner, so that it would exclude as meaningless what we want to regard as meaningless, while preserving what we want to regard as meaningful. This was no easy task. In the first place, there was the problem of deciding what was meant by 'empirical', and the positivists differed on this question. According to some, a sentence like 'I see an apple falling' would describe an empirical observation. But others, less generous in their interpretation of what is observable, would claim that this sentence is one we *infer* from more direct observation-sentences. Reports of these more direct observations might be reports about colours, shapes, smells, etc, from which we then infer the existence of material objects. Or they might be reports about essentially private sense-impressions, from whose occurrence we infer the existence of outside objects like apples. We shall not let these differences concern us.[6]

For what all the positivists agreed upon was that empirical observation is what we do through the normal senses or introspection. They differed as to *what it is*, physical objects, properties, or sense-impressions, that we do observe through the senses. We need not judge on this tricky issue. Let us take the principle as claiming that a sentence is only meaningful if it can be verified through the use of the normal senses or introspection.

In the second place, and more serious, was the problem of deciding what was meant by 'verifiable'. Two things, at least, were clear. First, in saying that a meaningful sentence must be verifiable, it was not meant that it should be verifiable *in practice*. To insist upon that would be to rule out as meaningless such perfectly acceptable sentences as 'Life exists in other galaxies' or 'Caesar ate a boiled egg for breakfast on the Ides of March' – sentences which we are in no practical position to verify. So what was demanded was that meaningful sentences should be verifiable *in principle*. Provided we can describe the observations which would verify a sentence, then whether or not we are in the position of actually making the observations, it is meaningful. As one writer put it:

It must be emphasized that when we speak of verifiability we mean the *logical* possibility of verification, and nothing but this.[7]

As we shall see soon, this notion of verifiability in principle is by no means clear.

A second thing was clear, too. By 'verification' we cannot mean strict, conclusive verification amounting to proof. If I say, 'All unsuspended bodies fall', I am talking of a possibly infinite number of occurrences. So, however many times I may have observed unsuspended things falling, it is always possible that the next unsuspended thing will not fall. Again, however many times I may fail to observe a unicorn, I shall never conclusively falsify the sentence 'Unicorns do exist' by future observation. These two sentences are plainly meaningful, despite the fact that the one is not conclusively verifiable, and the other is not conclusively falsifiable. (Note that there are some sentences which are neither conclusively verifiable nor conclusively falsifiable: *eg* 'There exists a unicorn which never falls down'.) Positivists, therefore, retreated to the notion of 'weak' verifiability. It was suggested that a sentence was meaningful provided that some observations would count as *relevant evidence* for or against its truth.[8] Thus 'All unsuspended bodies fall' will be meaningful, since certainly some observations are relevant evidence for its truth. But this will not do, for what is meant by 'relevant evidence'? Presumably even the wildest metaphysician or pseudo-scientist would insist that some observations are relevant to their claims. And certainly religious believers could claim the same. The trouble is that, lacking an account of what is meant by 'relevant', we are in no position to reject these claims. Other attempts were made by positivists to tighten up the notion of weak verifiability, but it is generally admitted that none of these attempts were successful.[9] So it seemed that, while the demand for strong, strict, or conclusive verification ruled too much out, the demand for weak verification let too much in that the positivists would be loath to let in.

Of course the failure of the positivists to devise an adequate criterion does not, by itself, mean that no such criterion can be found – though it should make us sceptical about the possibility. What I wish to do now, though, is to offer some general reasons for supposing that no satisfactory statement of the principle could ever be given. The claim that all meaningful sentences must be verifiable is misguided in whatever sense of 'verifiable'. What we want is not amendment of the principle, but its exorcism.

[1] Suppose there is a civilization of the blind, and that one day a citizen stands up and says: 'There exists in each of us the potential for sensing things in a quite novel manner. If we were to sense in this way we should no longer have to rely upon touch and hearing to gauge the distance of objects from us.' If he is asked to describe these potential experiences, he cannot, of course, give any answer, since he has never had any such sense-experiences. No doubt the positivists in this civilization of the blind would accuse the man of talking meaningless nonsense. But they would be wrong. For suppose that one day, as a result of atmospheric change, each of the citizens woke up able to see. Here is the new sense predicted by the man. What he said was true, so it cannot have been senseless. However, and this is the essential point, at the time he made his prediction he was quite unable to give any sort of description of the observations that would confirm the potential for seeing. Equally, it is not senseless for me to postulate the potential for humans to sense in a manner which is at present unimaginable and indescribable. There is no reason to believe me; but I might be right.

[2] The emergence of previously indescribable sense-experiences is not the only kind of emergence that poses a problem for positivists. Take the claim, made by followers of Wilhelm Reich, that the universe is governed by 'orgone-energy'. As critics of Reich rightly point out, the orgone-energy enthusiasts do not say enough about it for us to be able to test for its presence or absence by empirical methods. To that extent, the claim is unverifiable. Suppose, though, that there occurs in the future a revolution in scientific thinking comparable to quantum physics. It may be that previously unsuspected data, totally unpredictable at present, will be unearthed. And it might be the case that the new phenomena can be explained and interpreted in the light of the little that Reichians have said about orgone-energy. After all, if someone in 2000 BC had put for-

ward a theory resembling modern quantum physics, what he said would have been quite unverifiable. He, and others, would be totally unable to describe the sorts of observations which 4,000 years later were the crucial observations in establishing quantum physics. Surely, though, it is peculiar to call his theory meaningless, since it turned out to be pretty nearly true. The point is, in the case of the Reichians and of the precocious quantum theorist, that hypotheses can be formulated which the proponents are unable to defend in terms of any imagined observational confirmation. But still, it may be that unsuspected data will be discovered, so that on reflection the data are seen to confirm the hypotheses.

The possibility of these forms of emergence cripples the notion of verifiability in principle as a test for meaningfulness. Something is verifiable in principle if, *at the time it is put forward*, it is possible to describe the possible verificatory observations. This overlooks the possibility of hypotheses being confirmed by later observations which the hypothesizers were in no position to predict. Many concepts have a so-called 'open texture'; that is, they do not allow us to specify in advance all the observations which might show that the concepts are or are not applicable.[10] So we can see that the demand for describing what observations would confirm or disconfirm a hypothesis is too strong a condition for meaningfulness. (I should add that I am in no way defending the orgone-energy theory. But I would prefer to say that it is false, rather than meaningless gibberish.)

[3] Positivists usually speak as if it was a single sentence, or a single hypothesis, that is verifiable by observation. But this is a crucial mistake. It is never a single sentence or hypothesis that is confirmed or disconfirmed in isolation from all else. It is only in conjunction with other sentences or hypotheses that a single one can come up for verification. Take the hypothesis that all unsuspended bodies fall. Suppose we observe an apple being tossed in the air, and then fail to observe it fall. Does this falsify our hypothesis? Not at all; there are plenty of alternative explanations. It might be that the apple did fall, but that we did not notice it due to bad observational conditions. Or it may be that, unknown to us, the apple was suspended by a gravitational field in the atmosphere. Now it is only if we make certain assumptions concerning the absence of interfering conditions, or the adequacy of observational circumstances, etc, that we could regard the failure to observe the apple's falling as falsifying our hypothesis. Now the failure to make the predicted observation can cast as much doubt upon these supplementary assumptions as upon the hypothesis itself. So, as W. V. Quine says, 'Our statements about the world face the tribunal of sense experience not individually but only as a corporate body.'[11]

This causes trouble for the principle of verification. The principle claims that a sentence is meaningful only if we can describe the observations which would verify it. But, as we now see, no observation need be taken as verifying a particular sentence. For we could take any observation as verifying or falsifying some supplementary hypothesis or assumption, rather than the sentence in question. Let me give an actual historical example. A geologist named Gosse claimed that the world began in 4004 BC. Apparently this is easy enough to falsify by geological and archaeological evidence. Gosse, however, preferred to treat the observations of such scientists not as falsification of Genesis, but of the various hypotheses, assumptions, and theories concerning the nature of fossils, dinosaur bones, or rocks. By doing this, he immunized his own claim against possible falsification through observation. Any recalcitrant observation would be handled, not by rejecting his claim, but by making an adjustment to some other hypothesis, or perhaps, by bringing in some completely new hypothesis concerning, say, God's having sprinkled the newly created world with dinosaur bones.

The point can be generalized: any sentence at all can be totally immunized against possible verification or falsification by handling any confirming or disconfirming observation through adjustments in our other hypotheses, or through the introduction of new hypotheses. People who treat certain sentences, like 'The world began in 4004 BC', in this way can be accused of dogmatism, stupidity, fanaticism, and intransigence. But they cannot be accused of speaking meaningless nonsense. We might express the point like this: whether or not a sentence is verifiable is partly a function of the *attitudes* people take towards it. They can decide not to make it verifiable or falsifiable. But the meaningfulness of the sentence is not similarly a function of their attitude towards it.

[4] If all our claims about the world had, as their purpose, to state verifiable facts about it, then we could criticize any claim if it fails to be verifiable. But is there any reason to suppose that it is the purpose of all claims to state something which is verifiable? We can promise, warn, encourage, and guarantee, as well as state. And within the realm of statements, is it to be supposed that each has the same function? It would seem that the positivists must admit that there is at least one statement which is meaningful, but which is neither verifiable nor analytic – namely, the statement of the principle of verification itself. If we say that the principle is sensible because it has a different sort of function from scientific hypotheses, then we have opened up the flood gates. For it is open to other philosophers, and to theologians, to insist that their statements have special functions, and may be sensible within the terms of these. A philosopher defending some thesis could argue, for example,

that his thesis serves to lend coherence to otherwise disorganized phenomena, or that it simplifies what otherwise seems complex, or that it
relieves certain mental cramps people have felt, or that it lays bare the
presuppositions of some of our talk, and so on. If his thesis does
serve such functions, then why should we condemn it as meaningless just because it is not empirically verifiable? William Alston
writes:

> If there are such entities as properties existing independent of their
> exemplifications and an omnipotent spiritual creator of the physical
> universe, there would be no reason to expect them to manifest them-
> selves in the details of our sense experience ... Again, I could not
> expect my sense experience to be any different whether other people
> are really conscious or whether they are simply intricate machines ...
> To adopt the verifiability criterion is to rule out even wondering
> whether such things are so; and it would seem that any principle that
> would prevent our recognizing the fact that a certain sort of thing
> exists is unreasonable. Thus, to show that a certain supposed assertion
> cannot be empirically tested is not to show that it is not an assertion;
> it is simply to show that it is a very different kind of assertion
> from scientific hypotheses ... And it is hardly surprising that
> metaphysics and theology should turn out to be very different from
> science.[12]

It would seem, then, that when a positivist calls sentences meaningless
he is saying little more than that they do not closely resemble scientific
hypotheses. But then why should all sentences resemble scientific
hypotheses? If, as might be said of some theological talk, utterances can
comfort, provide a picture of the universe, stimulate communal effort,
or whatever, it is difficult to deny that they must have some significance.
Only an arbitrary definition of 'meaning' in terms of verification –
which is unacceptable on other grounds – could permit us to treat all
such utterances as senseless.

It may well be that a great deal of unverifiable talk is senseless. But,
as Sir Isaiah Berlin remarks, 'A statement is unverifiable because, when
examined, it turns out to be meaningless, and not vice-versa'.[13] There is
not, in fact, likely to be any simple test, like verifiability, of meaningfulness. There is no reason to suppose that utterances which fail to be
meaningful all fail in the same way. It seems that there is no substitute
for taking different utterances on their own merits, seeing what they are
supposed to do, and whether they do it. The principle of verification –
however healthy the wielding of it may have been in philosophical dead
wood – can provide no universal and automatic means for ruling out all
that we want to rule out. Nor is any comparable principle likely to provide it either.

2 Emotivism

A philosophically influential view about meaning, especially in the fields
of ethics and aesthetics, has been the view that there is something called
'emotive meaning'. Historically, most of those who have postulated the
existence of emotive meaning have regarded meaning as a function of the
responses which utterances typically produce. Now since certain
utterances typically produce responses which could be described as
'emotional', it seems natural to conclude that these utterances have
emotive meaning.[14] Here is how one 'emotivist', Professor Stevenson,
defines 'emotive meaning' along these lines:

> The emotive meaning of a word is a tendency of a word, arising through
> the history of its usage, to produce (result from) affective responses
> in people. It is the immediate aura of feeling which hovers about a
> word . . . Because of the persistence of such affective tendencies (among
> other reasons) it becomes feasible to classify them as 'meanings'.[15]

Now, in Chapter 2, I argued against the view that meaning is a function
of responses to words; in which case the mere fact that certain words
tend to produce emotive responses does not show there is emotive meaning. However, the claim that there is emotive meaning can be stated
independently of this dubious, general view of meaning. The claim would
be this: in defining certain words, reference must be made to the emotive
attitudes typically associated with those words, whatever the nature of
this association might be. For example, it has been said that reference to
favourable, or 'pro-' attitudes must be made in explaining the meanings
of words like 'good', 'heroic', 'marvellous', 'pleasant', or 'hurrah'.
Similarly, reference to unfavourable, or 'con-' attitudes must be made
in explaining the meanings of 'bad', 'nasty', 'limey', or 'boo'. Such
words, it is claimed, are very different from words like 'triangle' or 'cat',
in whose definitions no reference to emotive attitudes need be made. It
would, supposedly, be gross blindness to think that all words are meaningful in the way that 'triangle' and 'cat' are.

Why, apart from the rejected assumption that meaning is a function
of response, have philosophers and linguists supposed that there is
emotive meaning? There are at least two reasons.

[1] There is an argument for emotive meaning that logical positivists
seem committed to giving. (Historically, emotivism was an integral part
of logical positivism.) The positivists insisted that a sentence had meaning only if it was analytic or verifiable. But, then, what about lines of
poetry? 'My love is like a red, red rose' is not analytic. And to set about
verifying it by the use of botanical instruments would seem to miss the
point of the line. More important, what about ethical utterances, like
'Stealing is bad'? This is not analytic; but nor does it seem to be em-

pirically verifiable. However hard you look at, sniff at, or listen to, a man in the act of stealing, you do not detect by the means of your senses some property called the 'badness' of the act. Certainly you cannot verify that stealing is bad in the way you can verify that stealing is the most common form of crime in the USA. If poetic and ethical utterances are neither analytic nor verifiable, it seems, by the principle of verification, that they are meaningless. Yet surely this is an absurd conclusion. One cannot dump ethics and poetry into the trash-can alongside the gibberish of some metaphysicians and pseudo-scientists. Most of the positivists realized this. Their normal manoeuvre was then to distinguish between two dimensions of meaning – 'cognitive' and 'emotive'. A verifiable sentence, like 'This rose is red', will have cognitive meaning; while poetic, or ethical utterances, though lacking cognitive meaning, nevertheless have emotive meaning. They serve to express and influence people's feelings. According to Ayer:

> In saying that a certain type of action is right or wrong, I am not making any factual statement, not even a statement about my own state of mind. I am merely expressing certain moral sentiments.[16]

Other philosophers, like Stevenson, stressed the way ethical utterances influenced the feelings of others, rather than their role in expressing the feelings of the speaker. The argument, then, is this: unless we ascribe emotive meaning to certain utterances, including ethical, they would, by the principle of verification, be meaningless. Since they are not meaningless, they must possess this emotive dimension of meaning. Naturally this argument will only greatly appeal to one who is already committed to the assumptions of logical positivism.

[2] A second argument for emotive meaning, one that is not confined to any particular philosophical outlook, runs as follows: consider the following pairs of sentences:

(a) Harry is an Englishman.
   Harry is a limey.
(b) Johann is a German.
   Johann is a kraut.
(c) Romeo and Juliet had carnal knowledge of each other.
   Romeo and Juliet made love.

Intuitively, one feels like saying that the sentences in each pair do not mean the same thing. But, equally, one feels like saying that each conveys the same factual, or 'cognitive', information. In that case, there must be some dimension of meaning other than the cognitive. For if two sentences are cognitively identical, yet differ in meaning, this can only be because there is some other type of meaning, emotive, which

distinguishes them. So, for example, 'Harry is a limey' does not mean
the same as 'Harry is an Englishman', because the former must be
defined in terms of emotive factors, but not the latter.

It is going to be of considerable philosophical importance to decide
if there is emotive meaning or not. In particular, if we follow Ayer and
Stevenson in saying that moral judgments have emotive meaning, it
seems that we are committed to some form of ethical subjectivism. For
if 'Stealing is bad' is simply a way of expressing, or influencing feelings,
it is difficult to see how it can be true or false – any more than 'hurrah' or
'boo' can be true or false. As Ayer explains, if in calling something
'good', I am merely expressing my sentiments, then

> the man who is ostensibly contradicting me is merely expressing his
> moral sentiments. So that there is plainly no sense in asking which of
> us is in the right. For neither of us is asserting a genuine proposition.[17]

So there is no accidental connection between accepting the notion of
emotive meaning and taking a subjectivist line in ethics or aesthetics. I
shall not be dealing here with the specifically ethical implications of
emotive meaning. That there are such implications, though, has partly
encouraged the hot debate over emotive meaning.[18]

Nobody, I take it, would wish to deny that many words and utterances
have emotive *force*, that they can be used to express and influence feelings. The question, though, is whether these emotive aspects of words
should be counted as part of their meanings.[19] Now in Chapter 2 we
saw how many senses of 'meaning' there were; and, no doubt, it would
not actually be false to speak of emotive meaning in some sense or other
of 'meaning'. Indeed, I mentioned the example of the word 'Cossack'
having emotional effects upon the peasants, and so we could call these
effects part of the meaning of 'Cossack'. However, I stressed that this
is not the central sense of 'meaning' we would be concerned with, and
I preferred to call it 'connotation'. The interesting question is not 'Is
there any sense of "meaning" in which we can speak of "emotive meaning"?' The interesting question is 'Should reference to emotive factors
enter into the meanings of words *in the central sense of "meaning" with
which we are concerned*?' I tried to sketch what that central sense was in
terms of what philosophers have said about meaning (*p* 19) and through
examples exhibiting the uses of 'meaning' that interested us (*p* 18).

I want to argue that there is no such thing as emotive meaning in this
central sense. Philosophers and linguists who talk of emotive meaning
have not discovered a new dimension of this central meaning, but are
using 'meaning' misleadingly to talk about what could be talked about
in better ways. It is worth noting that some philosophers who talk of
emotive meaning are aware of the non-central use of the term 'meaning'
involved. Stevenson says:

I chose the term (emotive meaning) in the spirit of choosing between two evils . . . I might have chosen a term that was wholly unfamiliar; but that would have been opaque and might have given a pretentious, technical appearance to a relatively simple distinction. So I diverted the word 'meaning' to my purpose, hoping that I had chosen the lesser evil.[20]

I want to show that Stevenson chose the greater evil – and, moreover, that the alternative need not be to employ 'pretentious, technical' terms. It seems to me that if we regard reference to emotions as explaining the meanings of some words, in the way that reference to properties explains the meanings of words like 'triangle' or 'cat', then we are in two kinds of trouble. First, I think we make the concept of meaning quite unworkable and unmanageable. Second, we should make it impossible to say some of the things we want to say, and usually do say, about meaning in its central form. So, even if it is not, strictly speaking, *incorrect* to talk of emotive meaning, I think it is most unwise, and inconvenient to do so.

The first point is this: the mere fact that a given utterance, on some occasion, produces an emotive effect upon a person is no reason for introducing reference to that effect into the meaning of the utterance. Take the sentence 'there is a green book on the shelf'. Obviously no paraphrase of this would include reference to anyone's feelings. But it is quite possible that, on some occasion, this sentence should have an emotive effect. If I am a spy whose life depends upon finding a microfilm hidden inside a green book, then hearing the sentence 'There is a green book on the shelf' might produce all sorts of hopes and fears in me. But the effects produced in me have nothing to do with the emotive meaning of the words, but with the fact that I am a spy in a precarious position. If we were to say the sentence had emotive meaning just in virtue of its effects on me, we should be committed to some extraordinary conclusions. For example, no one could ever know what that sentence means, since no one could know of all the possible effects it might have upon people. Second, the sentence would be amazingly ambiguous, since it is capable of producing the most diverse effects upon people, depending upon context.

This point, as it stands, will not worry the philosopher who insists there is emotive meaning. For he will reply that a sentence only has emotive meaning if it is *typically* associated with emotive factors. He would say that the difference between 'There is a green book on the shelf' and 'Harry is a limey' is that the latter typically expresses or influences emotive attitudes. But – and here is my second point – this is not enough to show there is emotive meaning. For there are sentences which *definitely do not* have emotive meaning which, nevertheless, typically produce emotive attitudes. Take the sentence 'There is a poisonous snake behind you'. A paraphrase of this sentence would make no reference to fear or horror; yet, presumably, an utterance of this sentence would typically produce fear and horror. Again, we do not need to suppose that the words have some special emotive meaning to explain why the sentence has this effect. The explanation is much simpler: most people hate snakes. If we did insist that reference to fear and horror should be made in giving the meaning of sentences containing 'snake', we should be in the odd position of not being able to talk of snakes without thereby exhibiting, or producing, fear and horror. This would be particularly awkward for snake-lovers, who would then have to invent some other word to apply to their beloved serpents. So, then, there is no reason to say that utterances have emotive meaning just because they may typically exhibit or influence emotive attitudes. Some further condition would be required which the emotivist has not yet given.

My third point is this: not all the uses to which language can be put can be described as cognitive or emotive. I may use words to get you to do something, rather than to make you think or feel something. I can use words to make objections, guarantees, promises, bets, and so on. Now if we are going to say there is emotive meaning just because sentences can be used to influence feelings, should we not equally speak of 'objection meaning', 'guarantee meaning', 'promise meaning', 'bet meaning', and so on, since sentences can be used to perform these various things? Must we not introduce a new dimension of meaning corresponding to every use to which words can be put? But, if we do this, the concept of meaning has become useless. For we will have entirely lost the distinction between what a sentence means, and some of the diverse uses to which it can be put. We will no longer be able to discuss the meaning of a sentence except in connection with each and every context in which it might be used in different ways. Further, any sentence will become incredibly ambiguous, since almost any sentence could, given the right contexts, be used to perform any number of functions. To include all the uses of a sentence in its meaning would be like including all the uses to which a hammer could be put in its function. But when I hit someone over the head with a hammer, I am not using it in its proper function. The only reply the emotivist could make is that there is some special reason why the emotive use of language, and not other uses, should be included in meaning So far as I know he has given no such special justification.

It is worth noting, in passing, that people may have been tempted to include various uses of sentences in their meanings because they have failed to distinguish between [1] what a man means (*ie* intends) by his words, and [2] what the words he uses mean. I can say 'When he said "It's late", he meant it was time for you to go'. This may make it look as if his using the sentence to get you to go is part of the meaning. But this is not so. No paraphrase of the sentence, or translation of it into a foreign language, would make mention of you going. It is not the words that mean you should go; but what he meant (*ie* intended) by uttering those words. Similarly we should distinguish between the emotive effects meant (*ie* intended) by a person in using certain words, and the meaning of the words themselves. (For more on this point, see section 3 of Chapter 8.)

My final, and most important point, is this: emotive meaning, if there were such a thing, would lack the most salient and essential characteristics of meaning – so it is best not to speak of emotive meaning at all. Some properties belong to a thing in virtue of the meaning of the word used to refer to it. For example, a triangle has the property of being trilateral, in virtue of what 'triangle' means. Other properties, like the redness of some triangles, do not belong to things in virtue of meaning. Now where a property belongs to something, X, in virtue of what 'X' means, it is impossible to refer to something as being X and then to deny that it has the property in question. It would, for example, be absurd to say 'This is a triangle, but it is not trilateral'. It would not be absurd, though it might be false, to say 'This is a triangle, but it is not red' since being red is not part of what 'triangle' means. This point – that one cannot deny that a thing has those properties which belong to it in virtue of meaning – shows what is an essential part of our concept of meaning. Now consider the following pairs of sentences:

(*a*) Harry is an Englishman, but he is not a male.
    Johann is a German, but he is not of any nationality.
(*b*) Harry is a limey, but I like Harry and most other Englishmen.
    Johann is a kraut, but I admire all Germans.

The first two sentences are absurd and necessarily false. They are absurd because one is denying that Harry and Johann have properties which are part of the very meanings of 'Englishman' and 'German' – those of being male, or of having some nationality. Now, if feelings of loathing, hate, disrespect, or irreverence were part of the meanings of 'limey' and 'kraut', as emotivists would claim, the second two sentences should also be absurd and necessarily false – for one would be denying of Harry and Johann what is entailed by the very meanings of one's words, namely that one loathes them, has no respect for them, etc. Yet it seems plain to me that neither of the second sentences is absurd, or necessarily false. If one calls a man a 'limey', then, no doubt, one's audience will naturally conclude that you don't like Englishmen. However, you, the speaker, can easily disclaim that this is your attitude towards the English. You could then be accused of being misleading; but you could not be accused of contradicting yourself. In other words, a person can certainly deny that he has those emotive attitudes which the audience take his words to be expressing. On the other hand, a person cannot deny what is entailed by his using words like 'triangle', namely that the things he is talking about are trilateral, etc. The connection, then, between 'limey' and certain attitudes is not at all like the connection between 'triangle' and trilateralness. If the latter connection is paradigmatically one of meaning, then it is highly misleading to regard the former connection as one of meaning. As Max Black says:

> The crucial point is that we can *understand* emotive language whether or not we are swayed by it: we don't need to share the feelings expressed in 'bitch' or 'kraut' (happily enough) in order to discern the intended force of these derogatory epithets.[21]

We could not understand 'triangle' unless we shared the view that triangles must be trilateral. Let me summarize the point: where reference to B is part of the meaning of A, one cannot say, without contradiction, 'This is an A, but not a B'. Since one *can* say things like 'He's a limey, but I like him', or 'He's heroic, but I hate heroes', attitudes such as like or dislike cannot be part of the meanings of 'limey', 'hero', etc.

I suggest, then, that [1] there are no good reasons for introducing emotive meaning, [2] that if we did introduce it, the value of the concept of meaning would be completely undermined, and [3] that talking of emotive meaning would contradict a most salient and essential feature of our concept of meaning. We can, as far as I can see, explain all that needs explaining in terms of emotive *force*, or emotive *impact*, which some words, for some reasons, acquire. We should then keep apart meaning from force or impact. I suggest, for example, that 'limey' and 'Englishman' have the same meaning (though different connotations). They differ in that people will usually employ the former only if they want to express or influence a hostile attitude towards the English. But this fact should not make us speak of the emotive meaning of 'limey', any more than the fact that 'snake' makes lots of people shiver should make us speak of 'snake' having emotive meaning. I am aware, of course, of the oddity of saying that 'limey' and 'Englishman' mean the same. But I think it sounds odd only because we are confusing different senses of 'meaning'. The oddity is more than compensated, I believe, by making clear distinctions between types of meaning, and by insisting that, in the most central sense of 'meaning', there is no such thing as emotive meaning.

Let me make this final point. It is sometimes suggested that there are some words which are indubitably emotive in meaning, whatever may be the case with the vast majority. I am thinking of words like 'hurrah' and 'boo'. Surely, it is argued, when these are uttered at theatres or dinners, they have no cognitive meaning, but serve purely to express or arouse feelings. My reply is this: it is essential to distinguish between 'hurrah' as a *word*, and *hurrah* as something we shout at the theatre. When I yell *hurrah* at the theatre, I am no more uttering the word 'hurrah' than a bee which is buzzing is uttering the word 'buzz'. The word 'hurrah' is the name of the noise we make at theatres, just as 'buzz' is the name of the noise bees make. There is all the difference between using the word, as in the sentence 'I don't like people who hurrah loudly', and making the noise *hurrah*, to show my appreciation. In the first case, I don't hurrah, but utter the word 'hurrah'. In the second case, I don't utter the word 'hurrah', but make a noise which is onomatopoetically similar to the word. It may well be that hurrahing is simply a way of expressing or arousing feelings. But the word 'hurrah' is no more emotive than the word 'buzz' is. It is useful to point this out since some philosophers, assuming that there are these indubitably emotive words, have supposed that there may be plenty of other less obviously emotively meaningful words. As far as I can see there are no words at all which have emotive meaning.

3 Paradigms and polarity

There were two types of philosophical argument which were highly influential for several years. Even when philosophers did not make explicit appeal to these arguments, much of what they had to say on such diverse topics as free will, knowledge, validity, and probability, rested upon acceptance of one or other. The arguments are usually referred to as the arguments from paradigm cases, and from polar opposites, respectively. Both arguments rest solidly upon certain views about meaning – which is why I deal with them in this chapter. Since there is considerable resemblance between both arguments, I treat them together in one section. The arguments are, I believe, fallacious – and it is generally accepted that they are fallacious. To ignore them, however, would be to ignore an important chapter in recent analytic philosophy.

A: THE ARGUMENT FROM PARADIGM CASES

Consider the following reasoning designed to show that there must be such a thing as freedom of the will: in order to understand what the expression 'act of free will' means, it is necessary to be able to point out the sorts of cases to which people would unhesitatingly apply that expression. For example, a paradigm case of a free action might be that of a young man marrying the girl he loves under no parental or social pressure. To know what 'act of free will' means one has to know that it is applicable to that sort of case, and not to the case of a man marrying when a gun is at his back. If this is so, it must be absurd to deny the existence of free will, as determinists have. For to deny free will is to deny that people ever do get married under no pressure – and this denial is palpably false. If I admit that men do get married under no pressure, but then deny there is free will, this will show that I don't know what 'free will' means.[22]

The above argument is an example of the argument from paradigm cases. The form of the argument is: if an expression can only be understood in terms of actual cases to which it is unhesitatingly applied, then that expression must be genuinely applicable. So, if 'act of free will', or 'knowledge', or 'validity' are among such expressions, then we prove very neatly that there must be acts of free will, that there is such a thing as knowledge, and that some arguments must be valid. Philosophers in the past who have denied the existence of such things have simply failed to understand the meanings of the terms. Specifically they have failed to realize that these meanings are inextricably tied to actual cases of the words' applications. Professor Flew states the argument as follows:

> If there is any word the meaning of which can be taught by reference to paradigm cases, then no argument whatever could ever prove that there are no cases whatever of whatever it is.[23]

If this form of argument is valid, then we do have a powerful tool to use against determinists, sceptics, and indeed anyone who challenges our commonsense beliefs.

Unfortunately, it is not clear what the argument is. Proponents of it alternate between speaking of the meaning of an expression being 'given in terms of paradigm cases', being 'defined in terms of paradigm cases', being 'elucidated' in terms of them, and being 'taught by reference to paradigm cases'. Now these ways of speaking are not at all equivalent; and, as we shall see shortly, it does make a considerable difference to the force of the argument which of the formulations we accept.

There are certainly some connections between the meaning of a word and paradigm cases of its application. First, one of the best ways of teaching a person what a word means is to point out to him clear-cut examples of what that word applies to. If, in teaching logic to a class of freshmen, I want to show them what 'valid argument' means, one of the best things I can do is to list some arguments which logicians unhesitatingly call 'valid'. Second, where a word is unhesitatingly applied to certain cases by people, the onus is very much upon a person who denies that the word has genuine application to demonstrate why. If he can give no reason at all why the word should not be applied as it always is, we can conclude that he does not know its meaning. So, certainly, the *presumption* must be that where a word is commonly applied to certain cases, it is correctly applied to them. It is, for example, up to the sceptic to show why 'knowledge' applies to nothing, rather than up to us to show that it does apply to some cases.

Neither of these connections between meaning and paradigm cases, however, can support the claim that where a word is applied to paradigm cases, it *must* be correct to apply it to them. In the first place, it is possible to teach a word's meaning by employing *bogus* examples; cases to which the word does not really apply at all. For example, a child may learn the meaning of 'spy' by watching the antics of actors in James Bond films, but the actors are not really spies. Again, I might learn the meaning of 'courage' by seeing certain actions; but I might, on later reflection, decide that these were not genuine cases of courage after all, but only cases of 'Dutch' courage, or of mock bravado. So one cannot conclude from the fact that 'X's meaning was learned by reference to cases A, B, and C, that 'X' must genuinely apply to them; they may all be bogus examples.

As for the second connection, while it is true that the onus is upon one who wishes to deny that a commonly applied word genuinely applies to demonstrate this, we cannot rule out the possibility that he may succeed. To take an example: in the Dark Ages most men regarded trial by ordeal as a valid method of establishing guilt or innocence. So the onus was upon those who denied the validity of trial by ordeal to prove their point. But, as we all know, they did prove their point. They showed that applications of 'valid' to trials by ordeal were not genuine or correct applications of the word.

For the argument from paradigm cases to work, and to help reach such conclusions as that there must be free will, knowledge, or validity, the connection between meaning and paradigm cases must be stronger than the two so far mentioned. For the argument to work, the following must be true: definitions of the relevant expressions must contain reference to paradigm cases of their applications. Only then would it be logically absurd to deny that the expressions genuinely apply. Only, for example, if the very definition of 'act of free will' makes reference to actual cases of actions, like some marriages, will it be a travesty of the meaning of the expression to deny that it ever applies. If paradigm cases serve only as useful teaching devices, then it will not be absurd, though it may be false, to deny that the words taught through them have genuine application.

The question is: are expressions defined in terms of paradigm cases? It seems that there may be some expressions which are defined in this way. It is often suggested, for example, that 'metre' means 'length of the standard bar kept hermetically sealed in Paris'. Here the word is defined in terms of a specific object to which it refers. Given this, it would be absurd, rather than false, to deny that the standard bar itself is a metre in length. Or take the word 'Romantic' as used in literary studies. It is arguable that this word just means Keats, Shelley, Byron, etc. Anyone who did not know that Keats, etc were to be called 'Romantics' would not know what the word meant. Other possible examples are words which express the so-called 'simple' properties – like 'red', 'green', or 'sweet'. It has been argued that such expressions cannot be given verbal definitions at all, since they are not analysable. Asked what 'red' means a person can do little more than refer to examples of red things. If this is so, no conflict can arise between how people apply the words, and the definitions they give of them. If the only test of what 'red' means is to see what it applies to, then it would seem absurd to deny that it has any application.

The trouble is that expressions like these are the exception rather than the rule. It is not true that most expressions are defined in terms of examples of their application. Certainly it does not seem to be true of the important expressions like 'act of free will', 'knowledge', or 'validity'. If it is possible to define a word without making reference to paradigm cases, then it is not clear why the word *must* apply. For it is always logically possible that nothing at all falls under the definition of the word. To illustrate this, consider the word 'miracle'. In earlier times, in some societies, the word 'miracle' was unhesitatingly applied to violent storms, or superabundant harvests. However, it is perfectly possible to deny that the storms or the harvests were miracles. It is possible because 'miracle' means 'act of divine intervention'; and it is possible that there are no genuine cases of divine intervention. However commonly people may have called things 'miracles', they may have been wrong in their beliefs; beliefs which are encapsulated in the use of the word 'miracle'. No doubt the word had a use in such societies, and served to refer people to events like storms and harvests; and so, even for an atheist, it might be useful and convenient to speak of these events as 'miracles'. Still, one can perfectly well refuse to accept the natives' interpretation of what they call 'miracles'; and to the extent that one does refuse this, it is perfectly sensible to say that 'miracle' has no genuine application.[24]

It is surely the case that philosophically interesting terms like 'act of free will', and 'knowledge', are not defined in terms of paradigm cases. 'Act of free will' means (roughly) 'act which the agent could have avoided'. It might turn out that there are no acts which people can avoid; and if so, it would be sensible to deny that there are acts of free will. The art of the determinist, indeed, consists in trying to show that, in a perfectly good sense, nothing is avoidable. No doubt the onus is very much upon him to show this, and the fact that people do unhesitatingly speak of some actions being avoidable is evidence against him – but it does not clinch the case against him. The general point is this : what makes a word genuinely applicable is that there are cases falling under some description that appears in the definition of the word. It is this, and not the mere fact that people do unhesitatingly apply the word, that makes it genuinely applicable. Let us leave the final word to Professor Watkins:

> The specification ... of the expression now comes first, and the satisfying examples (if indeed there are any) follow ... The possibility will remain that the alleged paradigm examples were bogus ones which did not fit the specification.[25]

So it seems that the argument from paradigm cases cannot serve as the neat and powerful weapon with which to repel attacks upon our commonsense.

B: THE ARGUMENT FROM POLAR OPPOSITES[26]

Consider the following reasoning designed to show that, despite the claims of the sceptic, there must be such a thing as *knowledge* of empirical matters of fact: sceptics have often claimed that empirical truths can only be probable, but never certain. However, this is to overlook that the word 'probable' is in polar opposition to the word 'certain'. We call some things 'probable' precisely to contrast these cases from those which we can call 'certain'. If this is so, then we cannot say that *all* empirical truths can only be probable; for we would thereby lose the point of calling them 'probable', which is to contrast them with others which we call 'certain'. By refusing to call any truths 'certain' we deprive 'probable' of sense. As Professor Malcolm puts it:

> It is essential to the meaning of 'probable' and 'highly probable' that probability is contrasted with certainty ... if the application of 'certain' to empirical statements was abolished, the word 'probable' would also cease to apply to them.[27]

So sceptics who deny that we can attain certainty in empirical matters are saying something necessarily false, or perhaps senseless.

The form of the above argument is as follows: often two words, 'A', and 'B', are polar opposites, in that the one word only has sense by way of contrast with the other. Where this is so, it must be false to insist that there are no A's, or no B's, for to deny that 'A' has application is to deprive 'B' of its sense and function, and vice-versa. Many arguments of this form have been used in philosophy. An early example is Leibniz's claim, at the beginning of his *Monadology*, that some things must be simple if other things are complex – for it would make no sense to call something 'complex' except by way of contrast with calling others 'simple'. Again, it has been argued that not all actions can be determined, since the sense of calling an action 'determined' consists in contrasting it with those that can be called 'free'.[28] Finally, it has been argued that those philosophers of history who insist that all historical research is subjective in nature, are saying something absurd. For it only makes sense to call some research 'subjective' if we can call other research 'objective'.[29]

Several problems arise for this argument from the extreme vagueness with which it is usually stated. The first is this: when it is said that certain words are polar opposites, what sort of opposites are they, for there are certainly different sorts? In the case of some sorts of opposites, it is not even faintly plausible to suggest that each of the words in the pairs *must* have application. Take, for example, the pair 'secular' and 'spiritual'. It would be silly to argue that since, in some society, men perform secular jobs, others must perform spiritual ones. The society might be quite Godless. It is also necessary to distinguish between pairs of words like 'heads'/'tails', or 'odd'/'even', which are exhaustive, and pairs like 'good'/'bad', or 'hot'/'cold' which are not exhaustive. What I mean is that whereas a coin must either be heads or tails, and a whole number either odd or even, it is not the case that an action must be either good or bad, or that water must be either hot or cold. Now if two opposites are of this latter, non-exhaustive sort, it need not be at all plausible to insist that each of them has genuine application in some field. It is this consideration that partly vit...tes Malcolm's argument to the effect that some beliefs must be certain if others are probable. It might be that no beliefs are certain, but that 'probable' can still function to contrast some cases from others – from those which are doubtful, improbable etc. A belief need no more be either certain or probable than water need be either hot or cold. And just as 'hot' could distinguish some water from other water which was lukewarm, even if none of it was cold, so 'probable' could distinguish some beliefs from others, even if none of them were certainly true.

A second problem arising from vagueness of statement is this: what is the field of application that is meant, when it is said that each of two polar opposites must have application? If we take certain fields of application, it will not be at all plausible to say that each of two opposites must have application within *them*. For example, 'hard'/'soft' are opposites; yet it would be absurd to argue that since some emeralds are hard, other emeralds must be soft. Within the field of emeralds, that is, there is no reason to suppose that both 'hard' and 'soft' must apply. The failure to see this point has vitiated several instances of the argument from polar opposites. Recall the claim that some historical research must be objective if other historical research is to be described as 'subjective'. Now it may be that if some research is subjective, other research must be objective – but why should the distinction be found within the field of *historical* research? It might be the case that the objective methods which characterize research in physics or chemistry are never found in historical research. This point also vitiates Malcolm's argument about certainty. Even if we admitted that some beliefs must be certain if others are sensibly to be described as 'probable', why should the distinction be found in the field of empirical beliefs? It might be argued that the certainty of mathematical truths never characterizes empirical beliefs. So just because there is a distinction between certainty and probability does not mean that the distinction is to be found in the limited field of empirical beliefs rather than in some wider field of beliefs.

The two above objections do not hit at the principle underlying arguments from polar opposites, but rather at certain uses of it which have been vitiated by the failure to make the distinctions noted. There is a strong objection to be made against the whole style of argument, however, and it is not dissimilar from the one levelled against the argument from paradigm cases. I illustrated the objection to the latter argument by considering the word 'miracle'. I shall illustrate the present objection by taking the pair 'natural'/'supernatural'. Someone might argue: since 'natural' and 'supernatural' are polar opposites, then it can make no sense to say that all events are natural, for it would make sense only by way of contrast to those events which are supernatural. I feel that few scientists would be impressed by this *a priori* attempt to show that scientific knowledge cannot be all-embracing – and quite rightly so. It may well be true that a person cannot understand the meaning of 'natural', unless he also understands the meaning of 'supernatural'. It in no way follows, though, that 'supernatural' must genuinely apply to any events. 'Supernatural' means (roughly) 'type of event inexplicable by the sciences, now or ever'; and it may just be the case that there are no such events. No doubt the point of calling events 'natural' in the past was to distinguish them from those *believed* to be supernatural. But that belief may just have been false. If so, the statement 'All events are natural' is certainly sensible, and may well be true.

For the argument from polar opposites to work, it is not enough that polar terms must be understood in terms of one another. It must also be the case that one of the words is defined in terms of actual cases of the application of the other. Only then could it be absurd to say that the first word alone has application. Now there is no reason to suppose that many polar opposites are like this. We have already seen that 'natural' is not defined in such a way that it entails the existence of supernatural events. Nor, as far as I can see, do the definitions of 'probable', or 'determined' include reference to actual cases of the applications of 'certain' and 'free' respectively. It may well be that a person only understands 'determined' if he knows what it would be like for an action to be free – but it does not follow that any action actually is free. If we decided that all actions are determined, this would no doubt remove part of the point of calling any of them 'determined' – but it would not make it false, or senseless, to call all of them 'determined'.

There are in fact some polar opposites which are such that if one term has application, so must the other. For example, if some dogs are mongrels, then other dogs must be, or must have been, pedigrees, since 'mongrel' means 'mixture of pedigrees'. Again, if some people are parents, others must be children. These, however, are special cases; and there is no reason to suppose that all polar opposites are like these, including philosophically interesting ones like 'certainty'/'probability', or 'determined'/'free'.

The arguments from paradigm cases, and from polar opposites, involve the same mistake – that of illicitly generalizing from what is only true of certain, special cases. It is true that some words, like 'metre', can be defined in terms of instances of their application – but it should not be supposed that this is true of many words, including philosophically interesting ones. And we have just seen that the application of some polar terms entails the application of their opposites – but this cannot be generalized. In the vast majority of cases, words have application not *because* they are unhesitatingly applied to paradigms, not *because* their opposites entail such application, but because there are cases falling under the descriptions involved in their definitions.

Professor Gellner called these two arguments two of the pillars of linguistic philosophy.[30] This is an exaggeration; linguistic philosophy has not tumbled down as a result of rejecting the arguments. But it is no exaggeration to say that a great deal of fairly recent philosophizing has been vitiated by reliance, explicit or implicit, upon the arguments. With this I conclude my discussion of how doctrines about meaning have influenced philosophy. None of these doctrines have been correct; but the philosophical research they stimulated has been fruitful. We might hope that this research will be even more fruitful once we lay bare the faults in these doctrines about meaning. We shall see, in fact, how some preferable views about meaning have heavily influenced philosophy in section 2 of Chapter 8.

Notes

1 'Meaning and verification', in *Theory of Meaning*, ed A. and K. Lehrer. Prentice-Hall, 1970. *p* 100. Originally published in *Philosophical Review*, 45, 1936, 339–69.
2 *ibid*, *p* 103.
3 The difficult question of analytic truth will be discussed in Chapter 7.
4 Performative sentences will be discussed as part of the theory of speech acts in Chapter 8.
5 *Language, Truth, and Logic*. 2nd edn. Dover Books. Chapter VI.
6 For discussions of these issues, see *Logical Positivism*, ed A. J. Ayer. Free Press, 1959.

7 M. Schlick, 'Meaning and verification', in *Theory of Meaning*, ed A. and K. Lehrer. Prentice-Hall, 1970. *p* 108.

8 See Ayer's Introduction to *Language, Truth, and Logic*. 2nd edn. Dover Books.

9 For detailed arguments against various positivist attempts to state a coherent notion of weak verifiability, see I. Berlin, 'Verification', *Proceedings of the Aristotelian Society, 39*, 1938–39, 225–48. Reprinted in *The Theory of Meaning*, ed G. Parkinson. Oxford University Press, 1968, and G. Hempel, 'Empiricist criteria of cognitive significance', in his *Aspects of Scientific Explanation*. Free Press, 1965.

10 For the important notion of 'open texture', see F. Waismann, 'Verifiability', *Proceedings of the Aristotelian Society (Supplementary Volume), 19*, 1945, 119–50.

11 'Two dogmas of empiricism', in his *From a Logical Point of View*. 2nd edn. Harper & Row, 1961. *p* 41.

12 *Philosophy of Language*. Prentice-Hall, 1964. *p* 81.

13 'Verification', in *The Theory of Meaning*, ed G. Parkinson. Oxford University Press, 1968. *p* 34.

14 This seems to be the view of C. K. Ogden and I. A. Richards, *The Meaning of Meaning*, Routledge & Kegan Paul, 1930, J. R. Firth, *The Tongues of Men*. Watts, 1937, and C. L. Stevenson, *Ethics and Language*. Yale University Press, 1944.

15 *Facts and Values*. Yale University Press, 1963. *pp* 21–2.

16 *Language, Truth, and Logic*. 2nd edn. Dover Books. *p* 107.

17 *ibid, p* 108.

18 It is said that more traditional Oxford dons in the 1930s would refuse to dine with a certain Logical Positivist because of what they took to be his total amorality.

19 It should certainly not be *assumed*, as it is by several linguists, that these features are best treated as part of meaning. The German pioneer, K. O. Erdmann, for example, simply assumes that the 'feeling-tone' of words is one of the three dimensions of meaning. See *Die Bedeutung des Wortes*. Leipzig, 1925. His view is discussed in S. Ullmann, *Semantics*. Blackwell, 1962.

20 *Facts and Values*. Yale University Press, 1963. *p* 163.

21 *The Labyrinth of Language*. Mentor Books, 1968. *pp* 134–35.

22 For this argument, see A. Flew, 'Divine omnipotence and human freedom', in *New Essays in Philosophical Theology*, ed A. Flew and A. MacIntyre. Macmillan, 1955.

23 'Philosophy and language', in *Essays in Conceptual Analysis*, ed A. Flew. Macmillan, 1963. *p* 19.

24 For a similar point, see A. J. Ayer, 'Philosophy and language', in *Clarity is Not Enough*, ed H. D. Lewis. Allen & Unwin, 1963.

25 J. W. N. Watkins, 'A reply to Professor Flew's "Comment"', *Analysis, 18*, 1957, *p* 42.

26 For a fuller discussion of this argument, see my 'Polar opposites', *Methodology and Science, 1*, 1969, 1–12.

27 'Certainty and empirical statements', *Mind, 51*, 1942, *p* 38.

28 See for example J. L. Austin, *Sense and Sensibilia*. Oxford University Press, 1962, where he argues that words like 'determined' or 'forced' 'wear the trousers', and lend sense to the word 'free'.

29 For this argument, see C. Blake, 'Historical objectivity', *Mind, 64*, 1955, 61–78.

30 E. Gellner, *Words and Things*. Gollancz, 1959.

Chapter 4

Reference and predication

If language is to be used to communicate about the world, it is not enough that our words have meaning. We require, too, that some of the words can be used to refer to things around us, and that others can be used to describe what there is around us. I could devise a 'language' in which each symbol was defined in terms of other symbols. But if none of these referred to anything beyond other expressions, my 'language' would be useless for communicating about the world. To understand language, then, it is just as necessary to understand reference and predication as it is to understand meaning. Indeed, it is arguable that reference and predication are the most basic tasks to which language is put. For the simplest type of sentence we commonly employ is one in which we first refer to something, and then describe what we have referred to. When I say 'Mother is coming', or 'London is foggy', I first refer, and then I predicate.

The notion of reference, in particular, has always fascinated linguists, logicians, and philosophers. The linguist studies it as he must study any pervasive feature of language. The logician studies it, not only because he must be interested in pervasive features of natural languages if his artificial ones are to be of relevance, but also because of the numerous 'paradoxes of reference', of which more later. Philosophers are interested in reference for other reasons. In referring, words relate directly, so to speak, to the world; and any thesis about reference is also going to be a thesis about what there is in existence to refer to. To deny, for example, that 'the average man', or 'virtue', refer is to deny that there exist such entities as the average man or the universal, virtue. In the last chapter we saw how a whole philosophical school, logical positivism, was founded upon a doctrine about meaning. In this century it is equally the case that philosophical schools have been founded upon doctrines about reference – particularly so-called 'logical atomism', which we shall return to.

In the first section I consider some of the paradoxes which have persuaded some philosophers to deny what seems to be the obvious – namely that reference is a common, pervasive feature of our language. Bertrand Russell, in particular, argued with great plausibility that we rarely, if ever, refer with our words. And he, and others, have followed up such a denial with some startling metaphysical conclusions. I hope to show that these doubts about reference are unfounded, and in section 2 discuss the nature of reference in detail. What, quite, is it for a person to refer to something? In section 3 I consider a particularly important class of referring expressions – proper names. These may be the paradigms of referring expressions, but they are peculiarly tricky to understand. Finally, in section 4, I discuss reference's stable-mate – predication. When I say 'Mother is coming', I use 'Mother' to refer to someone; but what about '. . . is coming'? Again, we shall see that some odd results can be reached if we do not properly understand the role of predicates.

1 Does reference take place?

First, a note on terminology. I shall speak of 'referring expressions'. Among these are 'John Smith', 'London', 'the present Queen of England', 'the girl I like', 'his mother', and 'she'. Since it is the purpose of this chapter to decide just what a referring expression is, it is not simple or convenient to fix upon any sharp definition for the moment. It is best to think of referring expressions in terms of my examples of them, and by way of contrast to other, non-referring expressions, such as 'if', 'happy', or 'a queen'. These expressions either make no possible pretence at referring, or do not serve to pick out just one thing or person. When I say that 'a queen' does not serve to pick out one person, I mean that a man could say 'a queen is dead' without having any idea which queen it is. It is the role of the expression 'the queen', however, to pick out one person the speaker has in mind. More of this distinction between *the* and *a* later. I shall call anything supposedly referred to by a referring expression, a 'particular'. Thus if my mother is being referred to by the expression 'mother', she is the particular referred to. It should be noted that some philosophers have used 'proper name' instead of 'referring expression'. But it is surely wiser, because more in conformity with usage, to restrict 'proper name' to a certain subclass of referring expressions – those which, like 'John Smith' or 'London', always appear capitalized. These will be discussed in section 3. In this section, and the next, I shall be concerned with expressions of the form '*the* so-and-so'. Let us call them 'descriptive referring expressions'.

It would seem plain that there are any number of genuine descriptive referring expressions serving to pick out particulars. But it needs to be said, straight away, that some expressions which have the *form* of referring expressions are not ones of this sort at all. Consider the following sentences:

[1] The average man has 2·3 children.
[2] The whale is a mammal.
[3] The non-existent is non-existent.

When a person says the average man has 2·3 children he does not mean to refer to some strange man who has two children, and one-third of another child, in his family. Rather he means to be talking of all men, and of the ratio between these and all children. Again, if I say that the whale is a mammal, I am probably not talking about a particular whale in the Miami Seaquarium. What I say is a stylistic variant of 'All whales are mammals', or 'If anything has the property of being a whale, it has the property of being a mammal.' Finally, when I say that the non-existent is non-existent, I am not referring to a particular object, named 'non-existent'. Obviously there could be no such object; for if there were, it would not be non-existent. What I say is, rather, a stylistic variant of 'Whatever does not exist, does not exist'.[1]

So it would be going too far to suppose that expressions of the form 'the so-and-so' always serve as referring expressions. Still, it would seem that expressions of this form very often do serve to refer. Some philosophers, however, have argued that this is not so; that expressions rarely, if ever, serve to refer. Such philosophers would insist that 'the queen of England' or 'my mother' are no more referring expressions than 'the average man' or 'the non-existent'. These arguments are to be found at their strongest in some writings of Bertrand Russell.[2] The arguments have the form: if we treat the vast majority of expressions of the type 'the so-and-so' as referring expressions, we find ourselves entangled in intolerable paradoxes. The only sensible escape from the paradoxes is to deny that these expressions are referring ones.

What are the paradoxes Russell thinks we shall be involved in if we treat most 'the so-and-so' expressions as referring? There are at least three of them.

[1] Suppose I say 'The first man born in a light bulb does not exist'. What I say is surely true. But if 'The first man born in a light bulb' is a referring expression, I can be asked 'To whom are you referring?' I cannot reply that I am referring to the first man born in a light bulb; for I should then be contradicting myself if I go on to say that this man does not exist. In general, that is, I can only claim to be referring to A if I believe that A exists; but if I do believe this, I cannot then say that he does not exist. Nor can I reply to the question 'To whom are you referring?' by saying that I am referring to no one. For then I should be

trying to say something about nothing at all; and it is mad to try to say anything about nothing at all. I cannot, in general, say 'I am not referring to anything, and by the way, the following is true of what is not there to refer to . . .'. So on the assumption that 'The first man born in a light bulb' is a referring expression, it follows either that I am contradicting myself, or that I am talking gibberish, when I say of him that he does not exist.

[2] Suppose I say, 'The present king of France is bald'. Plainly this is not true, for there is no present king of France to be bald. But nor is the denial of this sentence true, for there is no present king of France to have hair. Yet, if 'The present king of France' were a referring expression, then surely it would be either true or false of what is referred to that he has hair. To deny this would be to deny the law of the excluded middle, on one plausible reading of that law (either something has a property or it does not have that property). I cannot say that I am referring to no one; for then I should be insane to try to say of no one either that he was bald or that he had hair.

We could present this paradox in a different way. According to Russell, anything we say is either true, false, or meaningless. If 'The present king of France' is a referring expression, it must be either true or false of what is referred to that it has hair, or it must be meaningless to say it has hair. We have already seen that it is neither true nor false. Now surely it is not meaningless, in any sense of 'meaningless' we have encountered. So, then, 'The present king of France' cannot be a referring expression at all.

It might be thought that this argument only shows that an expression like 'The present king of France' is not a referring one. But what about 'The present Queen of England'; since there is such a person, why cannot this expression be a referring one? The answer is as follows: if I say 'The present queen of England is bald', the *meaning* of what I say is the same whether or not there actually exists such a queen. If she had died just previous to my uttering the sentence, this sad fact would not alter the meaning of my sentence. Now if she had died, if there was no longer a queen, then by Russell's argument concerning the king of France, the expression 'The queen of England' could not be a referring one. If it were, it would have to be true or false of the person referred to that she is bald; but it isn't, since there is now no such person. Now if 'The queen of England' is not a referring expression when there is no queen, nor can it be one when there is a queen – since the meaning of the expression is the same in either case.

In general, if 'The A' is not a referring expression when there is no A, nor is it a referring expression when there is an A, since 'The A' means the same in either case.[3]

[3] The third paradox is stated clearly by Russell himself:

> If *a* is identical with *b*, whatever is true of the one is true of the other, and either may be substituted for the other in any proposition without altering the truth or falsehood of that proposition. Now George IV wished to know whether Scott was the author of *Waverley*; and in fact Scott *was* the author of *Waverley*. Hence we may substitute *Scott* for *the author of 'Waverley'*, and thereby prove that George IV wished to know whether Scott was Scott. Yet an interest in the law of identity can hardly be attributed to the first gentleman in Europe.[4]

Russell's point is this: if both '(The) A' and '(The) B' refer to the same particular, it cannot make any difference to the truth value of what we say which of the expressions we employ. However, it is possible to turn a true sentence, like 'George IV wished to know if Scott was the author of *Waverley*', into a false one simply by replacing one apparently referring expression, 'the author of *Waverley*', by another, 'Scott'. Hence it cannot be the case that both expressions really are referring expressions; for, to repeat, if they were it could make no difference to the truth of a sentence which of them we employed. (The principle, incidentally, that it can make no difference to the truth of what we say which of two referring expressions having the same reference we employ, is often known as 'Leibniz's law'. The defence of it, presumably, is that since the names we give a thing can make no difference to any other facts about it, it cannot matter which of the names we use.)

There, then, are three of the paradoxes which supposedly arise if we insist on treating 'The so-and-so' expressions as referring. If we do insist upon this then, to summarize, we shall have to deny [1] that sentences of the form 'The so-and-so does not exist' can ever be true [paradox 1], [2] the law of the excluded middle [paradox 2], [3] the principle that whatever we say is either true, false, or meaningless [paradox 2], and [4] Leibniz's law [paradox 3]. Certainly there have been philosophers who have been willing to deny each of these, rather than give up the view that 'The so-and-so' expressions are referring ones. Russell, though, prefers what might well seem the less expensive course of giving an alternative analysis of apparently referring expressions which reveals that they are not referring expressions at all. This analysis is usually called 'Russell's theory of descriptions'. I shall first state the theory; then remark upon its salient characteristics; then show how it is meant to solve the above paradoxes; and finally show how it paves the way for an elaborate metaphysical view of the universe.

According to Russell's theory, the correct analysis of 'The king of France is bald' is: there exists one and only one entity which is a king of France, and which is bald. More generally, any sentence of the form

'The A is B' is to be analysed as: there exists one and only one entity which is an A, and which is B.[5] We can describe what is done by such an analysis in a variety of ways. In the first place, no expressions occur in the analysis which are even *apparently* referring ones. No longer do we have expressions of the form '*The* so-and-so'; for note that in the analysis of 'The king of France is bald', we no longer have the expression '*The* king', but the general term '*A* king', which is not even a referring expression in appearance. We might express what has happened in a different way. In the analyses, apparently referring expressions give way to expressions which express properties, not particulars. We could have written out Russell's analysis of our sentence in the following form: there exists one and only one entity which has the property of being a French king, and which also has the property of being bald. So what Russell is saying is that sentences which apparently serve to refer to particulars are really assertions about properties; assertions to the effect that certain properties are or are not to be found instantiated in the world. We saw earlier that the sentence 'The whale is a mammal' is a concealed statement about properties. According to Russell, it turns out that, in a more subtle way, all sentences containing 'The so-and-so' expressions are concealed statements about properties, and how they are combined in the world.

What is gained by such an analysis? Supposedly, that each of the paradoxes can now be dissolved. Let us take them one by one:

[1] 'The first man born in a light bulb does not exist' becomes 'There does not exist one and only one entity which is a man, and which was first to be born in a light bulb'. In the analysis there is no expression, 'The first man . . .', of which we can ask 'To whom does it refer?' So we are not forced into saying that we are referring to someone, but that the someone does not exist. Nor are we forced to say that we are referring to nothing, and therefore are trying to talk about nothing. On Russell's account, we are talking about properties, and asserting quite truly that these properties are not found instantiated in the world – for it is not the case that anything has the property of having been born in a light bulb.

[2] Russell, as we have seen, analyses 'The king of France is bald' into 'There exists one and only one entity which has the property of being a French king, and which is bald'. Now this sentence is straightforwardly false, since there is nothing which has the property of being a French king. So we avoid having to say that the sentence is neither true, nor false, and so meaningless, as we had to say when we treated 'The king of France' as a referring expression.

[3] Russell analyses 'George IV wished to know if Scott was the author of *Waverley*' into (roughly) 'George IV wished to know if there was one

and only one entity which wrote *Waverley*, and who was Scott'. In this analysis, there does not appear an expression like '*The* author of *Waverley*'; no expression, that is, for which we could substitute 'Scott'. It was only where there was such an apparent referring expression that we could transform George IV's query into the imbecile one as to whether Scott was Scott. It would seem, then, that if Russell's analyses are correct, they do provide us with the most simple way of dissolving the paradoxes raised by the assumption that 'the so-and-so' expressions refer.

Before we assess Russell's theory of descriptions, it is worth glancing at the metaphysical directions in which such a theory can push us, and in which Russell allowed himself to be pushed. During the First World War, Russell elaborated a philosophical system which he called 'logical atomism'. At least one of the main influences behind this system was the theory of descriptions. Let us see how this is so. One implication of what Russell says is that any *genuine* referring expression *cannot fail to refer*. We saw that 'The queen of England' is not a genuine referring expression, since although there is a queen of England, there does not *have* to be in order for the expression to be used meaningfully. Since it can be used meaningfully in the absence of a queen, it is no more a referring expression than 'The king of France,' and is to be analysed into a statement about properties when it appears in a sentence like 'The queen of England is bald'.

So the question 'What genuine referring expressions are there?' becomes the question 'What expressions are such that they cannot, logically cannot, fail to refer?' It is no easy matter to find any. For example, 'The desk in front of me' will not qualify; since it is logically possible that I am deluded, and that no actual, physical desk is there at all – yet still the expression can be used meaningfully. According to Russell

> The only words one does use as names [*ie* referring expressions] in the logical sense are words like 'this' or 'that'.[6]

He adds immediately, however

> It is only when you use 'this' quite strictly to stand for an actual object of sense, that it is really a proper name [*ie* referring expressions].[7]

He means this: when I use 'this' in 'this is white' to refer to something in the outside physical world, I may fail, for I may be mistaken as to the existence of anything in the outside world. It is only when I use 'this' to refer to my sensation, or 'sense-datum', of white that I cannot fail to refer. For, according to arguments popular from Descartes on, I cannot be mistaken about the nature of my own experiences. If I think I am having a white sense-datum, then I *am*, however wrong I may be about the relation between it and the outside world. So, according to

Russell, it is only if 'this' is meant to refer to a sense-datum, that it cannot fail to refer; and, therefore, only then can it qualify as a referring expression.

Now recall that a particular was defined as what is referred to by a genuine referring expression. So it follows that the only particulars in the universe are sense-data, since only these are what genuine referring expressions refer to. Apart from sense-data, the only things which exist will be the properties which sense-data have – whiteness, sweetness, etc. What, then, has become of the familiar world of material objects – tables, dogs, human bodies? Don't they exist? Russell does not want to deny, in any straightforward manner, that these exist; but nor does he want to say that they do. Instead he speaks of them as being 'logical fictions'. He seems to mean the following: talk of the average man can be regarded as shorthand. for talking about actual men. There is no average man over and above actual men. To that extent the average man is a fiction; it is useful to treat him *as if* he existed. Somewhat similarly, says Russell, talk about material objects is mere shorthand for talk about our private sense-data, and their properties. For if Russell is right in what he has said so far, all we can directly talk about are sense-data and properties; so anything else we talk about must ultimately be understood in terms of the sense-data and properties. Men, tables, and mountains, therefore, have no existence over and above sense-data and properties; and to that extent they are, like the average man, fictions. Real men stand to sense-data as average men stand to real men. Russell employs the term 'logical atom' to apply to those entities which cannot be analysed any further, but in terms of which all else is ultimately reducible. Since talk about anything is reducible to talk about sense-data and properties, these are the logical atoms of the universe. [8]

We have arrived at a theory highly reminiscent of the empirical idealism of Berkeley and Hume, according to whom all our knowledge about the world is reducible to our knowledge of the 'simple ideas' of experience. Only we have reached these conclusions, not as they did, by reflecting upon the nature of our psychology, but by reflecting upon some facts about the nature of linguistic reference. No wonder Russell is able to say:

> The point of philosophy is to start with something so simple as not to seem worth stating, and to end with something so paradoxical that no one will believe it. [9]

Of course, it is not the theory of descriptions alone which leads us to logical atomism. Russell puts the theory in harness with a theory of perception that can be, and has been, severely criticized. Still, it has been worth showing how a doctrine about reference can play its role in the development of a broad philosophical system.

The fact that Russell's theory pushes us into somewhat bizarre directions provides added impetus for examining the adequacy of his account of reference. I hope to show that his arguments against the commonsense view of reference are unfounded. In this section I do not try to show that Russell's analyses of 'The so-and-so' expressions are false; but I do try to show that the motivation behind these analyses is unwarranted. The motivation was the three paradoxes discussed. It seems to me that, given the right assumptions, these are not paradoxes at all, in which case the grounds for Russell's denial of commonsense, and for his theory of descriptions, are completely eroded.

What are the faulty assumptions behind Russell's views? First, he assumes throughout that it is *expressions* which refer if anything does. However, it is not expressions, strictly speaking, which refer, but *we* who refer with the use of expressions. Consider the word 'he'. It cannot be said that this word refers to any particular person, for it can be used to refer to any number of different people on different occasions. I may use it at 2.30 pm to refer to Hercules; you may use it at 2.40 pm to refer to Attila the Hun. The significance of this point is as follows: if we insist that it is expressions that refer, and then discover that a given expression refers to nothing at all, it seems we must deny that it is a referring expression – since it cannot both refer and not refer. Indeed, on Russell's faulty assumption it is sufficient to rule an expression out as a referring one if it *might* fail to refer – as we saw in the case of 'The queen of England'. Once we stress that it is *we* who refer, we do not face the same difficulty. For we can say that an expression is a referring one provided that it *could* be used by us to refer. This does not mean that we must, on every occasion of its use, succeed in referring to anything. If I use 'The present king of France' today, I fail to refer to anyone. However, it is an expression capable of referring, and persons using it in 1660 were referring to someone with it, Louis XIV. A hammer need not have been used to drive in nails in order to be a hammer; it is enough that it is designed so that it could. Equally an expression can be a referring one provided it could be used to refer, regardless of whether or not it always, or ever, is used to refer.

A second faulty assumption of Russell's is that any sentence is either true, or false, or meaningless. A sentence *per se*, taken in abstraction from the context in which it was uttered, is neither true nor false. The sentence 'I am bald', *per se*, is not true or false; since it might be uttered by one man to say something true, and by another to say something false. It is only the sentence as uttered in a certain context that is true or false.[10] The sentence *per se*, though, is certainly not meaningless; and it is meaningful because it could be uttered in context to say something true or false. This point has the following significance: Russell argued that if 'The king of France' were a referring expression, the sentence 'The king of France is bald' would have to be meaningless, since it is certainly not true or false of anyone referred to that he is bald. So, to avoid the silly conclusion that the sentence is meaningless, Russell denied that 'The king of France' was a referring expression. We are in a position, though, to avoid the silly conclusion in a different way. The sentence 'The king of France is bald' is not meaningless, though it is, *per se*, neither true nor false. However, it is capable of being used to say something true or false. Someone uttering it in 1660 would have said something false, since Louis xiv had hair. Just because someone using it in 1972 fails to say something either true or false does not impugn its meaningfulness. Equally, just because a hammer is not used in a certain year to drive any nails in, it does not thereby cease to be a hammer.

In the light of these revised assumptions, we can see that Russell's paradoxes are not genuine paradoxes at all – so there is nothing we have to escape by denying that 'The so-and-so' expressions are referring ones.

[1] The first paradox ran: how can anything of the form 'The A does not exist' be true, since if 'The A' refers the sentence must be false, and if it refers to nothing, the sentence is gibberish? We can now reply: it may well be that in the sentence 'The A does not exist', the words 'The A' are not being used to refer. However, that does not prevent them being a referring expression since, as we have seen, what makes an expression a referring one is its ability to be used to refer, not its being actually used to refer on all occasions.

[2] The second paradox, concerning the king of France's pate, has already been dealt with. It does not follow from the fact that 'The king of France' is a referring expression that 'The king of France is bald' is meaningless, since it is not true or false. Provided it could be used to say something true or false, it is perfectly meaningful.

[3] The third paradox concerned George iv's wondering if Scott was the author of *Waverley*. Russell denied that 'The author of *Waverley*' was a referring expression, on the grounds that it could not, without absurdity, be interchanged with 'Scott'. Instead, though, we can say that it is a referring expression, but that in the sentence in question, 'George iv wished to know . . . etc', it is not being used to refer. It is clear, after all, that referring expressions are not always used to refer. Consider the sentence '"The author of *Waverley*" consists of four words'; here the relevant expression does not serve to refer. Similarly, we might insist that expressions filling the blanks in sentences of the form 'A wished to know if . . . was ——' are not being used to refer. Again this does not matter, since they are capable of being used to refer.[11]

None of this shows that Russell's analyses of 'The so-and-so' expressions are actually mistaken. It shows, though, that the motivation behind those analyses is unwarranted. In the next section I shall argue that Russell's analyses are mistaken. I have tried to establish in this section only that there is such a thing as reference to discuss at all.

2 The nature of reference

Reference occurs, then, and it occurs very often. Quite what, however, is it to refer? Or, as I prefer to ask: what are the necessary and sufficient conditions for a successful act of reference? The word 'successful' needs stressing here, since 'refer' is used in different ways. Sometimes when we speak of a man referring, we mean no more than that he tried to refer. We might say of someone 'When he said "the Fuehrer" he was referring to Stalin, not Hitler. He made a mistake'. On other occasions we can speak of a man referring even when he had no intention of referring to that particular. We might say to someone 'I know you meant to refer to Stalin, but you actually referred to Hitler'. Finally, sometimes when we speak of a man referring, we mean both that he intended to refer to a certain particular, and that he actually managed to. This seems to be the central sense. For if I say without any qualification that someone referred to Hitler, my hearers will take it that the man in question meant to and successfully managed to refer to Hitler. Reference in this final sense is what I call 'successful' reference. If we can explain what this is, it will be easy enough to deal with other uses of 'refer'.

Our problem is this: how does a series of words, or even a single word, allow us to pick out one and only one particular from the innumerable particulars there are in the universe? This is no mean task for a series of words to perform. We can best reach some answers by considering some informative defects in Russell's analyses of referring expressions.

[1] If Russell is right, part of what I do when I say 'The king is bald' is to *assert* the existence of the king (see *p* 74). But Russell seems to be wrong here. Surely all I assert is that the king is bald. His existence is not something that I assert in the sentence, but is, rather, something *presupposed* by what I say.[12] Unless I already believed there to be a king, I would not say of him that he was bald. We can see this by reflecting that if Russell were right, and if there were no king, then my sentence would be straightforwardly false – for part of what I assert, that there is a king, would be false. Most of us, though, would not regard 'The king of France is bald' as being false; at least, not straightforwardly false. If someone were to assert this, the normal reply would not be 'That's false', but 'What are you talking about? There isn't a king of France'. We might put it this way: if Russell's analysis were correct, bachelors would have no trouble answering the old chestnut 'Have you stopped beating your wife lately?' For the bachelor could reply 'My wife is no longer beaten

by me', and by Russell's analysis, this would mean 'There does not exist any entity which is my wife, and who is beaten by me' – which would be perfectly true. But bachelors do have trouble answering this question, and the answer just mentioned is not one they give. The reason that the question causes trouble is that it *presupposes* what is not the case – namely that there is a wife to be beaten.[13]

The point can be strengthened by considering the falsity of the analysis that Russell would have to give of the sentence 'Is the king bald?' For him the question must be equivalent either to (*a*) 'Is there one and only one king, and is he bald?' or (*b*) 'There is one and only one king; is he bald?' Against version (*a*) it can be argued that I am surely not asking two questions every time I ask a quesion of the form 'Is the A such-and-such?' You do not, in reply, have to say 'Yes. And yes' instead of just 'Yes'. Against (*b*) it can be argued that it is most peculiar to suppose that part of what I do when I ask a question is to assert that something is the case. That would imply that questions have a true or false component – which, surely, they do not.[14]

Finally, some purely linguistic considerations further strengthen this point. Take the sentence, 'I went to a cinema: the cinema was two miles away'. Any normal person hearing this would take it that 'cinema' was being used to refer to the same cinema in both cases. But if this is so, then the use of 'the cinema' in the second part of the sentence presupposes the existence of the cinema mentioned in the first part of the sentence. If it did not, there would be no reason for hearers to suppose that the two cinemas are the same. In general, we can say that expressions of the form 'The so-and-so' refer back to something mentioned earlier in the conversation, or to something the hearer is likely to be acquainted with through the context of the conversation. In either case, the question of the supposed existence of something to refer to has been settled before the utterance of the referring expression, and so is presupposed by it.

So we reach the first necessary condition of successful reference. In any sentence of the form 'The A is such-and-such', 'The A' can only be used to refer successfully if the existence of an A is presupposed by the speaker, and an A does actually exist.

[2] A second defect in Russell's analysis is this: it is not the case, as his analysis would have it, that 'The king of France is bald' is true if and only if there exists one, and *only one*, king of France. For there might be any number of kings of France; yet the sentence might be true, provided one of them was bald. It is sometimes the case, but by no means always, that the nature of the referring expression guarantees that it could be applied to only one particular. Thus 'The first man to marry Cleopatra' necessarily refers to one and only one person. Normally, though, the referring expressions we use can be used to refer to more than one person

on different occasions. 'The king' might be used to refer to Louis XIV one day, and to Og of Persia on another. So, although 'The so-and-so' expressions do express uniqueness in some way or other, the uniqueness does not consist in an assertion to the effect that there exists one and only one particular falling under some description, as Russell would have it.

How is it then that an expression like 'The king', which can be used to refer to different people, nevertheless refers to just one on a single occasion? One popular answer is that it is *context* which permits such an expression to refer uniquely on an occasion. 'Context' is to be given a generous interpretation here, and is meant to include at least the following:

(*a*) the physical surroundings – as when, standing in front of a certain girl, I turn to my friend and say 'The girl is hideous'.

(*b*) previous parts of a conversation – as when, having already mentioned that I met a girl yesterday, I say 'The girl was hideous'.

(*c*) the beliefs or thoughts of the hearer – as when, guessing that my friend is reminiscing over an old flame, I say 'The girl was hideous'.

The suggestion is that aspects of context, like these and others, will serve to guarantee that the referring expression refers to just one particular. It is context which enables us to determine which particular is being referred to.

No one would deny that context is often of great value in getting a hearer to recognize what particular is being referred to by the speaker. One has only to think how much more misunderstanding arises during telephone conversations than in face-to-face conversations because of the lack of shared surroundings. However, it cannot seriously be maintained that it is a necessary or sufficient condition of successful reference that context determines the referent. That it is not a necessary condition can be seen from the following examples:

(*a*) It may be that no aspect of context is relevant to my identifying a particular by using a referring expression. If, walking along a country path, I say 'The king is dead', there may be no aspect of context, like those listed above, which serves to determine to whom I am referring.

(*b*) It may be that the referring expression leaves no doubt as to who is being referred to; so that context plays no essential role in determining this. Since there was only one French emperor who lost at Waterloo, then my saying 'The French emperor who lost at Waterloo wore funny hats' contains a reference to Napoleon, whether I am standing in front of a bust of Napoleon or a bust of Cleopatra.

Nor could context be sufficient to determine the referent. It might be that all hearers in a given situation would take it that when I use 'the emperor', I am referring to Napoleon – I am, say, standing in Les Invalides, and the preceding discussion has been about Napoleon. Yet I could truly deny that I am talking of him, and insist that I am referring to Franz Josef. You could accuse me of being most misleading, but you cannot insist that I am referring to Napoleon just because the context made it look as if I was.

So what is it, if it is not context, that guarantees uniqueness of reference? Let us try the following suggestion: I successfully refer to a single particular by using 'The A' only if I am able to replace 'The A' by a longer expression which is applicable to just that one particular. (There will, of course, be an exception; namely, where 'The A' is already an expression, like 'The first husband of Cleopatra', which is applicable to only one particular. In such a case there is no need to replace it by another.) For example, when I say 'The king is bald', I only succeed in referring to a particular king if I am able to replace 'The king' by some expression, say 'The king who was over seven feet tall, and who conquered Macedon', which is applicable to only one person. Let us call an expression which, on any occasion of its use, applies to only one person an 'identifying expression'. It follows that a referring expression is either an identifying expression, or an expression which the speaker is able to replace by an identifying expression. To see that I fail to refer unless I am able to replace my referring expression by an identifying expression, consider the following case. I say 'The king is bald'. 'Which king?' you ask. I reply 'The king who was over seven feet tall, and who conquered Macedon.' You then ask 'Which one? There were two kings over seven feet tall who conquered Macedon.' Suppose I was unaware of this, and am unable to say anything which would distinguish the one tall conqueror from the other. I must then admit that I do not know who I am talking about; which one was bald. Consequently I must amend my original sentence from 'The king is bald' to 'A king is bald'.

This point is supported by some linguistic considerations. We saw that a normal person hearing the sentence 'I went to a cinema; the cinema was two miles away', would take it that 'the cinema' referred to the one already mentioned. He would read the sentence, that is, as meaning 'The cinema which I went to, was two miles away'. Unless both speaker and hearer are willing to fill in some such relative clause after an occurrence of 'The cinema', it is impossible to see how either of them can understand what is being referred to. There would, that is, be no reason for the hearer to suppose that the cinema that is two miles away is the one the speaker had already referred to. Now the function of relative clauses like '. . . which I went to, . . .' – so-called 'restrictive' relative clauses – is to restrict the field of particulars that I might be referring to, to just one. In actual practice it is not normally necessary to fill in such a relative clause. Context might make it clear which relative clause is to be filled in if one were to be filled in. However, that such a relative clause could be filled in appears to be a precondition for successful reference.[15]

We can bring this point in line with what was said before by saying that an identifying expression is one which could have the form 'The X, which is . . .', where the relative clause mentions properties which only one X has.

So far, then, we have two necessary conditions for successful reference; first that the existence of something be correctly presupposed, and second that the referring expression can be replaced by an identifying expression (unless it already is one). These conditions are not sufficient, however. Suppose I say 'The French emperor, who was five feet tall and wore funny hats, lost at Sedan.' The referring expression I use is applicable only to Napoleon I; yet I am trying to refer to the emperor who lost at Sedan, Napoleon III. If so, it would be odd to say I had referred to Napoleon I, despite the fact that I have provided an identifying expression which applies to him alone. This is not to deny that we could say 'Whoever you were trying to refer to you actually referred to Napoleon I.' But as I have already pointed out, it is worth employing a concept of *successful* reference. I can only succeed where I intended or tried. So we must add as a further necessary condition of successful reference that the speaker intended to refer to whoever his identifying expression actually applies to.[16]

This is not to suggest that it is always easy or possible to decide to what a person intends to refer. Indeed, one might wonder how a person can intend to refer to Napoleon III if the expression he employs is applicable to the uncle. The answer is that he must have in mind some other identifying expression, which he regards as more essential, which does really apply to Napoleon III. It may happen, though, that we are forced to say that the person did not know to what he intended to refer. Suppose he says 'The emperor wore no clothes', and in reply to our question 'Which emperor?' offers the four following identifying expressions: (*a*) 'The emperor who married Josephine', (*b*) 'The emperor who went to Elba', (*c*) 'The emperor who lost at Sedan', and (*d*) 'The emperor who invaded Mexico'. Here, the first two expressions apply to Napoleon I, while the second two apply to Napoleon III. Unless the speaker regards one of these expressions as more basic than the others, or unless he is able to provide more identifying expressions applying to only one of the emperors, we must conclude that he does not know to whom he is referring. Still, while it is not always easy or possible to decide what the speaker's intention is, we can hold that having the right intention is a necessary condition of successful reference. Where the intention is confused or unclear, then to that extent his act of referring is not fully successful. It need not be a total failure. Reference need not be a hit-or-miss affair, any more than writing a book need be a total success or a total failure.

I believe that the three necessary conditions I have listed are jointly sufficient. Let me put the position more formally: a person successfully refers by using 'The A' if and only if (a) he correctly presupposes the existence of the A in question, (b) 'The A' is an identifying expression, or could be replaced by an identifying expression by the speaker, and (c) the speaker intends to refer to that which 'The A', or the identifying expression which replaces it, actually applies to.

I shall conclude by considering an objection that might be levelled against what I have said. The objection is that a further necessary condition must be added. In its strong form, the objection is that an act of reference is successful only if the *hearer* succeeds in identifying the particular referred to by the speaker. In its weaker form the objection is that the speaker must at least intend that the hearer identifies what is being referred to.[17] It seems to me that both suggestions are misguided. The stronger suggestion is clearly too strong. I do not fail to refer successfully simply because my audience is too stupid, or too hard of hearing, to realize what I am referring to. And what if one of my hearers does, and another does not, identify the referent? Then we should have to say that I have both succeeded and failed in my referring. It is wiser, surely, to make a distinction between *referring to*, and *referring someone to*. We can then say that, while I may fully succeed in referring to something, I may nevertheless fail to refer someone in my audience to it, because he is stupid, or hard of hearing, or whatever.

The weaker suggestion is also misguided. I do not see why, when I refer successfully, I should intend a hearer to identify anything. In the first place I may be soliloquizing, and as part of this, referring. Here there is no hearer who I can even try to refer to something. In the second place, consider the following example: I may, as a private joke, like to hear my friend accidentally sing the praises of someone he detests. Suppose he detests Mary, but loves Cynthia. Suppose, too, he mistakenly believes that Cynthia is the secretary of the Young Communists. I ask him 'What do you think of the secretary of the Young Communists?', referring in fact to Mary, who is the real secretary. My friend replies 'She's a marvellous girl, isn't she?' Here I have successfully referred to someone, Mary, and I have successfully referred my hearer to somebody, Cynthia. Yet, as we see, the person I refer to is not the person I even intend my friend to identify. It follows that it is not a condition of successful reference that I should intend my hearer to identify the particular to which I am actually referring.

There are problems about reference with which I have not dealt – for example I have only touched upon the complex question of referential expressions appearing in opaque contexts. I hope, though, to have shown that there is such a thing as reference; and to have shown the basic ingredients in that mechanism of language which is called 'reference'. We can see more clearly, I hope, how we bring our words 'down to earth', and relate them directly to that world.

3 Proper names

There is a class of words, like 'The so-and-so' expressions, whose primary function is to refer to single particulars. These are proper names, like 'Attila', 'London', 'John Smith', and so on. I have reserved discussion of these for a separate section for two reasons. First, not everything I have said about other referring expressions can be automatically applied to proper names. Second, there is a traditional philosophical problem that arises in connection with proper names, which does not arise in connection with other referring expressions. The problem is that plausible arguments can be marshalled to show that proper names have meaning, and others to show that proper names do not have meaning. There are *prima facie* reasons for and against the view that they have meaning. The *prima facie* reason for saying that proper names do have meaning is this: how on earth could words having no meaning serve a systematic function in language? 'Blug' and 'grumb', which are meaningless, have no systematic function after all. The *prima facie* reason against saying that proper names have meaning is that we do not, as a matter of fact, talk of them as having meaning. If you say 'John Smith is a necrophiliac', I might ask 'What does "necrophiliac" mean?' but not 'What does "John Smith" mean?'[18]

Since the notion of meaning is so slippery, we must tighten up our description of the problem in order to see what is at issue. The question is this: can a proper name, say 'John Smith', mean the same as some longer descriptive expression, say 'the man with the longest nose in Christendom', which alone applies to the thing referred to by the proper name? Or, if you like, can proper names be regarded as abbreviations of longer descriptive expressions? If they can, there is no special problem about proper names, since we have already explained the role of such descriptive referring expressions in the last section. If not, we must offer some alternative account of how proper names function.

The view that proper names cannot mean the same as longer descriptive expressions was urged by John Stuart Mill, in his *System of Logic*. According to him, proper names are 'unmeaning marks', which have 'strictly speaking, no signification'.[19] He argues, first, that even if a proper name was originally applied to something in virtue of some descriptive properties possessed by it, this fact soon becomes irrelevant to how the proper name is to be used. Thus 'Dartmouth' was originally applied to that town because it stood at the mouth of the river Dart. The town no longer stands at the mouth because of silting. Nevertheless, it is still perfectly correct to call the town 'Dartmouth'. In this way proper names differ from meaningful expressions like 'the triangle'. We can refer to something as a triangle only if it continues to possess certain properties, like three-sidedness. If it loses this property, we cannot call the figure a 'triangle'.

Second, Mill argues, proper names do not express properties because we cannot infer what properties a person has from the mere fact that he has a certain name. If all I know about a certain person is that his name is 'Horace', then I can know nothing else about him. Whereas if I know that a figure is correctly called a 'triangle', I can infer several properties which the figure must possess. Since, according to Mill, to have meaning is to express properties, it follows that proper names do not have meaning.

Both of Mill's arguments are extremely weak. In the first place, it is not only proper names, like 'Dartmouth', whose origins become irrelevant to their later use. The word 'philosopher' in its Greek form was originally applied to people who were 'lovers of wisdom'. But if Professor X of a philosophy department is motivated by love of money, rather than love of wisdom, he does not cease to be a philosopher. In other words, there is no reason to suppose that proper names have no meaning just because the original reasons for their use cease to be reasons for their continued use. Mill's second argument fares no better. Let us admit that 'His name is "Horace"' does not allow us to infer what other properties he has. Equally the sentence 'He has gone to the bank' does not allow us to infer what properties the place he has gone to has. The reason is that 'bank' is ambiguous. If we do not know whether it is a river bank, a commercial bank, or a blood-bank he has gone to, we are in no position to infer the properties of the place. Similarly, anyone who holds that proper names have meanings will admit that proper names are usually ambiguous. He will insist, though, that once a proper name is disambiguated – ie once we know which person or thing it refers to – then we can list the properties implied by the name. Just as we can list the properties expressed by 'bank' once we know which sense of 'bank' is meant, so we can list the properties expressed by 'Horace' once we know which Horace is being referred to.

Not only are Mill's arguments against the view that proper names have meanings weak, there also seem to be strong arguments in favour of saying that they have meanings. Here is one of them. If 'Tully' and 'Cicero' have no meaning, then they cannot differ in meaning. In that case the two sentences 'Tully is Tully' and 'Tully is Cicero' cannot differ in meaning, since the only difference between them is that one occurrence of 'Tully' has been replaced by 'Cicero'. Surely, though, the two sentences do differ in meaning, it is argued. The first is utterly trivial and uninformative; whereas the second one is informative. But if they do differ in meaning, then this must be because 'Tully' and 'Cicero' differ in meaning. The suggestion might be that 'Tully' means the same as 'the greatest Roman orator', and 'Cicero' the same as 'the author of *The Laws*'. If so we can see why 'Tully is Cicero' is informative; it tells us that two descriptions apply to the same person.[20]

This argument, it might seem, clinches the case for saying that proper names do have meanings. It would have to be admitted, on this view, that proper names are ambiguous in at least two ways. First, as we have seen, a proper name will mean something different each time it applies to a different individual. Second, if a proper name means the same as some descriptive expression which applies to the individual, then since there might be many descriptive expressions which uniquely apply to that individual, the proper name will have as many meanings as there are descriptive expressions applying uniquely to the individual. So 'Napoleon' will mean, *inter alia*, 'the French emperor who lost at Waterloo', 'the French emperor who married Josephine', etc. Still, it will be argued, this multiple ambiguity does not matter if, in fact, we are able to operate successfully with proper names. At any rate, it is better to say that proper names have meanings, albeit ambiguously, than to insist, with Mill, that they have no meanings. Here, too much is better than too little.

I am going to argue that there are good reasons for rejecting this view that proper names have meanings. And I am going to argue this despite the fact that at least one popular argument against the view is indecisive. It runs: if 'Aristotle' meant 'the teacher of Alexander, the pupil of Plato, and the author of the *Metaphysics*, who was born at Stagira', it would follow that Aristotle did not exist if it turned out that there was no one of whom the descriptive expression was true. It would follow just as it would follow that no bachelor is in the room if it turned out that no one unmarried was in the room. But surely, it is argued, it would be absurd to say that Aristotle did not exist if it was discovered, say, that no philosopher was ever born at Stagira. We would, rather, continue to speak of Aristotle and conclude that we were mistaken in believing that he was born at Stagira. In that case 'Aristotle' cannot contain as part of its meaning 'born at Stagira'. Nor, so the argument goes, could it contain any particular fact about Aristotle as part of its meaning, since any particular fact about him might turn out not to be a fact at all – and this would not make us refuse to apply the word 'Aristotle'.[21]

I do not find this argument convincing. As far as I can see, it only shows that there are some descriptions which 'Aristotle' cannot mean the same as, and does not show that there are not descriptions of a different sort that it could mean the same as. Suppose we said that 'Aristotle' means 'the man who possessed a *sufficient* number of the following properties :

teacher of Alexander, pupil of Plato, . . ., born at Stagira'. In that case, there would be no contradiction in saying that Aristotle was not born at Stagira – for it would only be if a *sufficient* number of Aristotle's supposed properties turned out to be true of no one person that we should have to say he did not exist. Being born at Stagira is not a sufficient number of such properties. No doubt it is not easy, or even possible in some cases, to decide in advance what a sufficient number of properties is. Suppose that forty per cent of the properties we believed to be true of Aristotle should turn out to be true of no one person, or not true of the person who really has the other sixty per cent of the properties. Would we say that there never was such a person as Aristotle, or would we say that there was, but that we had been radically mistaken about him? I do not know. But all this shows is that the meaning of 'Aristotle' might be vague. It is not only proper names which may be vague. 'Vehicle' has meaning, yet it is difficult to decide in advance just what properties a thing can lack before we would cease to call it a 'vehicle'. Again, 'woman' has meaning but that does not make it any the easier for officials at the Olympic Games to decide just who is and who is not a woman.[22]

I do not, then, accept at least one popular argument against the view that proper names have meanings. It must be admitted, though, that this argument does force the proponent of the view to hedge a little, and to say that proper names do not have meanings in such a straightforward way as other words. It might, therefore, be better if we could explain the functioning of proper names without saying that they mean the same as longer descriptive expressions. I think, too, there is one good reason for denying that proper names have meaning. On the view being considered, recall, a name like 'John' will have a different meaning each time it names a different person. This does turn proper names into a pretty odd bunch. For the same principle, that names have as many different meanings as there are things named, does not hold in the case of other referring expressions. The expression 'the king' surely means the same, whether it is being used to refer to Louis xiv, Og of Persia, or Saul. It is absurd to suggest that 'the king' has as many meanings as there are kings, actual or possible. For this reason, we may want to deny that proper names have meaning; since, if they do, they must have it in a radically different manner from other referring expressions – so radical that it seems best not to speak of meaning. Perhaps it does not matter much what we say; whether proper names have meaning but in a very funny way, or that they do not have meaning at all. If we do say the latter we must give an account of how they function without appealing to meaning. Further, we must be able to cope with the argument about Tully/Cicero that seemed to show proper names must have meaning. Both tasks are not insurmountable, I believe.

We may explain the relation between a proper name and a descriptive expression which might replace it as follows: when a speaker refers with a proper name, he does so with the willingness and ability to replace that proper name by some longer descriptive expression that applies uniquely to the referent. This is not to say that 'Aristotle' means the same as 'the philosopher who taught Alexander, etc . . .'. Saying that involves us in problems, as we have seen. We need not say this in order to see how 'Aristotle' can be used to refer. Instead we can explain it in terms of the speaker's being able to replace the proper name by the descriptive expression. We have now brought the account of proper names into line with the account already given of other referring expressions. When we explained how 'the king' can be used to refer to just one individual, we did this in terms of the speaker's being able to expand 'the king' into an identifying expression, like 'the king who was over seven feet tall, conquered Macedon, etc . . .' which applies to only one person. It was not suggested – and it would be absurd to suggest – that 'the king' means the same as this longer identifying expression. Now while it is not equally absurd to suggest that a proper name means the same as some identifying expression, there is no need to suggest this. We can explain the relation between a proper name and an identifying expression in the same terms as we explained the relation between 'the king' and 'the king who was over seven feet tall, etc . . .'.

Let us see how we might deal with the Tully/Cicero example. How, it was asked, can 'Tully is Cicero' and 'Tully is Tully' differ in meaning, unless 'Tully' and 'Cicero' differ in meaning, and so possess meaning? First, it is worth noting that the two sentences need not differ in the amount of information they provide. If I already know that Tully is Cicero, then 'Tully is Cicero' gives me no new information. Indeed, if all I know of Cicero is that he is Tully, then 'Tully is Cicero' tells me no more than that the person who is Tully is the person who is Tully. Second, though, we can explain why 'Tully is Cicero' is likely to be more informative without appealing to differences in meaning between the two names. It may be that a person would be willing to replace 'Tully' by a longer descriptive expression which is not the same as he would be willing to replace 'Cicero' by. In that case, if we tell him that Tully is Cicero, he is being given the information that the two descriptive expressions apply to the same man. So it is not the different meanings of 'Tully' and 'Cicero' that make 'Tully is Cicero' informative; but the fact that people tend to associate different descriptive expressions with the two names.

One last, but important point: it is easy to canvass support for the view that proper names have meanings if we regard, as the sole alternative, that proper names are *meaningless*. But we are not forced to choose between 'meaningful' and 'meaningless'. From the fact that something does not have a meaning, it does not follow that it is meaningless. My nose does not have a meaning, but it is not meaningless.[23] 'Meaningless' is a pejorative term which, when applied to words, implies that they have no use, function, or purpose. In that case, proper names are certainly not meaningless. What is being overlooked is that words can have uses without having meanings. It is not clear, for example, that 'ouch', said when I am stung, has a meaning; but it certainly has a use and purpose. At any rate, since 'meaning' is such a slippery term, it is best not to put the question about proper names in the bald form 'Do they have meaning or not?' What we should do is what I have tried to do – namely work out the relation that holds between a proper name and descriptive expressions. That relation can be explained without bringing in the notion of meaning at all.

4 Predication

Referring expressions occur most frequently in sentences which serve to tell us something true or false about what is referred to. Sometimes the sentences in question contain two referring expressions, *eg* 'Tully is Cicero'. This is an identity-statement. Insofar as I have already tried to deal with referring expressions, I shall say no more about identity-statements. More commonly, a sentence contains a referring expression and a different sort of expression, a predicate. In 'Socrates is bald' or 'Mother loves to cook', the predicates are '. . . is bald' and '. . . loves to cook' respectively. I shall call the expressions coupled with predicates the 'subjects' of the sentences. Thus 'Socrates' and 'Mother' are the subjects of the above sentences. Typically a subject will be a referring expression.

In attempting to understand the role of predicates, we enter into a field well-trodden by generations of philosophers. Plato's theory of forms or ideas can be regarded as a theory about predication; and I shall shortly say a little about the metaphysical problem of universals, which is closely connected with the question of predication. However, let us first look at two unsatisfactory attempts to explain how predicates function.

Perhaps the simplest and initially most appealing account of predicates would be this: just as referring expressions function by being used to refer to particulars, so predicates function by being used to refer to something else. It might, for example, be claimed that just as 'John' refers to John, so 'is bald' refers to the property of baldness. So, on this view which I shall call the 'reference' theory of predication, subjects and predicates differ only in the nature of the entities they refer to. Philosophers who have taken this line have differed as to what sort of entities predicates refer to. 'Universals', 'ideas', 'properties', 'concepts', or 'qualities' are some of the names philosophers have applied to these entities. For our present purposes, these differences are inessential, since any version of the 'reference' theory runs into similar trouble.

A good example of such a theory can be found in the works of the German logician and mathematician, Frege. According to him, a Concept, as he calls it, is 'the reference of a grammatical predicate' in just the way that a particular, or Object, is the reference of a subject.[24] A predicate can be defined, therefore, as that which refers to a Concept. This definition would fail to be helpful, of course, if it turned out that subjects can also refer to Concepts, for we should then have failed to distinguish subjects from predicates. Now it seems that subjects can indeed be used to refer to Concepts, for consider the sentence 'The Concept *horse* is an easy one to understand.' Are we not referring to a Concept by the subject 'the Concept *horse*'? Oddly enough Frege denies that we are doing this.

> The three words 'The Concept *horse*' do designate an Object, but on that very account, they do not designate a Concept, as I am using that word.[25]

Frege is forced to say this if he wishes to remain faithful to his definition of a predicate as that which alone can refer to a Concept.

There is a second reason why he is forced to deny that 'the Concept *horse*' refers to a Concept. If it did, then by Leibniz's law, we should be able to use it instead of any other name of the same Concept. Now, according to Frege, the words 'is a horse' in the sentence 'X is a horse' refer to a Concept, since they form a predicate. So we should be able to replace 'is a horse' by 'the Concept *horse*' if both referred to the same Concept. But if we do this, we end up with nonsense. The expression 'X the Concept *horse*' is not even a sentence. So, since we cannot interchange 'is a horse' and 'the Concept *horse*', one of them cannot be the name of a Concept.

Frege says that it is a mere 'awkwardness of language' that we are unable to refer to the Concept *horse* by the expression 'the Concept *horse*'.[26] But what Frege describes as an awkwardness, many would want to describe as a straight contradiction. If we can refer to the Tower of London by 'the Tower of London', why can we not refer to the Concept *horse*, whatever that is, by 'the Concept *horse*'? At the very least, the fact that Frege's definition of a predicate forces us to such paradoxical conclusions is good enough reason for making us look again.

There is, in fact, sufficient reason for rejecting the view that predicates serve to refer to abstract entities, including Frege's Concepts. We take our hint from what was said two paragraphs earlier. If a predicate refers we should be able to replace it by any other expression which refers to the same thing without affecting the truth or falsity of what is said.[27] Suppose that 'is bald' refers to an entity in 'Socrates is bald'. Let me

now invent another name for this entity; say 'Harry'. If we then replace
'is bald' by 'Harry', we end up with 'Socrates Harry'. This is not even
a sentence, let alone a true or false one. The general point is this: if predicates are names of entities, then subject/predicate sentences are pairs
of names, since subjects are names (or referring expressions). But a pair
of names is not a sentence at all; it is a mere list. Hence one of the expressions in a subject/predicate sentence cannot be a name. Since subjects certainly do name, then predicates cannot. So we must reject the
view that predicates function by being used as names of abstract entities.[28]

It would be an added criticism of the 'reference' theory of predication
to show that there do not exist the abstract entities to which predicates
are meant to refer. It is not necessary for us to show this, since even if
there are such entities, it would still not be the case that predicates
function by referring to them. Nevertheless, it is worth glancing at this
ontological question, because interest in predicates has largely been
motivated by the connection they might have with the existence of
abstract entities. Traditionally there have been realists, who insist upon
the existence of such entities (universals, concepts, properties, or
whatever), and nominalists, who insist that there are only particulars.
I shall not try to show, in such a short space, that there do not exist these
entities. I shall try to show only that our ways of talking do not establish
that there *are* such entities.

The reasons for saying that there do not have to be abstract entities,
like universals, are very similar to those given in section 1 of Chapter 2
for saying that there do not have to be entities called 'meanings'. First,
we saw that our use of noun-like expressions in no way entails believing
there are entities named by the expressions. We do not populate the
universe with entities called 'sakes' or 'nicks' just because we use expressions like '. . . for the sake of . . .', or '. . . in the nick of . . .'. Now
we do use expressions like 'redness' or 'wisdom' or 'virtue'; but we
should not therefore conclude that there must be abstract entities
named by such expressions. Socrates' wisdom might no more be a
separate entity than Socrates' death is. Second, we saw that sentences
containing noun-like expressions could often be paraphrased so that the
noun-like expression disappears, and with it the temptation to postulate
entities. 'Wisdom belongs to the few' means, presumably, 'few people
are wise'. 'Virtue is its own reward' means, presumably, 'people should
feel rewarded just by acting virtuously'. In the paraphrases, there are
no expressions which even apparently refer to abstract entities.

The point is not that it is *false* to say things like 'there is such a thing
as wisdom', or 'justice exists' – though some philosophers have spoken
as if this was the point. That they are not false can be seen from the fact
that they can be given adequate paraphrases which are true. Sentences
like these, though, are 'systematically misleading', to use Ryle's

phrase.[29] They are misleading in that they tempt people to search for entities answering to the nouns.

I am not insisting that there do not exist these various abstract entities. All I insist is that there is no compelling reason to suppose that there do. At any rate, this has been somewhat of a digression, since even if there are such entities, they cannot be used to explain the function of predicates. Predicates are not, as I have tried to show, the names of such entities.

There is a second inadequate account of predicates that I shall consider briefly. It might be said: a predicate is an expression which is used to assert something *about* what is referred to by the subject, in a way that the subject cannot be used to assert something about what is expressed by the predicate.[30] This account fails, of course, if it can be shown that subjects can say something *about* something in the way predicates do. It seems to me that this can be shown. I can do no better than quote P. F. Strawson's criticism of this account:

> Now certainly we could often say of someone who used the sentence ['Raleigh smokes'] that he was talking *about* Raleigh, that he made an *assertion about* Raleigh ... But it is also plain that there might be circumstances in which it would be correct to say of someone using the sentence that he was talking *about* smoking, and that one of the things he asserted about it was that *Raleigh* smoked or was a smoker. To this extent at least, and as far as the word 'about' is concerned, the name 'Raleigh' seems to qualify on the definitions as a [predicate].[31]

Suppose, that is, I was asked 'What is smoking? I do not understand the word.' I might, by way of reply, point to Raleigh and say 'Raleigh is smoking at this moment. That's what smoking is.' Here it would be natural to say that I had said something about smoking. But this does not make 'Raleigh' a predicate; so the account of predicates in question must be inadequate. Perhaps there is some sense of 'about' in which only predicates can be *about*; but if so, we need this sense explained to us.

When one turns to more adequate accounts of predication, including the one I hope to present, one is struck by their apparent triviality. While this may be something of an anti-climax, I am not sure that it should worry us much. In the first place, it seems that the 'problem' of predication is largely generated by asking the wrong question. If we ask 'To what entities do predicates refer?' we have the problem of finding an answer. Once we outlaw this question, it is not clear what the problem is meant to be. Can we do any more than state in commonsense terms what happens when a person predicates? And this may be pretty dull. Second, it seems to me that the 'problem' of predication reduces to other problems. It will be seen from my account of predication, which I shall give in a moment, that it involves notions of meaning, truth, and inclusion. All of these notions require explication, but insofar as they can be explicated, there is not, I feel, any special problem about predicates.

Let me suggest the following definition: A person successfully uses a predicate 'F' if and only if (a) he intentionally says something true about a referent by using 'F' with one of its proper meanings, and (b) the referent can be said to be included among the things which are F. I shall devote the rest of this section to expanding upon, and explaining, this definition.

[1] The definition will only be intelligible if we already have a grasp of such concepts as truth, intention, meaning, and inclusion. If someone is already puzzled about predication, this definition will probably not illuminate him, since his puzzle probably concerns one or more of these concepts.

[2] Why is it necessary to add the second clause about the referent being included among the things which are F? There are two reasons. First, we want to distinguish between subject/predicate sentences, and identity-statements like 'Tully is Cicero'. The latter sentence says something true about Tully, but it would be absurd to say that Tully is included among the things which are Cicero. Cicero does not contain anything in the way that a class does. For this reason '. . . is Cicero' does not qualify as a predicate. Second, the use of 'true' is vague. On one possible use of 'true' we can speak of a subject being true of a referent. I may say, for example, that 'The conqueror of Hannibal' is true of Fabius. If so, we could not distinguish subjects from predicates by the first clause of the definition alone. What we must do is restrict the sense of 'true' so that only predicates can be 'true of'. This I have done in the second clause by insisting that a predicate is true of something in the sense that the something is included among the things which are F.

Both of these reasons add up to the important point that there is an essential asymmetry between subjects and predicates. I have expressed this point by saying that, whereas the referent of the subject can be said to be included in the class of things which are F, we cannot similarly speak of the referent including the things which are F.[32]

[3] The definition lends support to the old dictum that particulars cannot be predicated of anything; that is, expressions referring to particulars cannot appear in the position of a predicate. The reason should be clear. A particular, like a single man or a chair, cannot include other particulars as members. Of course we might speak of John Smith containing his teeth, and say that his teeth are included in him. But this is obviously a different sense of 'inclusion' from the sense in which John Smith is included in the class of men, and his teeth are included in the class of teeth.

[4] I have included in the definition the demands that the speaker intends the predicate to be true of the referent, and that he is using the predicate with a proper meaning. I do this, first, to exclude cases where a person says something true by accident. I might believe that Socrates was Roman, and then lie by saying that Socrates was Greek. Second, it is to exclude cases where I say something true, but without understanding the meaning of what I say. I might for example say 'Socrates is wise', but believe that 'wise' means 'stupid'. In both cases, we could, no doubt, speak of the person having predicated. But it is useful, as it was in the case of reference, to distinguish between successful predication, and other cases of predication. It would certainly be strange to say in an unqualified way that a person had asserted that Socrates was a Greek, if the person was lying and believed that Socrates was a Roman.

The definition is incomplete to the extent that no complete accounts have been given of some of the crucial terms appearing in it. I claim no more than that the definition is correct, and that it avoids the pitfalls into which other accounts have fallen. With this I end my discussion of reference and predication, and with it my discussion of one of the most basic, if not *the* most basic, type of sentence we employ.

Notes

1 Some Existentialists apparently regard 'nothing' as the name of some weird kind of something, which has certain properties such as filling us with 'angst'. I leave it to the readers of Existentialist writings to make what they can of such talk. On the surface it seems comparable to the belief of that Christian sect which, reading in the bible that *nobody* was perfect, proceeded to worship this remarkable person.

2 See, for example, his 'On denoting' and 'The philosophy of logical atomism', in *Logic and Knowledge*. Allen & Unwin, 1968. These writings were originally published in 1905 and 1918 respectively.

3 My presentation of this argument does not exactly correspond to Russell's own. He relies upon an implausible 'Fido'-Fido theory of meaning which we rejected in Chapter 2. The point can be made, as I have made it, without relying on such a theory.

4 'On denoting', in *Logic and Knowledge*. Allen & Unwin, 1968. *pp* 47–8.

5 For those acquainted with the symbolism of the Predicate Calculus, this analysis of 'The A is B' reads:

$$(\exists x)((Ax \ \& \ (y)(Ay \supset (x = y))) \ \& \ Bx)$$

6 'The philosophy of logical atomism', in *Logic and Knowledge*. Allen & Unwin, 1968. *p* 201.

7 *ibid.*

8 It should be noted that other logical atomists, notably the early Wittgenstein in his *Tractatus Logico-Philosophicus*, did not share Russell's views as to the nature of the logical atoms.

9 'The philosophy of logical atomism', in *Logic and Knowledge*. Allen & Unwin, 1968. *p* 193.

10 In his article 'On referring', *Mind*, *59*, 1950, 320–44, P. F. Strawson distinguishes between *sentences*, which are mere series of words, and *statements*, which are the truths or falsehoods produced by using sentences. I have preferred to distinguish between sentences *per se*, taken in abstraction from context of utterance, and sentences taken in context – the latter being capable of truth or falsity. For the purposes of this chapter, it does not matter how we draw the distinction. There is a substantial issue involved, however, which will be taken up in section 3 of Chapter 7. 'On referring' is reprinted in *Essays in Conceptual Analysis*, ed A. Flew. Macmillan, 1963.

11 The problem of referring expressions which occur in so-called 'opaque' contexts such as 'A wished to know if . . . was ———' is still under intense discussion. Many philosophers take the course of denying that expressions in such contexts occur referentially. See, for example, G. Frege, 'On sense and reference', in his *Philosophical Writings*, trans M. Black and P. Geach. Blackwell, 1966, or W. V. Quine, *Word and Object*. M.I.T. Press, 1960. Others have preferred to insist that the expressions do occur referentially, and so have denied Leibniz's law. See, for example, L. Linsky, *Referring*. Routledge & Kegan Paul, 1967.

12 See P. F. Strawson, 'On referring', *Mind*, *59*, 1950, 320–44.

13 For this way of objecting to Russell's analysis, see P. Geach, 'Russell's theory of descriptions', *Analysis*, *10*, 1950. Reprinted in *Philosophy and Analysis*, ed M. MacDonald. Blackwell, 1954.

14 For this argument, see J. R. Searle, *Speech Acts*. Cambridge University Press, 1969. Chapter 7.

15 For further discussion of relative clauses in connection with reference, see Z. Vendler, *Linguistics in Philosophy*. Cornell University Press, 1967. Chapter 2.

16 Thus I would not go along with J. Meiland, *Talking About Particulars*. Routledge & Kegan Paul, 1970, *p* 44, when he writes that a person has, in an unqualified sense, referred to X when the expression he uses applies to X and nothing else. This pastes over the distinction between successful reference, which involves having the right intention, and a sense of 'reference' that requires qualification.

17 Searle, *op cit*, for example, includes as one of his rules of reference that 'S (the speaker) intends that the utterance of R (some referring expression) will pick out or identify X to H (the hearer)'. *p* 95. For more detailed criticism of Searle's account, see my 'Searle on intentions and reference', *Analysis*, *32*, 1972, 159–63.

18 Though see note 36, Chapter 2.

19 *A System of Logic*. Longman, Green, Reader & Dyer, 1886. *p* 21.

20 For this argument, see G. Frege, 'On sense and reference', in his *Philosophical Writings*, trans M. Black and P. Geach. Blackwell, 1966. *pp* 56–7.

21 For this argument, see J. R. Searle, 'Proper names', *Mind*, *67*, 1958, 166–73. Reprinted in *Philosophy and Ordinary Language*, ed C. Caton. Illinois University Press, 1963.

22 For more detailed arguments, see my 'Definition and "clusters"', *Mind*, *81*, 1972, 495–503, and J. Meiland, *Talking About Particulars*. Routledge & Kegan Paul, 1970.

23 Some Existentialists seem to have succumbed to the temptation of supposing that if something is not meaningful, then it must be meaningless. Thus Sartre, having argued that life as a whole has no meaning, concludes that life must therefore be meaningless, absurd, and pointless. (See his *Existentialism and*

Humanism. Methuen, 1948.) You may as well argue that since stones have no meaning, the poor things are therefore absurd.

24 'On concept and object', in his *Philosophical Writings*, trans M. Black and P. Geach. Blackwell, 1966. *p* 43.

25 *ibid*, *p* 45.

26 *ibid*, *p* 46.

27 Though we may have to make exception for where predicates occur in so-called 'opaque' contexts. See note 11 above

28 For this argument, see J. R. Searle, *Speech Acts*. Cambridge University Press, 1969. *pp* 102–3.

29 G. Ryle, 'Systematically misleading expressions', *Proceedings of the Aristotelian Society*, *32*, 1931–32, 139–70. Reprinted in *Logic and Language*, ed A. Flew. Blackwell, 1951. 1st Series.

30 See, for example, P. Geach, 'Subject and predicate', *Mind*, *59*, 1950, *circa p* 463.

31 *Individuals*. Methuen, 1961. *p* 144.

32 This way of making the distinction between subjects and predicates is quite close to Strawson's 'category criterion'. He writes: 'Two terms coupled in a true sentence stand in referential and predicative position, respectively, if what the first term designates or signifies is a case or instance of what the second term signifies.' ('Singular terms and predication', in *Philosophical Logic*, ed P. F. Strawson. Oxford University Press, 1967. *p* 83. Originally published in the *Journal of Philosophy*, *58*, 1961, 393–412.)

Chapter 5

Language and culture

It is a truism that language is interwoven with culture; that it affects how we think and behave, and is affected by how we think and behave. The aim, in this chapter, is to try to understand what the relationship is. In particular, I want to investigate a hypothesis about the connection between language and culture, which is extremely radical, and goes far beyond the truism we would all be ready to admit. According to this hypothesis, which is intimately connected with the names of Edward Sapir and Benjamin Lee Whorf, language is not just an element of culture which interacts with other elements; it is the very forge from which cultures emerge in the forms they do.

1 The Sapir/Whorf hypothesis

'Culture', says Sapir, 'may be defined as what a society does and thinks.'[1] When linguists, anthropologists, and philosophers study the relation between language and culture they are not, however, concerned with culture in such a broad sense as this. Certainly they are concerned with men's ideas, conceptions, and beliefs, but not with everything men do. For not everything men do could have an interesting connection with their language. If there were no animals in a society, the people would eat only vegetables; but that is not something that has been influenced by their language. But just about everything men do may be conceived of by them in certain ways. Now once a person's conceptions of what he is doing enter into how we should describe what he is doing, then we shall be concerned with the relation between his language and his activities. Our vegetarians, for example, might think of their carrots as gifts from God – in which case their eating takes on a significance with which language may well be connected. Still, this talk of 'culture', of 'what a society does and thinks', is much too vague for our purposes. Only examples can show what we are concerned with.

We have already been concerned with one aspect of the connection between language and thought, in section 2 of Chapter 2. There we asked what the relation between a given word, or given sentence, was with a given idea or thought. We decided that words and sentences are not labels given to some quite separate mental entities. But when Sapir and Whorf talk of the connection between language and thought, they are interested, not in the connection of a particular sentence with a particular thought, but in the connection between whole areas of language, and whole areas of human intellectual phenomena. For example, the connection between how men think about the nature of time, and the grammar of the language they use to talk about time.

Again, we have already been concerned with one aspect of the relation between language and behaviour, in section 3 of Chapter 2. There it was argued that very often one cannot identify what a man is doing independent of understanding the words he uses to describe it. This is not the sort of connection that interests Sapir and Whorf. They are concerned with how whole ways of talking affect whole modes of behaviour. (We shall, though, be returning to the question of how we identify what behaviour is going on.)

It is best to regard the Sapir/Whorf hypothesis as a challenge to a commonly accepted conception of the language/culture relation. It is commonly thought that language reflects a pre-existing reality of which men are pre-linguistically aware. Languages are then devised to describe that reality. Since this reality is pretty much the same for all peoples, since environment is fairly similar, one expects that all languages will be basically similar in their modes of describing that reality. Equally it is commonly assumed that while, no doubt, what we say often affects how we behave, the position is usually that what we say is determined by how we behave. Men first behave, and then describe how they behave.

These assumptions are strongly challenged by Sapir and Whorf. For them, language is no mere passive recording instrument, which reflects a pre-existing reality of which we are aware. Rather it is the essential factor in forging what our conception of reality is, and how we perceive it. Not only our conceptions and perceptions, but also our attitudes towards our fellow-men, and so our behaviour towards them, are largely dictated to us by the language we happen to possess. Nor is it the case that languages share any great similarities; they differ radically, and as a result, the ways in which men conceive, perceive, evaluate, and behave will differ radically. Put in an extreme form, the hypothesis is that it makes no sense to speak of reality. What reality is for a person will be a function of the language he employs, and there will be as many 'realities' as there are radically distinct languages. Since there is no super-language, from the standpoint of which we can judge actual languages, there is no way in which it is possible to choose between differing conceptions of reality, different forms of evaluation, and different ways of perceiving. We are committed to complete relativity, with no prospect of making objective tests of divergent systems of thought.

A few quotations from Sapir and Whorf will help give the flavour of the hypothesis:

Language is a guide to 'social reality'. Though language is not ordinarily thought of as of essential interest to the students of social science, it powerfully conditions all our thinking about social problems and processes. Human beings do not live in the objective world alone, nor in the world of social activity as ordinarily understood, but are very much at the mercy of the particular language which has become the medium of expression for their society. It is quite an illusion to imagine that one adjusts to reality essentially without the use of language and that language is merely an incidental means of solving specific problems of communication or reflection. The fact of the matter is that the 'real world' is to a large extent unconsciously built up on the language habits of the group. No two languages are ever sufficiently similar to be considered as representing the same social reality. The worlds in which different societies live are distinct worlds, not merely the same world with different labels attached. [Sapir][2]

... the background linguistic system of each language is not merely a reproducing instrument for voicing ideas but rather is itself the shaper of ideas, the program and guide for the individual's mental activity, for his analysis of impressions, for his synthesis of his mental stock in trade. Formulation of ideas is not an independent process, strictly rational in the old sense, but is part of a particular grammar, and differs, from slightly to greatly, between different grammars. We dissect nature along lines laid down by our native languages. The categories and types that we isolate from the world of phenomena we do not find there because they stare every observer in the face; on the contrary, the world is presented in a kaleidoscopic flux of impressions which has to be organized by our minds – and this means largely by the linguistic systems in our minds. [Whorf][3]

No individual is free to describe nature with absolute impartiality but is constrained to certain modes of interpretation even while he thinks himself most free ... We are thus introduced to a new principle of relativity, which holds that all observers are not led by the same physical evidence to the same picture of the universe, unless their linguistic backgrounds are similar. [Whorf][4]

Which was first: the language patterns or the cultural norms? In the main they have grown up together, constantly influencing each other.

But in this partnership the nature of the language is the factor that limits free plasticity and rigidifies channels of development in the more autocratic way.   [*Whorf*][5]

So it is being claimed that people in different societies perceive, behave in, conceive of, and take attitudes towards the world in radically different ways – and these differences are largely to be explained in terms of their possessing radically different languages.

No one, I take it, would deny that there are many variations in culture corresponding to variations in language. It is not a mere coincidence that the Eskimos have more words for snow than we do. Nor is there a chance correlation between the hippies' attitude to life and their use of a special vocabulary containing expressions like 'do your own thing', 'up tight', 'that's not my bag', and so on. Nor need we deny that, in many ways, we are free to classify what we perceive in different ways. For example, there is no necessity to divide up the spectrum in just the way we do with our colour vocabulary. Another language need contain no exact synonym for 'yellow'. We can further happily admit that some people lack some of our concepts, and that this will correlate with a lack of certain words in their language. Aboriginals, perhaps, have no concept of the electron, and no words for talking about anything faintly like an electron.

If the Sapir/Whorf hypothesis is to be interesting, it must be saying something far more radical than the above points, which everybody would happily admit. And they are saying something far more radical. They are saying that not only do different people classify what they perceive differently, but that they actually perceive differently as a result of having different languages. They say that not only do some people lack very sophisticated concepts, like that of an electron, but that some people lack such basic, central concepts as those of time, space, matter, and cause. They are saying that not only do certain attitudes vary with language, but that whole systems of norms and morals differ as a result of linguistic differences. It is at this point that the philosopher must take serious note of the hypothesis. For if it is true, many cherished philosophical doctrines must be jettisoned. For example, according to philosophers from Aristotle, through Kant, to a contemporary one like Strawson, all rational men must think in accordance with certain basic concepts or categories – including those of time, material object, and space. Yet, if Whorf is right, there are peoples, like the Hopi Indians, whose languages do not permit the expression of such concepts, so that there is no reason to say the peoples have them. Again, many philosophers have insisted that only humans, and creatures resembling humans in behaviour, can have minds.[6] Yet if Whorf is right, this only reflects the nature of our mental language. There are societies in which mental properties are systematically ascribed to inanimate objects – and who is to say that these ascriptions are wrong? There is no higher language which can serve as a perch from which to judge between the different languages.

Before we are in any position to assess the hypothesis, it must be knocked into more manageable shape. It must be specified more closely which aspects of language are meant to correlate with which aspects of culture. We can break language down into a phonetic aspect, a syntactic aspect, and a semantic aspect. This is, of course, a crude breakdown, but it will do for our present purposes to say that language can be looked at in terms of sound, or structure, or meaning. We can also break culture into three crude divisions – perception, norms or attitudes, and conceptualization. It is possible, that is, to make rough distinctions between men's perceptual, discriminatory abilities, the norms and attitudes involved in their behaviour towards one another and the world, and the concepts they employ in thinking about the world.

Accepting this rough breakdown of language and culture, it follows that there are nine possible relations holding between language and culture. These are:

1 *phonetics – perception*	4 *syntax – perception*
2 *phonetics – norms*	5 *syntax – norms*
3 *phonetics – concepts*	6 *syntax – concepts*

7 *semantics – perception*
8 *semantics – norms*
9 *semantics – concepts*

Nobody, as far as I know, has claimed that there is any interesting relationship between culture and language considered solely as a system of sounds. The nature of the noises we make, considered phonetically, is not something likely to influence how we perceive or think. So we can ignore the first three language/culture correlations. Attention, though, has been given to each of the other possible relationships. The bulk of the literature, however, has been devoted to investigating the last four of the possible relationships. It has been argued that there are significant connections between [1] the syntax of a language and the concepts of those speaking the language, [2] the vocabulary of a language and the perceptual abilities of those speaking it, [3] the vocabulary of a language and the norms of the society employing it, and [4] the vocabulary of a language and the concepts of those employing it. Whorf, for example, was most interested in the first and last of these four possible connections.

This rough breakdown of the possible connections between language and culture puts us in a better position to assess the Sapir/Whorf hypothesis. But we are still not in a very good position. Philosophers, we have seen, are interested in the hypothesis partly because of the implications

it has for traditional philosophical doctrines. But they also have a different sort of interest. This is the interest of philosophers as philosophers of
science. The point is that there are considerable methodological and
conceptual problems involved in the hypothesis, which must be ironed
out before empirical research can get under way in assessing it. An
empirical researcher who is unaware of these problems is likely to find
the value of his researches invalidated from the very outset. The remainder
of this section is devoted to illuminating these methodological/conceptual
difficulties.

Before we can establish that language causally influences culture, a
more modest point must be established – namely, that there are significant
correlations between linguistic differences and cultural differences.
Unless we can establish that cultural differences parallel linguistic
differences, there will be no reason to suppose that the latter are somehow
responsible for the former. The conceptual/methodological problems
about to be discussed concern the difficulty in establishing even this
more modest claim. There would undoubtedly be further conceptual
problems involved in establishing the stronger claim that language is a
causal determinant of culture.

The first problem is the problem of translation. Clearly we must
translate other languages properly before we can assert that these
languages differ in significant and relevant respects from our own. Where
we are dealing with an exotic language, like Hopi, this is no easy task.
One great danger in translation is that of over-literal translation. For if
we translate over-literally we may read into the thought of other peoples
what is not really there. Suppose a foreign anthropologist was to translate 'breakfast' as if it meant 'meal which breaks, or ends, a period of
fasting'. His readers would at once attribute pretty strange gastronomic
habits to Englishmen and Americans. The point is that, whatever the
etymology of the word 'breakfast', it no longer means a meal which
breaks a fast, but the first meal of the day. The anthropologist's translation
was over-literal. Whorf, it seems, is sometimes guilty of just this. In
his attempt to show that the Hopi do not conceive of time as we do, he
notes that they do not count days in our manner. Whereas we speak of
'four days' or 'ten days', they supposedly speak of 'day (or dayness)
for the fourth time' or 'day (or dayness) for the tenth time'. Whorf concludes that the Hopi do not think of days as discrete, separate stretches of
time, as we do; but of a single entity, dayness, which is continually
reappearing. Before we accept this reasoning, let us consider an analogy.
We speak of 'King Charles the First' or of 'King William the Fourth'.
The French, on the other hand, speak of 'Le Roi Louis Deux' or of 'Le
Roi Guillaume Six'. They count their kings, that is, by using cardinals
rather than ordinals. A French anthropologist, noting that we count
kings differently, might reason as follows: 'The English are a funny lot.

They do not speak of Charles Two or Charles Four, but of Charles for the second time, or Charles for the fourth time. Obviously they do not think of kings as being separate people, as we do in France. They must believe that there is a single Charles who keeps reappearing on different occasions through reincarnation.' This reasoning is quite analogous to Whorf's reasoning concerning the implications to be drawn from the Hopi talk of days. The point here is that the French anthropologist has over-literally translated English. The correct translation into French of 'Charles the Second' is not 'Charles le deuxième' but 'Charles Deux'. 'Charles the Second' has the same use in English that 'Charles Deux' has in French. It is because the anthropologist over-literally translated our talk of kings into French that he is tempted to ascribe weird beliefs about kings to us. Similarly, it may well be that the correct translation of Hopi talk about days would not render them as saying 'dayness for the fourth time' but 'four days'.[7] We shall see that there are other occasions on which linguists and anthropologists may have gone astray in ascribing cultural differences to peoples as a result of over-literal translation of their languages.

A second, even more serious methodological problem is this: if a significant correlation is to be established between A's and B's, it is necessary that the A's and B's be separately identifiable. There is a one hundred per cent correlation between actions done by bachelors and actions done by unmarried men – but since these are not separately identifiable types of actions, the correlation is insignificant. If it is claimed that linguistic differences significantly correlate with cultural differences, it must therefore be possible to identify the linguistic differences independently from the cultural ones. A great danger is that someone will define cultural differences in terms of linguistic ones. There will then be a correlation between language and culture, but of a completely vacuous, trivial sort. Suppose, for example, an African anthropologist claimed that the French conception of sex was importantly different from the American; and suppose he gave as his sole evidence that the French employ genders far more frequently than Americans. It will then follow that where the language of sex varies, so do conceptions of sex. But this is a trivial assertion; since all that is meant by saying that conceptions of sex vary is that the languages of sex vary. To establish a significant correlation, it seems we would have to have some non-linguistic criteria for establishing that there are conceptual differences – behavioural criteria, for example. Whorf, I believe, is often guilty of just the sort of error mentioned. At one point he says that the Hopi concept of time must be different from ours simply because they do not employ tensed verbs. But if differences in the language of time by themselves constitute differences in concepts of time, then it is utterly trivial to say that concepts vary with language. What is required for the correlation to become significant is that we should have some non-linguistic criteria, or linguistic criteria of a very different type, for deciding that the Hopi conceive of time differently. If by these other criteria, behavioural ones perhaps, we can establish that they do, then we are in a position to suggest that there is a significant correlation between the linguistic and the conceptual differences. Now it is no easy matter to provide this separate identification of linguistic aspects and cultural ones. The difficulty is especially chronic where we are trying to correlate linguistic differences with conceptual ones; for the best way to find out what a man's concepts are is to see what he says. We shall return to that point in the last section of this chapter.

In the next section I want to discuss two possible examples of significant language/culture correlation. These cases are more manageable than the more interesting connection there may be between language and conceptualization, which is the type of connection that is of prime philosophical interest. However, since they are simpler cases, and a good deal of work has been done upon them, they may serve as models for highlighting the problems which arise in establishing any sort of significant language/culture correlation.

2 Two test cases

A: COLOUR PERCEPTION

I shall start by seeing how there may be a significant connection between the vocabulary a person uses and his perceptual, discriminatory ability. This type of connection between language and culture is the one that is most free from the conceptual/methodological problems mentioned in the last section. For [1] it is relatively easy to translate perceptual, *eg* colour, words, since there are standard tests for deciding how people use them, and [2] it is relatively easy to provide separate identifications of how men speak and how they make perceptual discriminations. It is essential, of course, that we do provide this separate identification. We do not want to say that Eskimos perceive snow differently from ourselves simply on the grounds that they employ more words for talking about snow.

I shall concentrate upon colour terminology and perception, since the most work has been done in this area.[8] The first thing to realize is that colour terminology does vary considerably from society to society. This is not surprising. It is reckoned that the average human being is able to distinguish some seven million different colours on the spectrum; yet, in most languages, there is only a handful of colour words in common use. This means that our colour words label large chunks of the spectrum; chunks which contain many, many distinguishable shades. Now there is no reason to suppose that all peoples will divide up the spectrum in identical ways; that the labels they apply to chunks of the spectrum will exactly correspond. Indeed, we know that they do not. For example, the Welsh word 'glas' is applied to some things we would call 'blue', and to others which we would call 'grey'.[9] Again, they use the word 'llwyd' for some things we would call 'brown', but for other things we would not call 'brown'. So there is no exact correspondence between English and Welsh labelling of the spectrum. Where the Welsh can use a single word to apply to some colour, the English may have to use some compound expression, like 'greyish blue', or 'brownish with a touch of green' – and vice versa.

The second thing to realize is that perceptual abilities vary from society to society. Consider the following experiment: some English-speaking subjects were shown a coloured sheet, and a few minutes later were presented with a chart on which there were several coloured patches. They were then asked to identify on the chart the colour which they had previously been shown. Some Zulus were then put through the same test. It turned out that there were some colours which the Englishmen were better at reidentifying than the Zulus. Equally there were some colours which the Zulus were better at reidentifying than the Englishmen.[10]

The question is: is there any correlation between differences in colour terminologies and differences in discriminatory abilities? If there is, this is confirmation, in this area, of the Sapir/Whorf hypothesis. And it seems that there is such a correlation. It has been shown that people are better at reidentifying colours for which their language provides single-word, unambiguous labels. Where a colour has no single word for it in a language, the speakers of that language are relatively poorer at re-identifying this colour. Suppose, for example, that the coloured sheet is of a colour which most Englishmen would unhesitatingly describe as 'red', but which Zulus would have to describe with the help of some longer, compound expression. It turns out that the English are better at reidentifying this colour; and, moreover, that there is less disagree-ment between the judgments of the English. The conclusion is that there is a correlation between [1] the availability of single words applicable to certain colours, and [2] the ability to reidentify those colours better than other colours where no single words are available. Or, as Brown and Lenneberg put it:

> A given set of cognitive categories will be more available to the speakers of a language that lexically codes these categories than to speakers of a language in which the categories are not represented in the lexicon.[11]

Not only is there such a correlation, but it is plausible partially to explain it in Whorfian terms – in terms, that is, of the influence of language upon perception. It could reasonably be supposed, for instance, that memory, or the ability to reidentify, is aided by the subject's being able to describe what he has perceived in simple words. The shorter the description we can give of what we have perceived, the better we are at recalling it. (A student of mine, Mr B. Tedeschi, performed a useful experiment along these lines. He showed a coloured stick to two groups of children, A and B. He named the stick 'Da' to group A, and 'Danayanga' to group B. He found that children from group A were then significantly better at, and more interested in, picking the stick out from other ones.) This explanation is supported by other known facts. It is known, for example, that people are better at reidentifying shapes which resemble shapes for which they have simple names in their language. Thus I am better at reidentifying this shape ⬭ than this shape △ , because my language provides names for things resembling the first, eg 'dumbbell' or 'spectacles', or 'waterwings', but not for things resembling the second. Presumably, that is, I may employ words like 'dumbbell' or 'spectacles' to apply to the shape when I see it, and this increases my chances of reidentifying it, since I can now recall the word as well as the shape directly.

This sort of explanation of the correlation between linguistic and perceptual factors is not the only possible explanation. It may be that the reason the Zulus are good at reidentifying certain colours is not because they have a single name for each of them, but because those colours are very frequently encountered in Zululand. So it is their practice with these colours, rather than a fact about their language, which best explains their ability. But this sort of explanation will probably not do for all cases; since there are examples of differences in colour discrimination which do not correlate with differences in colour environments. At any rate, the main point is that there is a significant correlation between linguistic and cultural factors in the field of perceptual abilities. To that extent, we can regard it as a clear-enough model for the sort of correlations Whorf and others want to establish in different areas of language and culture.

B: KINSHIP TERMINOLOGY

I now want to discuss the possible connection there might be between [1] kinship terminologies, and [2] the various attitudes taken towards kinsmen, and the various norms governing inter-kin behaviour, which exist in different societies.

The first thing to note is that kinship terminologies do, in certain respects, definitely vary from culture to culture. For instance, the Ngaranyin of Western Australia, employ a single word 'wuniji' to apply to what we would describe as a man's father's brother-in-law, his own brother-in-law, his son-in-law, and his sister's son's child. And in Hungary, there are separate single words for the elder brother and younger brother, or the elder sister and the younger sister. It is unlikely, in fact, that any two kinship terminologies exactly overlap. One will probably find few languages which possess expressions which exactly parallel each of the English expressions, 'uncle', 'nephew', 'brother-in-law', etc.

The second thing to realize is that attitudes towards kinsmen certainly do differ, in certain ways, from society to society. In some societies, less respect is paid one's biological father than is paid to some other, older relative. In one society, at least, a person is not allowed to address his grandmother directly, but must do it through another person, or even animal. Incest taboos, furthermore, vary from society to society. What is regarded as condemnable incest in one society may be regarded as healthy family affection in another. Again, in some societies the relationship of cross-cousinhood is of paramount significance, while in others it is of minor importance.

That kinship terminologies and attitudes should vary in the above ways is not particularly startling or interesting. That people live in different ways is bound to have some effect on their attitudes and upon their vocabulary. The linguistic and attitudinal differences I shall be concerned with are of a much deeper, more far-reaching sort than those mentioned so far. It would be most significant and interesting to show that a natural assumption made by most Westerners is mistaken. The assumption is that, in any society, many attitudes will be governed by the fact that some people are *blood-related* to others. For most Westerners, perhaps, a kinship system is thought of precisely as a system of blood-relationships. Alongside this assumption is the assumption that any language will be bound to contain a battery of words whose essential role is to mark out, and express, blood-relationships. If these assumptions are correct, one is not going to find any very interesting correlations between differences in kinship terminologies, and kinship attitudes or norms, since all such terminologies and attitudes will be basically the same – both based upon a primary concern for blood-relationship.

These assumptions have been strongly challenged by some anthropologists and linguists in recent years. It is a gross error, according to these thinkers, to suppose that the kinship terminologies and attitudes in other societies have any great resemblance to our own. It may be that behaviour to blood-relations in other societies has a superficial resemblance to our own; but the significance that such behaviour has for other societies may be totally different.

It has been insisted by many anthropologists that kinship attitudes in other societies are not based essentially upon blood-relationships at all. Rather kinship attitudes are based upon *social* relationships between men. What makes a man your kinsman in some societies is not essentially that he is related to you by blood, but that he stands in a certain social relationship to you. Equally, it is insisted, kinship words in these societies do not have, as their main function, the marking out or expressing of blood-relationships, but the marking out or expressing of social relationships. Just as it would be a mistake to suppose that the king and queen in chess are related by marriage, despite their names, so it would be a mistake to suppose that words in other societies which parallel our kinship terms express blood-relationships.

One thing should be made clear. Anthropologists who argue in the above manner need not deny that kinsmen in other societies are blood-related. What they do deny is that being blood-related is what makes them kinsmen. As one writer puts it:

> Classes of relatives between or of whom particular behaviour patterns are expected are here grouped under the same name, so that the arrangement of kinship names runs to that extent parallel with the arrangement of behaviour patterns.[12]

His point is this: in our society a word like 'nephew' is applied to persons in virtue of their being blood-related to a certain person. As a result, no doubt, certain behaviour patterns will be expected towards nephews. In other societies, the position may be reversed. Certain behaviour patterns will be expected of, and between, certain individuals. These individuals will then be given a common name. Now it may well be that these persons are blood-related in any number of different ways. But this is largely coincidental. What groups them together under one heading, and what makes the blood-relationships have any significance, is that certain types of behaviour are expected of them, and towards them.

A good example of the view that kinship systems are essentially socially based rather than blood-based can be found in the works of the influential French anthropologist, Claude Lévi-Strauss.[13] For him kinship systems are special instances of exchange systems. Dealings between people in society, or between societies, can be carried on in various ways. One way is to exchange goods. Another way is to exchange persons through marriage. Just as there are rules governing and restricting how goods may be exchanged, so there are rules restricting how women may be exchanged. According to this somewhat unromantic view, kinsmen are regarded as units having significance in an exchange system. The rights and duties of kinsmen arise as do the rights and duties of businessmen – through contact and barter. Just as there are many ways in which a commodity market can function, so there are many ways in which exchange of persons can be arranged. Thus the variation in kinship systems from society to society. On this view, for example, what makes a group of men kinsmen of a similar sort is that wives of these men cannot be exchanged with another society. So it is not biology, but economics, that forms certain persons into a significant group, to which we apply a kinship term.

We have, then, two contrasting theses – the common Western assumption, and that of several anthropologists.[14] The first holds that all kinship systems are essentially based upon blood-ties, which in turn give rise to certain social attitudes and norms. The second holds that some kinship systems are essentially systems based upon social functions and roles; and this in turn dictates what we shall regard as the significant blood-relationships.

If the second thesis is correct, there are radically different types of kinship systems – blood and social. Further there will be radical differences in kinship languages – for in some the terms express blood-relationships, and in others, social ones. Assuming these differences correlate, this would seem to confirm a Sapir/Whorf hypothesis in the field of kinship. Or rather, it would confirm that there are significant correlations between language and culture; it would still be an open question as to whether the language factor is causally responsible in any way for the cultural. Is it, then, really the case that kinship languages vary in the radical way suggested; and that kinship attitudes and norms vary in the same way? These questions are very hard to answer – and largely because of the methodological/conceptual problems already mentioned. What I wish to do is to suggest considerations which at least cast doubt upon the view that kinship languages and culture vary in these radical ways. If I am right, it is not at all clear that confirmation for the Sapir/Whorf hypothesis can be found in this direction.

The first two considerations concern the problem of correct translation of foreign kinship terminologies. In the first place, it may well be that anthropologists have been guilty of over-literal translation. If so, this will have tempted them to overestimate the differences between how we think of kinsmen and how other societies do. I have heard the following argument: there is a Navaho term which applies to all of one's wife's relatives, and which means 'those for whom I carry burdens'. This is supposed to confirm the view that some kinship terms do not essentially express blood or marital relationships, but relationships of social obligations and rights. But is there any reason to suppose that this is the correct, as opposed to the over-literal, translation of the Navaho word? 'Grandfather', for example, does not mean 'father with grandeur'. Nor does 'godfather' mean 'divine father'. No doubt there are historical reasons for talking of *grand*- and *god*fathers; and similarly there may be historical reasons why the Navaho employ a term which is etymologically connected with talk of burdens to apply to certain relations. But these historical reasons may have nothing to do with the present meanings of the terms. Really, I am just offering a word of caution. From the fact that a foreign kinship word *can* be translated into words expressive of social rights and obligations, it does not follow that the foreigners think of their kinsmen in these terms, as opposed to marital or blood terms. For the translation may have been over-literal.

The second point concerning translation is more subtle and interesting. Take the word 'uncle'. In England and America this word is applied not only to parents' brothers, but also to older friends of the family. Some children, indeed, are encouraged to call anyone who is post-adolescent 'uncle'. Despite this, a visiting anthropologist who concluded that 'uncle' does not express a blood-relationship, would be making a grave error. For he would be failing to distinguish a central, primary sense of 'uncle' in which only a blood-relative can be an uncle, from an extended, secondary sense. Equally, a foreign anthropologist would be mistaken if, having heard trade unionists call each other 'brother', he concluded that 'brother' did not have a basically genealogical role. Terms like 'uncle' and 'brother' get used in extended ways because of analogies between how we treat (blood) uncles and brothers, and how we treat older friends of the family and fellow workers respectively.

Now it may well be the case that this problem has infected anthropologists' translations of exotic kinship terminologies. Sometimes, definitely, a foreign kinship term has a secondary use which must not be confused with its central use. In Australia, there is a tribe which uses a word to apply to wives, and also to the lands from which the wives come. Clearly, though, there is not a single sense of the word here, but a central and an extended sense. (Compare the way that 'father's land' becomes 'Fatherland'.) Suppose, then, we find a foreign word which applies to a wide variety of blood-relatives, and to some who are not even blood-relatives at all. Are we entitled to conclude that this word is not essentially expressive of some single blood-relationship, but of some social relationship? Not at all, without further investigation. For it may be that the word has a central role, in which it applies only to persons standing in a definite blood-relationship; and various secondary, extended roles in which it applies to a whole variety of blood-relatives and to men who are not blood-relatives at all. It may have been extended in a manner analogous to our 'uncle' and 'brother'. As Floyd Lounsbury puts it:

> I would assume rather that for kinship terms, as for the majority of other words, a term may have a primary sense . . . and various extended senses. For heuristic purposes, we might even go further in the case of kinship terms and say that the primary sense of each kinship term is to be found in its reference to the genealogically closest type of relationship which is found amongst the referents of the term. Following this line of thought, we might assume, again tentatively, that other more distant referents of a term represent extensions of its meaning and involve therefore an attenuation of that meaning.[15]

The significance, then, is this: it may not be that kinship terminologies vary radically in meaning. It may be that in each society the primary role of certain terms is to express various definite blood-ties. However, it is often the case that these words are applied to individuals having different blood-ties, or no blood-ties at all. But this is because the words are given secondary, analogical extensions. So once more we offer a word of caution against drawing inferences from variations in kinship terminologies.

My final consideration concerns the validity of inferences drawn from observation of apparently different behaviour adopted towards kinsmen in different societies. I pointed out, in section 3 of Chapter 2, that it is often a mistake to suppose that behaviour which resembles our own in observable respects is really the same behaviour. Equally, behaviour patterns may superficially differ from one another but be, in important respects, the same. We must insist upon a distinction between [1] behaviour towards kinsmen *qua* kinsmen, and [2] behaviour towards men who *happen to be* our kinsmen. Suppose that in a society it is customary for the younger brother to join the army, and for the older to join the church. Of course we will behave differently towards the two brothers. But the difference will be due, not to the one's being the elder and the other's being the younger brother, but to the fact that one is a soldier and the other a priest. From the fact that people in this society behave differently towards the two brothers, we cannot infer that they conceive of brotherhood in a special way.

Suppose, then, we find that men in an exotic society treat some blood-relatives very differently from how we treat those relatives. We are not entitled to conclude that they have totally different kinship attitudes – that, for example, they do not think in terms of blood but of social roles. For it may be that their attitudes are due to the fact that, in this society, the relevant blood-relatives have other characteristics or functions which determine that special attitudes shall be taken towards them. It need not be *kinship* attitudes that differ, as Lévi-Strauss suggests, but other attitudes due to the social arrangements in these societies. To take an analogy: if your father is a criminal and mine is not, you and I will treat our fathers differently. That does not show we have different views of fatherhood.

I conclude, then, that the study of kinship terminologies and attitudes does not lend any clear confirmation to the Sapir/Whorf hypothesis. Until much more work is done, it is not clear that terminologies or attitudes differ in radical ways at all. If they do not, there is no question of there being exciting correlations between differences in terminology and differences in attitude.

3 Language and conceptualization

We have discussed two test-cases for the Sapir/Whorf hypothesis. We have done so largely by way of leading up to the type of language/culture

connection that most interested these men – that between language, both
syntax and semantics, and conceptualization. Do concepts vary radically
in different societies, and does this variation correlate with variation in
languages? No one would deny that concepts vary at one level. It is
hardly a cause for wonder, as I mentioned, that the Aboriginals do not
have the concept of an electron. Matters become interesting when it is
argued that some of our most basic concepts, like those of time, space,
substance, or causality, are not shared by some peoples. For if this is so,
it puts paid to the cherished ideal of philosophers to discover a set of
concepts or categories which any rational human must employ in his
thinking.[16]

Here are some examples of language/concept correlations which have
been suggested:

[1] The Chinese ideal of the 'mean' – of the happy middle way which all
men and things strive to attain – is supposedly correlated with the fact
that adjectives in Chinese do not ascribe properties in a categorical way,
but instead serve to say that something is 'more or less' such-and-such.
The grammar, as it were, reflects or perhaps encourages an obsession
with the *relative* degree to which things have properties.'[17]

[2] Mobility is an especially important feature in the life of a nomadic
tribe, such as the Navaho. This correlates with the very widespread
existence in the Navaho language of nouns, verbs, and adverbs expressive
of movement.[18]

[3] Whorf suggests the Hopi lack our concept of time; and this is reflected or encouraged by the lack of tensed verbs in Hopi, and by their
lack of nouns denoting stretches of time, like our 'day' or 'month'.

[4] Whorf also suggests the Hopi lack our concept of space; and that this
is reflected or encouraged by the lack of words in Hopi even faintly
similar in meaning to our 'mile' or 'inch', or any of our words denoting
spatial stretches.

[5] Whorf also suggests the Hopi lack our concept of velocity. This
correlates with the fact that the Hopi do not have a word like our 'speed'
which applies both to things like horses, which move with respect to
their environment, and to things like chemical reactions, which do not.

[6] Finally, Whorf has suggested that many peoples do not share our
concept of mind – as something belonging only to higher animals, including humans. Rather they conceive of the entire universe as being
mind-impregnated. This supposedly correlates with the lack of a
vocabulary among these peoples which is used to speak about higher
animals alone.[19]

The main bulk of this section is devoted to general consideration of the
difficulties which arise in assessing the Sapir/Whorf hypothesis con-

cerning concepts. Towards the end, however, I shall return to some of the above examples, and discuss them in more detail.

The methodological/conceptual difficulties mentioned in section 1 are at their most intense when it comes to assessing the claim that there are significant language/concept correlations. In the first place, the problem of correct translation reaches its peak. Where we can safely assume that foreigners share our basic concepts, as we can with the French or the Germans, translation is not too difficult. But if we drop this assumption, as perhaps we should in the case of more exotic foreigners, we must be far more wary about our translations. If a Frenchman says 'C'est un lapin' wherever we would say 'That's a rabbit', it is reasonable to suppose the two sentences are nearly synonymous. But suppose we visit a new and strange land where the natives say 'Gavagai' when we would say 'That's a rabbit'. Are we justified in translating 'Gavagai' as 'That's a rabbit'? Well, only if we assume, *inter alia*, that the natives share our concept of a material object. It might be that they do not think in terms of discrete, particular material objects. It might be that a better translation of 'Gavagai' would be 'Rabbithood is revealing itself'. The natives, that is, might not think of there being separate entities, rabbits, but of a single abstract entity which sometimes reveals itself – rather as we might think of virtue as an abstract entity which occasionally reveals itself in actions. Or it may be that a better translation would be 'It is now rabbiting'. They may, that is, think in terms of events rather than of things – rather as we say 'It is pouring' rather than 'There is a pour'. So extreme caution is required in translating strange, new languages.[20]

The second problem, that of providing separate identifications of the linguistic and the cultural factors, is also at a peak. Obviously we do require some separate identifications. It would be absurd to say that the Hopi lack the concept of time simply because they lack tensed verbs. If we did say this, it would then be utterly trivial to say there was a correlation between conceptual and linguistic differences. What we want is some other test for deciding that the Hopi concept of time is not our own. The trouble is it is difficult to see what these other tests could be – for, as we saw in Chapter 2, a concept seems to be something essentially verbal. How do we find out what a man's concepts are except in terms of his language?

It might be suggested that we can identify a man's concepts by his behaviour. The difficulty with this suggestion is that, if we mean by 'behaviour' *actions*, as opposed to mere bodily movements, then it is impossible to know what the behaviour is without interpreting it properly. But to interpret it properly we must know how the agents conceive of it. As Peter Winch points out:

Conceptions according to which we normally think of social events . . .

enter into social life itself and not merely into the observer's description of it.[21]

For example, we could not know how to describe the behaviour of a man binding sheaves of wheat together – whether as 'preparing for future contingencies' or 'trying to influence the course of future events' – unless we had some idea how the man conceived of his relationship to the future, some idea of his concept of time. If this is so, it will be circular to try to test for concept differences in terms of behavioural differences.

A second point about behaviour is this: insofar as it is possible to recognize concepts through behaviour, it seems false to suggest that concepts vary at all radically from society to society. If, for example, we equate having a concept of time with the ability to notice change, with people not trying to cure others before they fall sick, with their not trying to get divorced before they get married, or with their not replying before they are asked, it is clear that everyone possesses the concept of time, and in a pretty similar fashion. Equally everyone possesses the concept of space, in similar ways, if by that we mean that they do not keep bumping into things, and are not always trying to put on clothes that do not fit them. So if we make behavioural features, like those mentioned, the test for whether men have certain concepts, then obviously all men do have concepts like those of time and space, and in near-identical manners.

It seems, then, that Sapir and Whorf cannot appeal to behavioural tests as the tests of concept differences. For either that appeal is circular, or it implies the falsity of the claim that basic concepts do vary radically.

We have to admit, I believe, that there can be no way of identifying what a man's concepts are except in terms of the language he uses. Conceptual ability is essentially linguistic ability. If this is so, we can no longer speak of there being a correlation between language and conceptualization, as Whorf and Sapir do. However, it is possible to restate their hypothesis in a less objectionable form. What we can try to do is to establish correlations between certain aspects of language, and those linguistic capacities which constitute conceptual capacities. Suppose we study the way the Hopi speak, and conclude, in some manner or another, that they do conceive of time differently from ourselves. We might then correlate this with certain aspects of Hopi grammar, such as their lack of tensed verbs. Here we are not correlating language with something else; rather we are correlating certain aspects of language, certain grammatical devices for example, with whole ranges and ways of talking about something; in this case, time.

How could we establish that concepts vary in terms of the ways men talk? One thing that would not be much use is to ask men 'What is your concept of time (space, matter, etc)?' While Einstein, Heisenberg, and their Hopi equivalents could give us interesting answers, the average taxi-driver or landlady could not. While the average man certainly does have a working concept of time, it is unlikely that he could make this concept explicit. So the questionnaire method of finding out if concepts vary is of little value. Anyway, Whorf himself is quite explicit that our deep concepts are possessed at an unconscious level. 'Thoughts are controlled by inexorable laws of pattern of which he (the ordinary man) is unconscious.'[22]

Once the questionnaire method is rejected, how shall we establish that concepts vary? It has been suggested that to possess a concept is to be able to use a group of related words properly.[23] To possess the concept of cause, for example, is to be able to use terms like 'cause', 'effect', 'if . . . then . . .', 'necessary', 'must' etc correctly. Let us take our cue from here. Groups of expressions, like the cause-group just mentioned, typically belong to larger groups. Take, for example, the pain-group of words, which will include such words as 'pain', 'agony', 'ache', 'excruciating', etc. This group belongs to a wider group, which we might call the sensation-group. That is, pain-words are used in connection with the same creatures, and the same sorts of things, sensations, as are words like 'itch', 'delicious', 'pleasant', 'tingle', 'twinge', etc. Distinct from the sensation-group of words would be what we might call the material property-group of words. This will include expressions like 'heavy', 'square', 'small', 'red', etc, whose main function is to express the properties of material objects.

I want to suggest the following: a concept X varies in two societies if the group of expressions connected with it belongs to different wider groups in the two societies. One could imagine a language, for example, in which pain was spoken of very much as we speak of colour. Whereas we speak of 'sensations of pain' or 'feelings of pain', men in this other community would speak of material objects possessing the property of pain in the way they possess the property of red or green. Just as we speak of perceiving the colour of a thing, they would speak of perceiving the pain of a thing when they are close to it. The world, for them, would contain patches of pain as it contains patches of colour.[24] In a language like this, the pain-group of words would no longer belong to the sensation-group, but to the material property-group. I am suggesting that because of this, it is reasonable to speak of them as having a different concept of pain from us. Put crudely, people who spoke of pain in this way would not be conceiving of pain as an inner, private sensation, but as a public property of the outside world which we sometimes, and unfortunately, perceive. We perceive the pain of the hot poker with our fingers in the way we perceive its solidity at the same time.

There is a second test I wish to suggest for establishing that concepts vary from society to society. When people explain concepts they very often employ analogies and metaphors. For example, our talk of time is very much based upon a spatial metaphor. We speak of 'rivers of time', 'stretches of time', 'points in time', and so on. Now it may well be that the analogies employed in other societies are radically different. Perhaps some people talk of time by way of analogy, not with space, but with emotions. If so, it would be plausible to suggest they have a different concept of time from us. For put bluntly, it would suggest that whereas we conceive of time as an objective, public, measurable, and quantifiable process, they think of time as an essentially private, personal, phenomenal process which may differ from man to man.

Naturally, these tests I suggest are very rough-and-ready. It is no easy matter to decide what words belong to a given group, and what groups belong to what wider groups.[25] Nor will it always be crystal-clear as to whether an analogy used by people has any great significance for how they think. But, admitting that the tests are rough, let us see how we might apply them to the cases that interested Whorf.

[1] *Time.* Whorf says that the Hopi

has no general notion or intuition of Time as a smooth flowing continuum in which everything in the universe proceeds at an equal rate, out of a future, through a present, into a past.[26]

On the other hand, the Hopi can get across what we would describe as temporal information – but they do so without using words that have any close correspondence to English words like 'after', 'now', 'future', 'ago', etc. How is this possible? According to Whorf the Hopi employ two basic concepts – those of the manifested and of the manifesting. The latter he also calls the concept of hope or hoping. This is

the realm of expectancy, of desire and purpose, of vitalizing life, of efficient cause, of thought thinking itself out from an inner realm (the Hopi HEART) into manifestation.[27]

Now, by employing words belonging to these categories the Hopi can get across 'temporal' information. For example, anything which we would call future will for the Hopi be in the realm of the manifesting – *ie* that which can be hoped for. What is past for us is, for the Hopi, in the realm of the manifested – *ie* that which cannot be hoped for. However, it must not be assumed that the Hopi talk of manifesting is at all similar to our talk of future. For, says Whorf,

the subjective or manifesting comprises all that we call future, but not merely this; it includes equally and indistinguishably all that we call mental and everything that appears or exists in the mind, or, as the Hopi prefer to say, in the HEART.[28]

Let us now relate this to what I said earlier about differences in concepts. The Hopi do have words which get across what we would call temporal information. But – and this is the essential point – the words they employ belong to a different group from the one to which our temporal words, like 'future', belong. The Hopi words belong to what might be called the mental-group. For, in getting across information about time, the Hopi thereby get across information about mental life – about hoping, what can be hoped for, etc. Clearly our temporal words belong to no such mental-group. In saying something is in the future, we say nothing about mental life. The point is reinforced if we consider the analogies employed by the Hopi in illustrating the notion of time. Our analogies, as I mentioned, are very largely spatial. We speak of 'rivers', 'stretches', 'lengths', etc, of time. The Hopi, though, talk of time in terms of tendencies, forces, intensities, and so on. These are terms which are appropriate for talking about the mind. Roughly, they seem to conceive of time, not on a parallel with space, but on a parallel with a mind which is maturing and developing, struggling to reveal and express itself. (Some readers may recognize shades of Hegel here.)

It might be said that it is one thing to suppose the Hopi can get across very broad information about past and future in terms of their manifested/manifesting dichotomy, and another to see how they can get across more detailed information – such as that one thing in the past occurred before another thing in the past. Before we can understand how they might do this, we must look at their concept of space.

[2] *Space.* According to Whorf, the Hopi cannot

refer to space in such a way as to exclude that element of extension or existence that we call 'time'.[29]

Rather, they have an overall concept of 'distance' which includes what we would call spatial and temporal elements.

Distance includes what we call time in the sense of the temporal relations between events which have already happened. The Hopi conceive time and motion in the objective realm in a purely operational sense – a matter of the complexity and magnitude of operations connecting events – so that the element of time is not separate from whatever element of space enters into the operations.[30]

The point seems to be this: where we speak of two events being separated by space or by time, the Hopi speak of the number of, and complexity of, the operations and activities that take place between the two events. We would speak of one town, for example, being a long distance from another. The Hopi would say that many complex operations must be undertaken in order to get from the one town to the other. Since these operations take time, it follows that the Hopi do not speak of spatial distance except in terms that involve the notion of time.

Once again we see that, while the Hopi can get across information we would describe as spatial, they do so by using words which belong to groups quite distinct from the groups to which our spatial words belong. In getting across spatial information, the Hopi also get across information about tasks, operations, difficulties, activities, and so on. When we speak of X being a long way from Y, no such reference to the tasks required to get from X to Y is involved. Hopi 'spatial' words belong, we might say, to the activities-group. Ours do not.

It is still hard, no doubt, for us to understand the Hopi ways of thinking and talking about time and space. Perhaps, though, the following consideration will help. Much of what, for the Hopi, appears to be *literal* talk, occurs in English as *metaphorical* talk. For instance, we speak of a generation *gap*, where we mean, not that there is actually some geometrical space between parents and children, but that communication between them is difficult. It is *as if* they were physically separated. Again, consider the phrase 'the world has become a smaller place since the aeroplane'. We do not mean that the earth has literally shrunk, but that there is less difficulty in crossing long distances. Similar examples can be found in connection with time. We might speak of parents belonging to a different *era* from their children; and we do not mean that pregnancies last for centuries, but that communication between the generations is about as negative as communication with men of centuries ago.

These metaphorical ways of talking in English correspond quite closely to what appears to be literal talk for the Hopi. Their word corresponding to our 'gap' seems to have as part of its literal meaning reference to difficulties in communication. It may be that just as we can say certain things by metaphorical extension from our literal ways of talking about space and time, so the Hopi can get across 'pure' spatial and temporal information by metaphorical extension from their literal talk about manifested and manifesting, and about difficulties and operations. At the risk of oversimplification, it may be suggested that the main difference between us and the Hopi is that what is literal for us is metaphorical for them, and vice versa. (Of course, the decision as to what counts as literal as opposed to metaphorical is a very tricky one which only very accurate translation can guide us in.)

How, then, shall we assess the Sapir/Whorf hypothesis with respect to language and concepts? We have seen that it is highly misleading to speak of there being a correlation between linguistic differences and conceptual differences among societies. That implies that language and conceptualization are distinct phenomena. In fact, though, concept differences consist in linguistic differences. More precisely, I have argued, concept differences consist in [1] the fact that certain words belong to very different groups in different societies, and [2] the fact that the explanatory analogies employed in different societies may be very different. But this is not to say that there are no correlations between aspects of language and conceptualization. It may be that the lack of tensed verbs in Hopi, for instance, correlates significantly with their concept of time. This is not a correlation between something linguistic and something non-linguistic, but rather, a correlation between one limited aspect of language and some wider aspect of language, the whole battery of terms and analogies employed in talking about time. Even if we do not want to speak of correlations between language and concepts, it is of the greatest interest and significance to show that concepts do differ; to show, that is, that ways of talking differ radically from society to society.

What of some of the larger claims of Sapir and Whorf, to the effect that language 'determines' our way of thinking, or that it is impossible for people from one society fully to understand those from another, or that no one is free to describe the world with impartiality? None of these big conclusions, as far as I can see, are warranted by what I have said about the connection between language and culture.

First, it is peculiarly self-defeating to insist that one cannot understand the concepts of another, radically different, society. For, if we are to believe anything Whorf has said about the Hopi, at least Whorf himself must have understood them. If the concepts of another society really are unintelligible to us, this is not something we could ever know. For to know it, one would first have to understand these concepts. If one finds it hard to understand the concepts of another society, the conclusion should be that we have not yet done enough investigation.

Second, it is surely an exaggeration to say that language 'determines' our thinking, in the sense that a person is incapable of thinking except in the terms dictated to him by his language. For, after all, many Western thinkers have arrived at very different conceptions of the world, yet they have been employing a common language. It may be that some Western thinkers have thought of the world in terms similar to the Hopi – yet they do not talk Hopi. (Hegel, as I mentioned, may be an actual example of this.) What is no doubt true is that certain novel concepts – say the theory of relativity – will be more difficult to absorb for some people than for others, depending upon how well-suited their language is for talking about the new concepts. For example, a language that lacks mass-nouns is a relatively unsuitable instrument for coping with the notion of substance. *Unsuitable*, it must be stressed, rather than impossible. I shall leave the final word on this issue to Charles Hockett:

Languages differ not so much as to what *can* be said in them, but rather as to what it is *relatively easy* to say. In this connection it is worthy of note that the history of Western logic and science, from

122 LANGUAGE AND CULTURE

Aristotle down, constitutes not so much the story of scholars hemmed in and misled by the nature of their specific languages as the story of a long and successful struggle against inherited linguistic limitations.[31]

To conclude: the Sapir/Whorf hypothesis is pregnant with suggestion and implication. It is also pregnant with difficulties as to its assessment. I have tried to iron out some of these difficulties, and to knock the hypothesis into a roughly testable form. Also, I have suggested that in some areas the hypothesis receives confirmation, though it may be that confirmation is received in the less exciting areas. Even where the hypothesis does receive confirmation, however, we must be on our guard against accepting some of the radical relativistic conclusions that its proponents have drawn from it.

Notes

1 *Language.* Harcourt & Brace, 1921. *p* 233.
2 Quoted in H. Hoijer, 'The Sapir/Whorf hypothesis', in *Language in Culture*, ed H. Hoijer. Chicago University Press, 1959. *p* 92.
3 *Language, Thought, and Reality.* M.I.T. Press, 1969. *pp* 212–13. This book is a collection of Whorf's papers, mainly from the 1930s.
4 *ibid, p* 214.
5 *ibid, p* 156.
6 See, for example, L. Wittgenstein, *Philosophical Investigations.* 3rd edn. Macmillan, 1969.
7 I owe this example to J. Greenberg, 'Concerning inferences from linguistic to non-linguistic data', in *Psycholinguistics*, ed S. Saporta. Holt, Rhinehart, & Winston, 1961.
8 See B. Berlin and P. Kay, *Basic Color Terms.* University of California Press, 1970.
9 I owe this example, and several others in this and the next sub-sections, to A. Capell, *Studies in Socio-Linguistics.* Mouton, 1966.
10 For a description of an experiment very like this, see R. Brown and E. Lenneberg, 'A study in language and cognition', in *Psycholinguistics*, ed S. Saporta. Holt, Rhinehart, & Winston, 1961.
11 *ibid, p* 490.
12 S. F. Nadel, quoted in A. Capell, *Studies in Socio-Linguistics.* Mouton, 1966. *p* 82.
13 See, for example, his *Les Structures Elémentaires De La Parenté.* Paris, 1967.
14 By no means all anthropologists would accept this thesis, and we shall shortly consider a criticism of it by the eminent American anthropologist, Lounsbury. Further, many who do stress cultural and linguistic diversity would not do so for Lévi-Strauss's reasons. See E. Leach, *Lévi-Strauss.* Fontana/Collins, 1970.
15 'Language and culture', in *Language and Philosophy*, ed S. Hook. New York University Press, 1969. *pp* 21–2.
16 One thinks especially of Kant's attempts in this direction in his *Critique of Pure Reason.*
17 C. Hockett, 'Chinese versus English: an exploration of the Whorfian theses', in *Language in Culture*, ed H. Hoijer. Chicago University Press, 1959.

18 See H. Hoijer, 'Cultural implications of some Navaho linguistic categories', in *Language in Culture and Society*, ed D. Hymes. Harper & Row, 1964.
19 Interestingly enough, Tacitus makes such a suggestion concerning the Germans of his day. *Germania*, ix.
20 I owe this example to W. V. Quine, *Word and Object*, M.I.T. Press, 1960. He claims that more than 'extreme caution' is required in translation, which involves 'radical indeterminacy'. It is impossible, that is, even in principle, to decide which the right translation is where several translations are compatible with all the observed facts of the natives' linguistic usage. Nor, he suggests does the notion of a *right* translation make sense in such a case. I shall not discuss this challenging view, since it could not be done justice in the space available.
21 *The Idea of a Social Science*, Routledge & Kegan Paul, 1963. p 95.
22 *Language, Thought, and Reality*. M.I.T. Press, 1969. p 252.
23 S. Hampshire, 'The interpretation of language: words and concepts', in *British Philosophy in the Mid-Century*, ed C. Mace. Allen & Unwin, 1957.
24 For this suggestion, see L. Wittgenstein, *Philosophical Investigations*. 3rd edn. Macmillan, 1969. Section 312.
25 Presumably the methods of 'collocational analysis' and 'field analysis', mentioned in Chapter 2, would help us out here.
26 *Language, Thought, and Reality*. M.I.T. Press, 1969. p 57.
27 *ibid, p* 60.
28 *ibid, p* 59.
29 *ibid, p* 57.
30 *ibid, p* 63.
31 'Chinese versus English: an exploration of the Whorfian theses', in *Language in Culture*, ed H. Hoijer. Chicago University Press, 1959. p 122.

Chapter 6

Grammar and mind

Except by way of passing, I have not yet discussed a basic element of language – the grammatical element. The word 'grammar' probably calls up memories of endless hours spent while we were children carving up, or parsing, sentences and giving labels like 'adverb', 'preposition', or 'noun' to the results of our dissections. If so, it is hard to imagine what great philosophical interest there could be in grammar. However, grammar as conceived of by contemporary linguists is a fruitful and exciting field of study – very different from what we did as children[1] – and full of implications for philosophy, not to mention psychology, computer science, and education.

There are several philosophical problems on which questions about grammar can impinge. Much of our enquiry into reference, for example, could be described as informal grammatical enquiry. And Wittgenstein liked to describe much of his investigation into the linguistic roots of philosophical problems as 'depth grammar'.[2] There is one traditional philosophical/psychological problem above all, though, to which recent study of grammar is of paramount importance. This is the old debate as to whether there exists 'innate' knowledge. Several philosophers have claimed that the human mind is equipped from birth, and independently of experience, with certain types of knowledge. This view has had little currency during the last few centuries. Empiricist philosophy, and stimulus-response psychology, have largely held the fort – and it is central to both these schools of thought that what men know they have learned; that there is no room for introducing the idea of innate, unlearned knowledge. In recent years, however, study of human grammatical abilities has suggested that the old innateness-hypothesis may contain a substantial element of truth; that the human mind is not at all as the empiricist philosophers, or stimulus-response psychologists, suppose. This exciting suggestion will be examined in sections 2 and 3 of this chapter.

It would be impossible to discuss contemporary grammatical theory except in conjunction with the name of the M.I.T. linguist, Noam Chomsky. His work, which came to notice in the mid-1950s, has since reached a very wide audience. At Oxford, in 1969, his lectures drew audiences of two thousand people or more, only a fraction of whom were students of linguistics. Part of his attraction, no doubt, is due to his political activism; but the size of his audiences reflects, also, the realization that Chomsky's work in linguistics may be of great relevance to many other disciplines – philosophy, psychology, computer science, anthropology, education, for example. It would be no exaggeration to say that Chomsky revolutionized the science of linguistics. Some would even say that he invented linguistics as a *science*. As one writer said of his first book:

> Chomsky's book on syntactic structures is one of the first serious attempts on the part of a linguist to construct within the tradition of scientific theory a comprehensive theory of language in the same sense that a chemical, biological theory is ordinarily understood by experts in those fields . . . [it is] a rigorous explication of our intuitions about our language in terms of an overt axiom system.[3]

In the next section I shall try to describe the sophisticated system which Chomsky, and those who have been influenced by him, have devised over the last few years. Later we shall see what wider implications this system might have.

1 Transformational grammar

A theory of language comprises, roughly, three components: the phonological, the grammatical (syntactic, including morphological),[4] and the semantic. Any full description of an English sentence, that is, would have to contain [1] a description of how speakers vocalize it, [2] a description of its grammatical nature, and [3] a description of its meaning.[5] We shall concentrate upon the second component. A grammar of a language may be regarded as a set of rules operating upon certain data for certain purposes. First, the rules of a grammar of English must generate all and only sentences in English. A fluent speaker of English is capable of recognizing an infinite number of strings of words as being grammatical sentences, and an infinite number of strings of words as being ungrammatical. The rules of the grammar must generate all and only those he would recognize as grammatical. No doubt there are many strings of words which some speakers would regard as grammatical sentences, and others would not – so there can be disputes at the margin as to which strings an adequate grammar should generate. But provided our rules allow us to generate the obviously grammatical strings, and forbid us to generate the obviously ungrammatical ones, then, with any luck, the rules will help us decide on the marginal cases where our intuitions fail us. Second, the rules of the grammar must enable us to exhibit the structure of grammatical sentences. A fluent speaker, for example, will recognize that in the sentence 'The boy hit the girl', the words 'the boy' form a single component in a way in which the words 'hit the' do not. Such recognition needs to be explained. At least these two conditions must be met by an adequate grammar of language. We shall come across other conditions later.

I shall begin by describing a type of grammar which, supposedly, does meet these two conditions. A grammar of a language of this type will be called a Phrase-Structure grammar.[6] One writer, writing in 1964, said of this type of grammar that it is 'the prevailing conception of syntactic description among modern linguists today'.[7] A Phrase-Structure grammar of English can be thought of as a sophisticated version of the sort of grammar you and I did at school, where our concern was to parse sentences into various components, and to assign these components to such categories as Noun, Verb, Adverb, etc. We shall soon see that a Phrase-Structure grammar of a language is highly inadequate; but we must understand its nature in order to see why a more advanced grammatical theory is required.

Take the sentence 'The boy hit the girl'. We could represent the structure of this sentence in the form of the following tree-diagram:

Fig 1

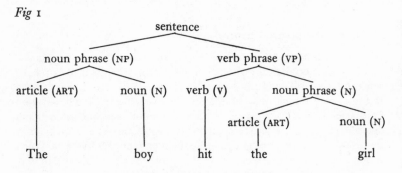

Let us call the structural description of a sentence, as represented in a diagram like *Fig* 1, the phrase marker (PM) of the sentence. The above PM informs us, *inter alia*, that a sentence can be composed of a noun phrase and a verb phrase; that a verb phrase can be composed of a verb and another noun phrase; that a noun phrase can be composed of an article plus a noun; and that among nouns are 'boy' and 'girl'. It serves, that is, to tell us which categories certain English words belong to; which higher categories these categories belong to; which higher categories the second categories belong to, and so on.

A PM can be regarded as a *derivation* of a string according to certain rules. What are the rules which allow us to derive the sentence 'The boy hit the girl' so that it can be represented in *Fig* 1? Any such rule will have the form X → Y. We read such a rule as telling us that a certain symbol, X, can be *rewritten as* another symbol or string of symbols, Y. So, the rule *sentence* → NP + VP tells us that the symbol *sentence* can be rewritten as the symbols NP + VP. Any rule of this kind will be called a Phrase-Structure rule (PS-rule). The following PS-rules will allow us to derive the sentence 'The boy hit the girl':

(1) Sentence → NP + VP
(2) NP → ART + N
(3) VP → V + NP
(4) ART → 'the'
(5) N → 'boy', 'girl'
(6) V → 'hit'

Given these rules, our sentence can be derived in the following way (the number of the rule employed in deriving each new stage or string is placed on the right):

Sentence	
NP + VP	(1)
ART + N + VP	(2)
ART + N + V + NP	(3)
The + N + V + NP	(4)
The + boy + V + NP	(5)
The + boy + V + ART + N	(2)
The + boy + V + the + N	(4)
The + boy + V + the + girl	(5)
The + boy + hit + the + girl	(6)

This derivation corresponds exactly to the derivation as represented in *Fig* 1, in that both the tree-diagram and the above presentation demonstrate the results of applying rules (1–6). By looking at either the tree or the presentation, we can tell that a NP can be composed of ART + N, or that 'the' is an ART, and so on.

We are now in a position, within the framework of a phrase-structure grammar, to define a grammatical sentence. Any line derived in accordance with PS-rules is a string. A string is well-formed only if each of its components or constituents can be traced back to the label *sentence* at the top of a tree-diagram. The last line of a PM is the terminal string. 'The boy hit the girl' for example is a terminal string. This is reached when there are no more PS-rules which would permit us to replace any of the constituents by some other symbol. We can now say that a terminal string is grammatical if and only if it is derived in accordance with the PS-rules of the grammar. Since the sentence 'The boy hit the girl' is a terminal string of a PM, then it is a grammatical sentence in English.

It is worth noting that PS-rules must usually be more complicated than those I have mentioned in at least two ways. First, a rule may be stated so as to give us a choice in rewriting. For example, we might have the rule:

(7) $\text{VP} \rightarrow \begin{Bmatrix} \text{v transitive} + \text{N} \\ \text{v intransitive} \end{Bmatrix}$.

This represents the fact that a VP can be composed either of a transitive verb together with an object-noun, or simply of an intransitive verb. Second, a PS-rule can be made 'context-sensitive'. Rules (1–7) tell us that one symbol may be rewritten as another, irrespective of what other symbols occur in the string to which the rules are applied. Normally, though, we want to say that it is only correct to replace one symbol by another if that symbol occurs in a string of a certain sort. For example, we can express the fact that English verbs must end in -s when the subject-noun is singular by the following rule:

(8) $\text{v} \rightarrow \text{v} + \text{s}$ / in the context NP singular + . . .

It should be clear that PS-rules are capable of generating a very large number of English sentences. This, as we shall see, is not an adequate defence of phrase-structure grammars.

It is now time to introduce a quite new type of grammatical rule, quite unlike the PS-rule. A grammar which employs rules of this new type will not, therefore, be a phrase-structure grammar at all. Consider the sentence 'The girl was hit by the boy', the passive of 'The boy hit the girl.' One would surely expect there to be some rule which would allow us to derive the passive sentence from the active, or some rules which would allow us to derive both sentences from one common root. And indeed we can devise such rules. The structure of the active sentence could be represented as $\text{NP}_1 - \text{V} - \text{NP}_2$. We may then have a rule which tells us that if a sentence having that grammatical structure is well-formed, then so is another sentence having the following grammatical structure, $\text{NP}_2 - \text{be} + \text{en} - \text{v} - \text{by} + \text{NP}_1$. (Here *be + en* is a string of morphemes which marks the passive; it would appear in an actual sentence as *eg* 'is seen'.) We have, then, a rule which allows us to transform an active sentence into a passive one:

(9) $\text{NP}_1 - \text{V} - \text{NP}_2 \rightarrow \text{NP}_2 - \text{be} + \text{en} - \text{v} - \text{by} + \text{NP}_1$.

The rule tells us to invert the order of the NPs; to transform the V in a certain way; and to insert 'by' before the last NP. Such a rule will be called a transformation rule (T-rule).

It is essential to realize that T-rules differ in several respects from PS-rules.

[1] A PS-rule only permits us to replace one symbol in a string at a time. As Chomsky points out,

> if this condition is not met, we will not be able to recover properly the phrase structure of the derived sentences from the associated diagrams.[8]

Suppose, for example, the string ART + N + VP was replaced by the string *The + boy +* VP. In such a case it would be impossible to tell whether 'The' had been derived from ART, or whether *The + boy* had been derived from N, and so on. The relevant part of the corresponding tree-diagram could be read in any of the following ways:

So we must only rewrite one symbol at a time. Further PS-rules do not allow us to alter the order of the symbols, but merely to replace any symbol by one or more symbols. That is, a PS-rule will always have one of the following possible diagrammatic forms:

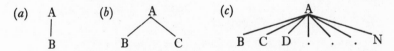

T-rules, though, obey no such restrictions. They allow us to change the order of constituent symbols; and there is no obligation to replace one at a time. This means, therefore, that the operation of T-rules cannot be represented in the form of tree-diagrams, as the operation of PS-rules can.

[2] Symbols like NP$_1$ or V, as they appear in T-rules, are *variables;* whereas, when they appear in PS-rules, they are *constants*. A PS-rule simply tells us that a certain symbol can be replaced by another symbol. But a T-rule tells us that *anything* which is of a certain grammatical form can be transformed into something of a different grammatical form. The active/passive rule mentioned, for example, tells us that any English sentence which is of a certain form can properly be transformed into a sentence which is of a different form. To that extent, T-rules differ from PS-rules in the way that algebraic rules differ from arithmetical ones. $2 + 2 = 4$ simply tells us that $2 + 2$ can be replaced by 4, and nothing

about any other numbers. $a+a=2a$, however, tells us something about all numbers. It tells us that whenever numbers are arranged in a certain way, they can also be arranged in a different way.

[3] Finally, T-rules can, and PS-rules cannot, make use of information concerning the *history* of a string's derivation. When we apply a PS-rule at a certain stage in a derivation, say the rule NP $\rightarrow$ ART + N, it is irrelevant how the symbol NP was itself derived at an earlier stage. However, if we look at the active/passive T-rule, it is only because I know that 'The boy' is the subject of the active sentence – only, that is, because I know it has been derived from NP_1 – that I am entitled to place it at the end of the passive sentence preceded by 'by'. It is only because I know that 'hit' in the active sentence is a transitive verb – only, that is, because I know it has been derived from v *transitive* – that I am entitled to transform it in a certain way and employ it in the passive sentence. J. J. Katz expresses this point in the following way:

> Transformational rules thus differ from phrase structure rules in that, while a phrase structure rule can only make use of information contained in the linear context of the symbol to be rewritten, a transformational rule can use any information in a phrase marker to which it applies.[9]

The importance of these differences between T-rules and PS-rules, and the bearing they have upon the preferability of a grammar containing the former, will emerge as we continue. Before continuing, though, it will be useful to take some more examples of T-rules, so that we may better understand their nature.

Example 1. Where each of the following sentences is grammatical

(*a*) He looked up the number.
(*b*) He called in the bets.
(*c*) He called up his brother.

so is each of the following

(*a'*) He looked the number up.
(*b'*) He called the bets in.
(*c'*) He called his brother up.

It is often the case, in English, that verbs are discontinuous, and where this is so one would expect a rule showing us how sentences in which the verb is used discontinuously (as in *a'* to *c'*) are systematically related to sentences in which it is not (as in *a* to *c*). Here is such a rule:

(10) NP $-v-$ particle $-$ NP $\rightarrow$ NP $-v-$ NP $-$ particle.

(Here I use v instead of v, to express that v (*eg* 'look' or 'call') is only part of the verb. The whole verb is 'look up' or 'call in'.) We see, again, that in this rule the symbols are variables, for we are being told that whenever a sentence has one sort of grammatical form, then a sentence having a different form is also grammatically well-formed. We can see also that the transformation of one string into another requires knowledge about the derivational history of the string. For only if I know that 'up' was derived from *particle*, and that this in turn was derived from v (by the rule v $\rightarrow$ v$-$*particle*) am I entitled to derive a' from a.

Example 2. Given the grammaticality of the two sentences 'The boy hit the girl' and 'The man hit the girl', we can predict the grammaticality of the sentence 'The boy and the man hit the girl'. Conjunction of subjects is a very common operation in grammar. What rule permits it? It is the following:

(11) NP_1-V-NP_2; $NP_3-V-NP_2 \rightarrow NP_1 + and + NP_3-V-NP_2$.

As our various examples show, there can be very different types of T-rules. It is of great interest to linguists to try to classify the various types. At the very least we should have to list [1] rules which alter the order of words (*eg* rule 9), [2] rules which delete certain words (*eg* rule 11), and [3] rules which add certain words (*eg* rule 9 again). The wealth of these different types of T-rules need not concern us.

It is now time to undertake the important task of showing why T-rules are required in an adequate grammar. A grammar which contains T-rules as well as PS-rules will be called a transformational grammar. The strongest way of showing that a phrase-structure grammar is inadequate would be to show that it is incapable of generating all and only grammatical sentences of the language. But it is not clear that this can be shown. As Lees says, there is 'no rigorous proof that a phrase-structure grammar is inherently impossible' in that way.[10]

However, there are other ways in which we could show the inadequacy of a phrase-structure grammar. Chomsky points out that

a weaker, but perfectly sufficient demonstration of inadequacy would be to show that the theory can apply only clumsily; that is, to show that any grammar that can be constructed in terms of this theory will be extremely complex, *ad hoc*, and 'unrevealing'.[11]

It seems that there are at least three ways in which phrase-structure grammars can be shown to be inadequate, of which the last is no doubt the most damning. I shall mention all of these ways, though.

[1] A phrase-structure grammar of a language will be unnecessarily, and absurdly, complex – in that it will contain far more rules for generating grammatical sentences than is required. Consider the case of passive sentences once more. There are a number of restrictions on what words

can appear in a passive sentence; (*a*) the v must be a transitive one – we cannot say 'He is slept by John'; (*b*) the first NP in the passive sentence must be one which can appear as the object of a transitive verb having an appropriate subject – we cannot say 'John was admired by sincerity'; and (*c*) the v followed by *by* + NP must utilize a certain form of the string of morphemes *be* + *en* – we cannot say 'John is eating by lunch'. Such restrictions, and plenty of others too, apply equally to the formation of active sentences. In an active sentence, for example, the object must be preceded by a transitive verb. Now if we employed a purely phrase-structure grammar, we should have to state the rules and restrictions twice over in slightly different forms – once in deriving the active sentence, and again in deriving the passive sentence. For example, the PS-rule derivation for 'The girl was hit by the boy' will have to contain a restriction on what v can be rewritten as, just as the derivation for 'The boy hit the girl' will. Such duplication of rules and restrictions is unnecessary. For, once we employ T-rules, we need state the restrictions only once – in deriving the active sentence. Then, by a single T-rule we derive the passive sentence. In being told that the passive can be derived from a grammatical active sentence, we are already being informed that all the restrictions mentioned above are being met with. There is no need to restate them all. We can see, then, that the introduction of T-rules into a grammar provides an enormous simplification in the grammar, in terms of the number of rules that is required.

[2] PS-rules are incapable of exhibiting the intuited interrelationships that hold between different sentences. There are clearly close interrelations between each of the following sentences:

(*a*) The boy hit the girl.
(*b*) Did the boy hit the girl?
(*c*) The girl was hit by the boy!
(*d*) Hit the girl, boy!
(*e*) If the boy hit the girl, then . . .

A phrase-structure grammar must provide separate PM's for each of these sentences; and as such there is no way in which the interrelationships between them can be exhibited. We can exhibit these quite easily, though, once we employ T-rules. For let us provide a single PM, in accordance with PS-rules, for just one of the sentences, the first. Then we can relate each of the other sentences to this one by showing how they can be derived from it by the application of single T-rules. (This remark will receive qualification at the end of this section.) Since the PM for the first sentence will reveal that 'The boy' is the subject, that 'hit' is transitive, etc, all such information will be naturally transferred to the interrogative, the passive, the imperative, and the conditional via the application of the relevant T-rules. It is as if, instead of having to describe ten photographs in detail to show their similarity to one another, we could say, simply, that they are all photographs of Harry. Each photograph is, as it were, a transform of Harry, and this explains their similarity.

Both of the above points are neatly summarized by Chomsky in the following passage:

> There are certain sentences (. . . simple declarative active sentences . . .) that can be generated by a constituent structure grammar in a quite natural way. There are others (*eg* passives . . .) that cannot be generated in an economic and natural way . . . but that are systematically related to sentences of simpler structure. Transformations that are constructed to express this relation can thus materially simplify the grammar when used to generate more complex sentences and their structural descriptions from already generated simpler ones.[12]

[3] Now for the most important set of considerations to show that phrase-structure grammars are inadequate. An adequate grammar should explain an enormous number of intuitions that speakers have about their language – including, for example, the recognition of ambiguities, of structural dissimilarities, or of underlying similarities between different sentences. A grammar which merely succeeded in generating all and only the grammatical sentences of a language would fail to explain a great deal that is involved in our knowledge of language. It can be demonstrated that a phrase-structure grammar of a language fails to explain more than a small segment of this intuitive knowledge.

Let us call the structure of a sentence as revealed by a PM solely in accordance with PS-rules the 'surface' structure of the sentence. So, for example, the surface structure of the sentence 'John is eager to please' will be represented in the following diagram, in accordance with PS-rules:

Fig 2

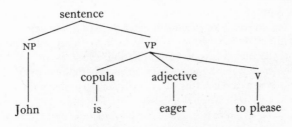

It is argued by Chomsky and his followers that we must go beyond the surface structure of sentences in order to explain our intuitive understanding of many aspects of language. We must, in addition, postulate

the existence of 'deep' or 'underlying' sentence structures. The claim
is that if we try to represent the structure of sentences in PM's derived
through PS-rules alone, we shall fail to explain a great deal of speakers'
understanding of sentences. Why must we postulate the existence of
deep structures? There are several reasons.

[1] First, as Chomsky says, 'the surface structure generally gives us very
little indication in itself of the meaning of the sentence'.[13] Consider, for
example, the sentence 'The love of God is good'. Plainly this is ambiguous. It could be paraphrased either as (a) 'It is good for people to
love God', or (b) 'God's love for people is good'. However, there is no
way of exhibiting this ambiguity if we represent the structure of the
sentence by a PM derived solely in accordance with PS-rules. For we
shall have the single PM:

Fig 3

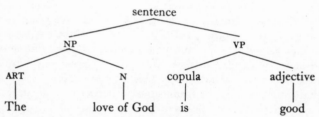

The surface structure of the sentence, that is, does not reveal its ambiguity. However, we can reveal the ambiguity at a deeper level, in the
following way. We can think of there being two different underlying
strings from which the sentence 'The love of God is good' can be derived
by different T-rules. The first underlying string will represent 'God'
as the object of the verb 'love'. This will be the string underlying the
sentence interpreted as meaning the same as 'It is good for people to
love God'. By a T-rule which permits us to transform the verb 'love'
into its noun form, we derive the sentence so interpreted from the
underlying string. The second underlying string will represent 'God'
as the subject of the verb 'love', and so will be the structure underlying
our sentence on its second interpretation. Once again we derive the
actual sentence from the underlying string by employing a T-rule.

Note that in a case like this we are justified in speaking of grammatical,
rather than of semantic, ambiguity. For the ambiguity is of a quite
systematic kind, and is not due to the idiosyncratic ambiguity of a single
word – as in the case of the sentence 'I went to the bank'. Other sentences
sharing the systematic ambiguity of our one would be 'The hunting of
lions takes place at sunset', and 'The hate of a woman can ruin a man'.
In each of these cases, we must presuppose two different deep structures

underlying the sentences, which are then related to the surface structures by different T-rules.

[2] Another case where surface structure may be a poor guide to meaning is where two sentences mean the same, but differ in surface structure. For example, the PM's representing the surface structures of the sentences 'They denied the existence of God' and 'They denied that God exists' would be different – yet the sentences mean the same. This can be explained at the deep level. Underlying the two sentences is a single deep structure, in which 'God' is represented as the subject of the verb 'exist'. Then, in the case of the first sentence, we derive the actual sentence by applying a T-rule which converts the verb into a noun. A different T-rule will derive the second sentence from the same underlying string.

[3] Next we have cases where the surface structure of two sentences is identical, but where there are intuitively felt differences in their syntax. Consider the sentences 'John is eager to please' and 'John is easy to please'. A moment's reflection shows that grammatically these are very different. The second can be paraphrased as 'It is easy to please John', while the first cannot be paraphrased as 'It is eager to please John'. The PM's, representing the surface structures of the two, however, are identical. *Fig* 2 on *p* 133, would represent either. This means that we must explain the difference between the two at the deep level. Underlying 'John is eager to please' is a string which represents 'John' as the subject of the verb 'please'. It might be something like 'John is eager for John to please someone'. Underlying 'John is easy to please' is a string in which 'John' is represented as the object of 'please' – something like 'It is easy for someone to please John'. The two underlying strings are then transformed into our two sentences by various T-rules.

[4] The last case I shall mention is where sentences do not, on the surface, contain constituents which must, nevertheless, be read into them if we are to explain how the sentences are interpreted. Consider the imperative sentence 'Help the man'. The surface structure of this is given by the following PM:

Fig 4

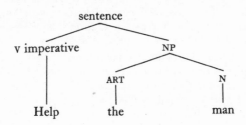

For a number of reasons, though, it is reasonable to say that underlying this sentence there is a string which contains 'You' as the subject of 'help'. These reasons include (*a*) everyone understands the command as directed towards whoever is being addressed – *ie* you, rather than they, from the speaker's point of view; (*b*) often commands are actually issued with the form 'You help the man' and seem to be synonymous with those of the form 'Help the man'; and (*c*) it is only correct to employ a reflexive pronoun as the object of a verb where the object is the same as the subject. That is, we can say 'John likes himself' but not 'John likes herself'. Now clearly we can issue the command 'Help yourself'; and this implies that 'You' must be occurring as the subject of 'help' in order to justify the use of the reflexive pronoun. And if 'You' must be postulated as the subject of 'Help yourself', it seems reasonable to postulate it as the subject of 'Help the man'. If so, we must regard 'Help the man' as having been transformationally derived from an underlying string in which 'You' appears as the subject. The effect of the T-rule in question is simply to delete the occurrence of 'You'. To take one more example of a similar sort: it is reasonable to suppose that, underlying the sentence 'John is better at chess than Bill', there is a string in which 'Bill' occurs as the subject of 'play chess'. Otherwise, how do we explain that people interpret the sentence as saying that John is better at chess than Bill is at chess, rather than as saying that John is better at chess than Bill is at water-skiing or at billiards?

The point of all these cases is the same. They show that the attempt to represent the structure of sentences by PM's, derived solely by PS-rules, leaves unexplained various intuitions we feel about sentences. To explain these intuitions, we must make a distinction between deep structures, which can be represented by PM's in accordance with PS-rules, and surface structures which are derived from the deep structures by the application of T-rules. To generate sentences by PS-rules alone would paste over information about their meanings which can only be adequately highlighted at the deep level.

For several reasons, then, we see the need to postulate new types of rules, T-rules. We are now in a position to summarize the nature of a transformational grammar of a language. Such a grammar is, allegedly, a set of rules adequate for generating all and only the grammatical sentences of that language. These rules will be of two distinct types. First, PS-rules which generate strings by successive stages of the rewriting of symbols. Second, while PS-rules serve to derive PM's which can be represented in tree-diagrams, T-rules then operate to convert these PM's into other PM's. 'A transformational rule is a rule that operates on a phrase marker converting it into another phrase marker.'[14] To take a simple example, we have the PM represented by the following tree:

Fig 5

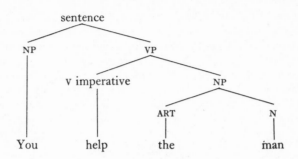

Then by a T-rule which allows us to delete the subject in imperative sentences we derive the PM represented in *Fig* 4. To stress an earlier point: we cannot regard the PM in *Fig* 4 as an adequate representation of the structure of 'Help the man', since it does not represent the fact that 'you' is its subject. That information is only represented in *Fig* 5.

I now want to make two points about transformational grammars, the second of which in particular will be important when we come to consider the philosophical/psychological implications these grammars may have.

[1] It will, to a large extent, be a matter of *decision* which grammatical operations we perform by PS-rules, and which by T-rules. Often we will have a choice between deriving a string of symbols directly through PS-rules, and deriving it from an underlying string through T-rules. Our decision will be dictated by considerations of simplicity, and the scope of illumination provided. In general, if there is some systematic relation between some string, X – Y – Z, and some other string, Z – H – X, we will prefer to generate just one of them by PS-rules and the other, from the one already generated, by a T-rule. Otherwise, we should have to duplicate unnecessarily the PS-rules required to generate both of them.

[2] Chomsky says 'in general, we cannot require that terminal strings be related in any very simple way to actual sentences'.[15] He also says 'the deep structure may be highly abstract: it may have no close point-by-point correspondence to the phonetic realization'.[16] What he means is that the underlying string derived by PS-rules alone, and from which we then derive an actual English sentence by T-rules, may have only a remote resemblance to the actual sentence, or to *any* actual English sentence. Some of the examples I have used make it look as if transformationally derived sentences are derived from other *sentences*. But this is not so. I have been oversimplifying. Rarely, if ever, are the strings from which sentences are derived by T-rules themselves *sentences*. As

Lyons puts it, '*no* sentences are generated without the application of at least a limited number of obligatory T-rules'.[17] So, for example, it is not that passive sentences are derived from active ones – but rather that both passives and actives are derived from similar underlying strings by different T-rules. Since fewer T-rules are required to derive the active sentence, this will more nearly resemble the underlying string than does its passive, whose derivations will require permutations of, and additions to, that string. To take another example: Chomsky says that the underlying string of the sentence 'A wise man is honest' can be represented as:

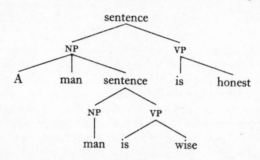

Here, the terminal string, *A – man – is – wise – is – honest*, is not a sentence, and is nowhere near to being one. To derive an actual sentence, several T-rules must be applied to this string – so that one occurrence of 'man' is deleted, and the first predicate is turned into a pronominal, or attributive adjective. Here, then, is a case in which the underlying string contains grammatical elements which receive no phonetic realization. And, in general, it will be the case that spoken English sentences do not directly represent, in phonetic terms, some of the grammatical constituents which appear only at the deep level. Often, the relation between the underlying string and the spoken sentence is very remote indeed (*ie* many T-rules are required to derive the latter from the former).

My account of transformational grammar has been a simplified one, since my concern is not with the detailed workings-out of such a grammar, but with its philosophical/psychological implications. No one would deny that there are many technical difficulties in working out an adequate transformational grammar within the framework laid down in Chomsky's early theory. Several transformational grammarians, including Chomsky himself, have proposed amendments, some major, to that theory.[18] There have, too, been more radical attacks made by the proponents of so-called 'Generative Semantics'; by, for example, Lakoff and McCawley.[19] One of their basic criticisms is that Chomsky draws an unwarrantedly sharp distinction between questions of well-formedness and of meaning. Semantic information, it is urged, is often, perhaps always, included in syntactic descriptions. (It has been argued, for example, that *Noun* is not merely a syntactic category, but also expresses the semantic concept of 'thinghood'.) It is also their contention, in opposition to Chomsky, that various phenomena of well-formedness cannot be economically explained without employing certain semantic notions in descriptions of underlying structures. For example, it has been argued that the notion of *presupposition* is required for economically explaining the syntactic behaviour of different verbs which take complements, such as 'think', 'know', or 'regret'. I do not discuss these views, partly because the technicalities involved are beyond the scope of this book, but mainly because the issues are not relevant to the particular philosophical/psychological questions to be dealt with in the next sections. As Katz points out, these critics 'share the view that sentences contain a level of grammatical structure which underlies surface form and is related to it transformationally'.[20] Since it is precisely this view which gives rise to the questions that will concern us, differences as to the nature of the level or of transformations are not to the point in the forthcoming discussion. Whether or not underlying structure is in fact the deep structure postulated by Chomsky is an extremely live issue in linguistics; but fortunately we can ignore it for our purposes. I mention generative semantics only to guard the reader against the impression that the account of grammar sketched in the previous pages is the only account, or even the generally accepted account.

2 Language and innate knowledge

James Beattie wrote in 1788,

> The principles of grammar form an important, and very curious, part of the philosophy of the human mind.

And Chomsky, writing very recently, claims that 'linguistics . . . is [a] subfield of psychology'.[21] It is not, of course, surprising that a study of language should reveal things about the nature of the mind. Language is man's most startling intellectual possession. But how, quite, can a theory of grammar relate to psychology and the philosophy of mind? The connection is this: a grammar of a language may be regarded not simply as a description of that language, but as a model which helps explain how people actually produce and understand language. A grammar, we saw, can be regarded as a set of rules in terms of which sentences can be generated. According to Chomsky we can regard men as being acquainted with such rules as they speak and listen. In his own words

> The person who has acquired knowledge of a language has internalized a system of rules that relate sound and meaning in a particular way.[22]

So when linguists study the rules of grammar, they are also studying an aspect of the human mind – for these rules are part of man's intellectual equipment.

There are indeed problems with the suggestion that speakers have 'internalized' a system of rules, and we will return to some of them in section 3. It is worth mentioning one of them immediately, however. According to Chomsky the rules men have acquired are rules like those discussed in section 1 – PS-rules, and T-rules. The reader might ask: granted that speakers have internalized some rules, why must the rules be of these types? Granted that these are the rules a linguist finds most useful to employ in describing grammar, does it follow that you and I actually employ them? This is a good question. The answer usually given is this: it is a fundamental presupposition of science that, given two theories both of which are capable of explaining the facts, we should choose the theory that is the simpler. Why else should we prefer an explanation of the apple's falling in terms of gravity to an explanation in terms of gravity *and* the desires of angels or apple-spirits? Because the latter introduces unnecessary complications, and does not advance explanation. Similarly, it is argued, we must regard humans' linguistic behaviour as explained by their following the simplest set of rules compatible with the observed data. Since a transformational grammar of the type described comprises the simplest set of rules required to explain the data, we should regard it as the model for human linguistic competence. As Lees puts it

> Granted that the so-called scientific method is valid, it is not too much to assume that human beings talk in the same way that our grammar 'talks'.[23]

Let us allow this answer to pass for the time being.

If we grant that speakers have internalized a system of grammatical rules, the question arises: what must the human mind be like in order for men to have internalized these rules? Chomsky's answer, crudely, is that we must attribute to the mind an innate, unlearned, complex structure in order to account for this internalization. It is at this point that what Chomsky says becomes of great interest to philosophers. For his claim sounds like the claim made by Descartes and Leibniz to the effect that there are innate ideas; that there is innate knowledge.

Let us now glance back at the debate over innate knowledge as it took place in the seventeenth and eighteenth centuries. It must be said straight away that both sides in the debate, the Rationalists and the Empiricists, have often been misrepresented – by one another, by historians, and in the popular imagination. Sometimes we are told that Empiricists believe the mind is incapable of any intellectual operations that do not, in some manner, derive from sense-experience. And sometimes we are told that Rationalists believe the mind is capable of intellectual activity in complete isolation from any sense-experience. That is how the Empiricist Locke interpreted his opponents. Both characterizations are extremely misleading. The Empiricists, despite their talk of the mind being a *tabula rasa* or an empty cabinet, had to ascribe certain unlearned abilities to the mind. For, at the very least, the mind must be innately equipped to learn from experience. It would be absurd to suggest that we must learn those abilities which are necessary conditions of our learning anything. For example, in order to learn at all one must at least be able to generalize. Second, it is clear that neither Descartes nor Leibniz believed men were capable of intellectual activity in complete isolation from sense-experience. Leibniz says of our innate ideas that 'without the senses it would never have occurred to us to think of them'. And he insists that sense-experience is 'necessary for all our actual knowledge'.[24] What he also insists, though, is that sense-experience cannot be sufficient to account for such knowledge. Against Locke's picture of the mind as a *tabula rasa* he pits the picture of the mind as a block of marble in which veins mark out a certain figure, which will not be clearly revealed until superfluous bits of marble have been chipped away. Sense-experience serves to reveal our innate ideas in the way that chiselling reveals the figure which belongs 'innately' to the marble.

We must, then, reformulate the terms of the debate in order to see what the real issue over innateness is. I shall do this, first, in general terms, with no specific reference to linguistic competence. Consider the following simple model, which is familiar in engineering:

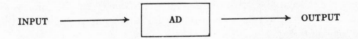

INPUT ——————————→ | AD | —————————→ OUTPUT

AD is some acquisition device capable of receiving input data and of producing some output. A typical AD would be a computer which receives and produces information. We may regard the human mind as an AD. The input into the human mind will be the data received through sense-experience – sounds, colours, etc. The output will be a wide range of intellectual activities – for example, the ability to operate with some concept, like that of causality. The question is: what must this AD, the mind, be like in order for an input of this sort to be transformed into an output of this sort? The Empiricist and Rationalist differ as to what must be ascribed to the AD. One might say that, according to a classical Empiricist like Hume, the only capacities ascribed to the mind are [1] the capacity to observe through the senses, [2] the capacity to associate elements in experience, and [3] the capacity for making inductive generalizations on the basis of observed associations. Let us take, by way of example, Hume's famous account of how we acquire the concept of causality. A person observes individual events taking place. Some of these events become associated for him, since they regularly take place in conjunction with one another. On the basis of this observed association, the person generalizes and concludes that these events will always take place in conjunction with one another. Consequently, whenever he observes one of the events taking place he always expects, on the basis of his inductive generalization, the other event to take place. If this expectation is sufficiently strong, he is regarding the one event as the cause of the other. For, according to Hume, to say that one event causes another is simply to say that events of the one type regularly precede events of the other type, and that people strongly expect the one event to be followed by the other. If Hume is right, he has explained our acquisition of the concept of causality purely in terms of our observations, associations, and inductions, of and from items in sense-experience.

A Rationalist, on the other hand, ascribes a richer content to the mental AD than those mentioned above. Kant, for example, argued that the mind must be innately equipped with some concepts or 'categories', to use his term – those, namely, which are the preconditions for having the sorts of sense-experiences we do. For him, the concept of causality cannot have been derived in the manner suggested by Hume – as a result, that is, of observing events in the world – since unless we already regarded the events as having causal properties we would not recognize them as events in the outside world at all. Rationalists, unfortunately, have been extremely vague as to what it is that is innate in the mind, and as to how the mind can possess innate equipment. To that extent it has largely been a negative thesis – the mere denial that the mind is as the Empiricists describe it. This partly explains the unpopularity of the Rationalist thesis.

In psychology, too, it is the Empiricists who have elaborated a theory of the mind and concept-acquisition. The dominant approach in psychology – until recently at least – has been some form of stimulus-response theory. This is an extreme Empiricist approach: the view that concepts are acquired through a process of stimulus-controlled learning, with minimal intervention by the AD, is but an extension of the Humean view. According to this approach, for example, one acquires the concept of food when one acquires the concept of what satisfies a sequence of goal-directed responses stimulated by hunger. And this is acquired on the basis of observed cases in which certain things, say eggs and bacon, have satisfied the goal-directed responses in question. Rationalists in psychology have been left with the negative thesis that, whatever explains the acquisition of concepts, it cannot simply be stimulus-response generalization.

The vagueness of the Rationalist thesis makes it all the more fascinating to study Chomsky's claims, since these represent one of the few attempts to work out in some detail an account of the innate possessions of the human mind. So let us turn to the problem of innateness as it relates to the specific question of language acquisition. First, what is the input to the language AD? It is not entirely clear what we should include – but we must at least include the utterances which the child has heard in its environment, especially those which his parents have made. Such utterances will include, moreover, explicit instructions as to how to produce and interpret grammatical sentences. We shall return to the problem of what counts as observable input-data later in this section.

Care must be taken, too, in deciding what counts as the output of the language AD. It is tempting to count the sum total of utterances the speaker makes as his output. But this would be unhelpful in at least two ways. First, a person is capable of producing and understanding infinitely more sentences than he in fact produces or hears. And his competence with respect to these possible sentences requires just as much explanation as the competence he displays with the actual sentences uttered in his life. Second, many, perhaps most, of the sentences a person produces are ungrammatical. But this is normally due, not to grammatical incompetence, but to such extraneous factors as slips of the tongue, lapses in memory, outside distractions, the occurrence of sudden thoughts, etc. Thus while the person often produces ungrammatical sentences, he nevertheless has the *competence* to have produced only grammatical ones. Were it not for interfering factors like those listed, he would have produced only grammatical sentences. It is useful to follow Chomsky here and distinguish between actual linguistic performance, and the speaker's underlying linguistic competence.

> We thus make a fundamental distinction between *competence* (the speaker-hearer's knowledge of his language) and *performance* (the actual use of language in concrete situations).[25]

Only in ideal circumstances – *eg* where there are no slips of the tongue, no distractions – will performance directly reflect competence. What is competence? It is supposedly, as described earlier, the person's acquaintance with a set of rules such that, if the rules are applied in ideal circumstances, the person will produce only grammatical sentences, and interpret any sentence properly. Thus the output of the language AD is the internalization of this set of rules.

It needs to be stressed that Chomsky is not supposing that people are consciously aware of the rules which they have internalized. That they have internalized them is something we postulate on the basis of their observed behaviour, not on the basis of their introspection. The notion of unconscious knowledge of rules is not without its difficulties, and we shall mention some of them in section 3. But, at first blush, the notion seems no worse off than the notion of unconscious motives which most

of us are happy to accept. So let us grant, for the time being, that people
do internalize a system of rules of which they are unconscious.

Well, what must the language AD be like in order for people to have
internalized these rules?

> The empiricist hypothesis claims that the language acquisition device
> operates essentially by principles of inductive generalization which
> associates observable features of utterances with one another and
> with other relevant sensory information to obtain an internalization
> of the rules of a linguistic description.[26]

Rules, for the Empiricist, are generalizations formed on the basis of
what we have observed about utterances in the past. On this account, I
understand a new sentence because it is observably similar to some
sentences whose meaning I have learned in the past. I do this by generalizing from what I have observed, and applying the generalization to the
new sentence. To take a very simple example, it might be said that I
recognize the grammaticality of the new sentence 'The boy laughs' and
the ungrammaticality of 'The boy laugh', because the first is observably
similar to sentences I have been told are grammatical in the past – 'The
boy speaks', or 'The boy rides', for example.

It is this account of language acquisition that Chomsky and his
followers hotly deny.

> Knowledge of language cannot arise by application of step-by-step
> inductive operations (segmentation, classification, substitution pro-
> cedures, 'analogy', association, conditioning, and so on) of any sort
> that have been developed within linguistics, psychology, or philo-
> sophy.[27]

Why does Chomsky insist upon this? Why does he claim that the mind
must be innately equipped with much more than the power to perform
inductive operations? It is possible to divide his reasons into two types:

[1] There is a set of empirical considerations which, supposedly, are
incompatible with the Empiricist hypothesis sketched.

[2] The nature of the rules internalized is such that, even in principle,
they cannot have been internalized through the procedures, postulated
by Empiricists, alone. (This is not to deny that, ultimately, it is for empirical reasons, like those discussed in the last section, that we suppose
the rules to have the nature they do.)

The second type of argument is, I believe, the more crucial. However,
I shall begin by sketching the empirical reasons – not only because these
are of considerable interest, but also because some writers, mistakenly I
believe, have regarded them as the crucial factors.[28] But according to
Chomsky, these empirical considerations merely '*lead one to suspect . . .*

that we are dealing with a species-specific capacity with a largely innate component'.[29]

The empirical considerations include at least the following:

[1] Compared with the number of sentences that a child can produce or interpret with ease, the number of seconds in a lifetime is ridiculously small. Hence the data available as input is only a minute sample of the linguistic material that has been thoroughly mastered, as indicated by actual performance.[30]

We are faced, that is, with the remarkable fact that, in a very short time, and on the basis of relatively few heard utterances, a child becomes a master of language. It is initially difficult to believe he could have attained this mastery solely on the basis of generalization from the small sample he has met with. It would be as if someone could become a chess-master as a result of having watched just one or two games of chess. So one is strongly tempted to suggest that the wide gap between input and output must be bridged by ascribing to the child a rich innate component.

[2] Not only is the input into the child tiny in relation to output, this input is also highly 'degenerate'. Most of the sentences a child hears are ungrammatical, due to slips of the tongue, etc, on the part of the speakers. If language rules were acquired solely by inductive generalizations, one would expect the child's competence to be infected with the mistakes he has heard, and would be expected to copy. Yet this does not happen. While the child will produce many ungrammatical sentences, the under-lying competence to produce the right ones is there. This suggests that the child brings with him to the data a mechanism which, as it were, allows him to disregard the innumerable mistakes he hears, when it comes to internalizing the rules.

[3] There is evidence to suggest that mastery of language, unlike mastery in intellectual fields whose subject-matter is entirely learned, is not radically affected by intelligence and environment. Children of low intelligence, brought up in a disadvantageous linguistic environment (eg a very taciturn family), are not deficient in grammatical skills to the extent one would expect upon Empiricist assumptions. The wealth and standard of linguistic input should make a very considerable difference to the speed and quality of the child's internalization of language on any Empiricist learning theory. But, apparently, they do not. This contrasts with ability at, say, history or philosophy, for other things being equal one's intelligence and intellectual environment are strongly determining factors. It is pertinent to point out here that while very stupid children can be very adept at language, the cleverest ape can be taught the use of symbols only at the most primitive level. These considerations suggest a species-specific, innate capacity for absorbing language.

[4] Unlike purely learned abilities, linguistic competence seems to be largely independent of the degree of motivation. In cases of learned skills, the greater the degree of the student's motivation to learn, the more quickly will they be acquired. In the case of language, though, those with a very high degree of motivation – immigrants to a new country, for example – are not more adept at learning language than young children without that degree of conscious motivation. This implies an innate mechanism that becomes impaired as age increases.

[5] The most commonly cited piece of empirical evidence is this: despite differences in languages, all known languages contain many basic similarities. These common features are normally called the 'universals' of language. All known languages, for example, contain structure-dependent rules like the T-rules discussed in the last section – despite the fact that it is easy to *imagine* a language which did not contain such rules. Given the fact that there are enormous differences in national environments, cultures, and methods of child-rearing, this should surprise those who insist that language is acquired solely on the basis of external input. It seems difficult to discover common features in environment which would explain the universals of language. As Katz says

> The only thing . . . that can provide the invariant condition that we want to correlate with the universal features of language as the causal antecedent is the common innate endowment of human language learners, *ie* some component of their specifically human nature.[31]

Surveying this battery of empirical evidence, one is forced to say two things. First, none of the evidence is conclusive. One might dispute some of the evidence, and one might also dispute the implication that Rationalists draw from it. For example, it might be suggested that human languages possess universals, not because of some innate endowment men have, but because all of the languages derive from some common language in the past.[32] Second, though, it is difficult to deny that, taken together, the evidence is impressive and strongly suggests the innateness thesis drawn from it. If we compare talking with walking, an innate ability, and then with writing, a learned activity, then in many crucial respects talking seems more like walking than writing.[33] So let us say that these empirical considerations certainly weigh the scales in favour of a Rationalist, versus an Empiricist, account of language acquisition.

Now I shall turn to what I take to be the more crucial argument in favour of the innateness hypothesis. The argument is that the nature of the rules and structural knowledge involved in understanding new sentences is such that, even in principle, they cannot have been internalized through inductivist procedures alone. The Empiricist's claim, remember, is that the child understands a new sentence because of the *observable* similarity between it and some sentences he has learned in the past. Or, to be more precise, he has learned that certain sounds, or phonemes, correlate with certain semantic elements. For example, he has learned that a certain set of sounds is appropriate for expressing the proposition that John is smiling. Then, when he faces a new sentence – a set of sounds in an order he has not heard before – he pairs these sounds with the meanings he has learned to pair them with, and so infers what the sentence as a whole means.

This account could be adequate *if* it was true that the new sentences we understand are always *observably* similar to ones whose meanings we have already learned. If this is not so, then the account falls down. Before we can decide upon this question, we must understand what the observable versus the unobservable features of a sentence are. In the narrowest sense, all I observe when you utter a sentence is a series of noises. In a slightly more liberal, and quite reasonable, sense I also observe the words and morphemes you produce. For since the noises you make *are* certain words, in that rules determine that the words should be vocalized in this way, there is a direct connection between the noises and the words which permits us to speak of observing words being uttered. In a yet more liberal, but again reasonable, sense we can speak of observing grammatical constituents in utterances. For since the noise you make is the word 'hit', say, and since the word 'hit' *is* a verb, in the sense that it can be derived from v by a PS-rule, there is a direct connection between v and the noise permitting us to speak of observing the occurrence of a verb in your utterance. Equally, since certain noises are the words 'the tall man', and since these words constitute a NP by PS-rules, we can speak of observing the occurrence of a noun phrase when you make these noises. We might, perhaps, follow Berkeley in making a distinction between *immediate* and *mediate* perception. According to him, what one immediately perceives are colours, sounds, shapes, etc, and only mediately does one perceive the physical objects which have these colours, sounds, and shapes. Similarly, we might talk of immediately observing the noises you make, and of mediately observing the occurrence of grammatical constituents, like verbs and noun phrases.

If we are going to grant to the Empiricist the observability of grammatical constituents in sentences, a very severe restriction, however, must be imposed. It is this: only those constituents are observable which are given phonetic realization in the utterance. Only if the constituent is directly related to certain sounds can we regard it as observable. For our only reason for saying that we observe a noun phrase is that certain words *eg* 'the tall man', occurred in the sentence, and that these words were actually given vocal form.

We have the means for putting this point more precisely. If any grammatical feature of a sentence is observable, it must be one that appears in the surface structure of the sentence as revealed by a PM.

For a surface PM represents the sentence as that sentence will actually be spoken once we apply rules for vocalizing the sentence – so-called phonological rules. That is, the terminal strings of PM's which represent surface structures are actual sentences. Consequently there is a direct correlation between the noises uttered, and the grammatical constituents of the surface structure – in that the terminal strings of the surface structure, which are related to the constituents by PS-rules, are those which receive phonetic representation in the utterance. Suppose the following is part of the surface PM for some sentence

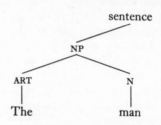

Since the terminal string, *The – Man*, is directly correlated with certain sounds, and since it is also directly correlated with the string ART – N (by PS-rules), and so with NP (by another PS-rule), we can speak of observing the occurrence of a noun phrase when we hear the utterance in question.

So, let us grant that when a person hears a new sentence he observes all of those grammatical constituents which would be represented by the surface PM for it. It should now be plain that a problem is emerging for the Empiricist. It follows from what has been said that two sentences are observably similar only if they are similar in surface structure. But, as we saw in the last section, understanding a new sentence almost invariably involves attributing *deep* grammatical features to the sentence. We saw, too, that the connection between surface and deep structure may be very remote, since several T-rules might be required to relate them. The implication is this: features of deep structure may have only the remotest connection with the actual sounds used in an utterance, in which case we cannot regard the deep features as observable at all. As Chomsky puts it

> The deep structure may be highly abstract: it may have no close point-by-point correlation to the phonetic realization.[34]

To remind ourselves of this by an example: recall that underlying the sentence 'Help the man' there is a deep structure in which 'You' occurs as the subject of 'help' – but this receives no phonetic representation, and so is an unobservable feature of the sentence.

So understanding sentences involves ascribing to them grammatical features which are not observable in the sense explained.

We must attribute to the speaker-hearer an intricate system of rules that involve mental operations of a very abstract nature, applying to representations that are quite remote from the physical signal.[35]

Let me spell out the implications of this, through examples, for the question of how children understand new sentences on the basis of old. We can agree that a child can only understand a new sentence because of its similarity with some he has learned in the past. But the crucial point is that this similarity is not, in many cases, observable similarity. Suppose we present a child with a sentence he has not heard before, 'John was persuaded to leave'. His understanding of this will include [1] knowing that it can be paraphrased as 'Someone persuaded John to leave', [2] knowing that it cannot be paraphrased as 'John's leaving was persuaded', and [3] knowing that it cannot be expanded into 'John was too persuaded to leave'. An Empiricist might claim that his understanding of the sentence in these ways is due to the observable similarity between it and the sentences 'John was forced to leave', or 'John was encouraged to leave'. It is true that these latter sentences share the characteristics of the sentence in question. However, in observable terms, the sentence 'John was persuaded to leave' is just as similar to the sentences 'John was pleased to leave', and 'John was expected to leave' as it is to the two sentences already mentioned. Yet these sentences just mentioned differ markedly from the others in important grammatical respects. Thus one cannot paraphrase 'John was pleased to leave' as 'Someone pleased John to leave'. Second, one can expand that sentence into 'John was too pleased to leave'. Again, one can paraphrase 'John was expected to leave' into 'John's leaving was expected'. The point is that in the case of 'John was encouraged to leave', 'John was forced to leave', and 'John was persuaded to leave', 'John' is the object of the verb. Whereas in 'John was pleased to leave', 'John' is the subject; and in 'John was expected to leave', it is not 'John' but 'John's leaving' that is the object. These are the differences which show why the sentences can be paraphrased and expanded in different ways from one another. But these differences in grammar are differences which exist at the deep level only. That is, the surface PM's for each of the five sentences mentioned would be the same. That 'John' is the subject in some of them, and the object in others, can only be represented in the underlying PM's. The point is this: if understanding 'John was persuaded to leave' was the result of inductive generalization from other sentences observably similar to it, we have no explanation of why people construe it as being grammatically like some and not others – for there are any number of sentences observably similar to it, but grammatically unlike it (eg 'John was pleased to leave'). That people construe it in one way rather than another can only be a result of their recognizing certain deep, and therefore unobservable, features of its structure.

It seems, then, that a child's ability to correctly interpret new sentences as soon as he is presented with them cannot be due solely to his noting observable similarities between these and others he has learned to interpret in the past. Often it is his recognition of deep similarities that is involved. He must be employing knowledge of grammatical constituents that are quite remote from the phonetic features of the utterances he hears. There is no use in the Empiricist saying that he understands the new by analogy with the old, for it is not observable analogy. 'To refer to the processes involved as "analogy" is simply to give a name to what remains a mystery'.[36]

To clarify the objection to Empiricism, it is instructive to glance at an imaginary language for which Empiricist explanations might work. Suppose in this language that passives were always formed from actives by placing the last word of the active sentence first – so that 'Mary John hit' would be the passive of 'John hit Mary'. And suppose in general that interrogatives, conditionals, imperatives, etc, were always formed by some similar simple change in word order. It could then be argued that a child understands any new sentence simply on the basis of its observable similarity with ones it has already encountered. For to know how to form a passive sentence, for example, is just a matter of recalling the observable fact that the last word of the active comes first. Our real languages differ radically from this imaginary language, though, in that our transformations are structure-dependent in a way that the transformations in the imaginary one are not. We transform one type of sentence into another by re-ordering the words according to the abstract grammatical categories they belong to, and not by simply changing the linear position of some words. We must possess, in a way that the speakers of the imaginary language do not, a recognition of the grammatical categories which determine the transformations we can make.

The thesis argued for so far has been negative, to the effect that inductive procedures cannot explain our understanding of sentences, and the internalization of the rules involved in that understanding. So far we have said nothing about the innate component we seem forced to postulate once we reject the Empiricist account. Whatever this innate component is like, it must be contained within certain crucial limits. First, it cannot be so rich as to include knowledge of the rules of English in particular, for then it would be impossible to explain how foreigners are equally adept at internalizing the rules of their grammars. But, second, it cannot be so impoverished as to contain no more than the inductivist ability ascribed by the Empiricist, for that would fail to explain our possession of rules dealing with unobservable features of sentences.

We must look again at the so-called universals of language, which were briefly mentioned on *p* 146. According to Chomsky there are two distinct types of linguistic universal – substantive and formal. These are universals in rather different senses. The substantive universals are abstract grammatical categories such that any known grammar contains a subset of them. Thus, while a given language might lack one of them, say the category of subject, it is out of these categories that any known grammar is formed. Thus English contains such grammatical categories as subject, predicate, verb, etc.[37]

> A theory of substantive universals claims that items of a particular kind in any language must be drawn from a fixed class of items.[38]

Formal universals are universals in a different sense. All known grammars contain rules whose formal, abstract properties are the same. These formal, abstract properties are the formal universals.

> Formal universals involve . . . the character of the rules that appear in grammars and the ways in which they can be interconnected.[39]

For example, all known grammars contain structure-dependent T-rules: so structure-dependence can be regarded as a formal universal. Linguists in the last few years have been searching hard for formal universals.[40]

Let us relate this to the question of innateness. The claim made by Chomsky and his followers is that the basis of the innate linguistic component is knowledge of these universals. We are asked to accept a picture of the child as being innately acquainted with a set of abstract categories which he will apply to the data of the language which he is learning, and with the abstract forms of those rules which he will internalize as he absorbs the data of his language. In more detail: given acquaintance with a set of substantive and formal universals, a child is capable of unconsciously formulating an indefinite number of hypotheses about how sentences are to be produced, interpreted, formed and transformed. The child then hears the utterances of the language he is to learn. He will find that many of the hypotheses he formulates are not compatible with the facts about English, say. Others he will find quite compatible. Eventually he will come to accept, again unconsciously, all and only those hypotheses which allow him to give correct interpretations of English sentences. At this point he has internalized the rules of his language, and has become a fluent speaker of it.

An analogy would be with how a scientist approaches his experimental data with a set of hypotheses as to the nature of the data. He will soon discover that some of these hypotheses fit the observed data, others do not. The compatible ones will form his scientific theory; or rather, those that are also recommended on grounds of simplicity, elegance etc. The data, of course, would mean nothing to him unless he approached them with a set of hypotheses which, as it were, tell him what to look for (see *p* 36).

In the case of the child, the crucial point to bear in mind is that he would be unable to learn his language, or internalize its rules, unless he approached the data of that language with a set of hypotheses framed in terms of certain innate universals. His acquaintance with these cannot be explained, however, in terms of his observations of his language, since as we have seen his knowledge of that language relies upon the recognition of deep aspects of grammar which are not open to observation.

It should be clear, then, that no denial of the importance of experience in the acquisition of language is being made. Without the hearing of utterances there would be nothing for the child's hypotheses to be tested against. Only when fed with the data of experience will the innate linguistic component be galvanized into action. I shall leave the last word on this account of Chomsky's ideas to Katz:

> The formal and substantive universals together permit the construction of a set of possible hypotheses about the linguistic description of a language. This set contains the systems of rules for each actual, natural language as well as systems for indefinitely many possible, but not actual, natural languages. Thus, we can regard this set of hypotheses, which we may refer to as 'initial hypotheses', as those from which the child selects in arriving at his internalization of the rules of his language . . .
>
> The role of experience is primarily to provide the data against which predictions and thus hypotheses are judged. Experience serves not to provide the things to be copied by the mind, as in the empiricist's account, but to help eliminate false hypotheses about the rules of a language.[41]

3 Some difficulties

As yet I have mentioned no criticisms that might be levelled against Chomsky's theory of language acquisition. Nor, in fact, do I intend to offer any substantial criticisms of my own. However, it would be misleading not to consider some of the objections which have been made – for the whole question is a hotly debated one. There are at least four directions from which Chomsky has been attacked:

[1] Some have challenged the accuracy of some of the empirical evidence adduced to support the innateness hypothesis.

[2] Some have challenged, not the empirical data, but the implication drawn from these to the effect that language acquisition depends upon a rich innate component.

[3] Some linguists have challenged Chomsky's linguistics, including the

all-important claim that any adequate grammar must contain a large number of T-rules.

[4] Philosophers have raised various conceptual objections against the claim that there can be innate knowledge of the sort described by Chomsky.

For example, it has been suggested that the existence of linguistic universals can be explained without reference to innate components, but in terms of the fact that all languages may have emerged from a common root. Again, it has been said that the speed of a child's acquisition of language is less startling once we reflect on the fact that he has already mastered a pre-verbal, gestural, silent language.[42] These would be criticisms of the second type. Some linguists have argued that a grammar employing only PS-rules can, with sufficient sophistication, provide an adequate description of a language.[43] This would be a criticism of the third type. I shall not be dealing with any but the fourth type of criticism – since the issues involved in the other types tend to be too technical to be adequately discussed here.

Criticisms of the last sort are those of most interest to philosophers, and concern the very intelligibility of Chomsky's thesis. Suppose we compress Chomsky's theory into the following form: linguistic competence or knowledge of rules partly owes to innate acquaintance with certain categories and forms, and so cannot be explained in terms of inductivist techniques alone. There are three crucial terms in this formulation, 'knowledge', 'innate', and 'inductivist'. Philosophers have challenged Chomsky's use of each of these terms, and have argued that if he had understood them properly he would not have proposed the theory he has. I shall say a little about innateness and induction, and rather more about knowledge.

One critic argues that, ever since Locke's attack on innate ideas in the seventeenth century, the claim that there are innate ideas has been seen to be unintelligible or patently false.[44] If the claim is that there are ideas in us of which we are conscious prior to any sense-experience, it is patently false: otherwise it is unintelligible. Consequently, if Chomsky's theory commits him to postulating the existence of innate knowledge, then that theory is either false or absurd. What we must do here is distinguish sharply between two different questions:

[1] Is Chomsky wise, and is he historically justified, in using the term 'innate' to apply to some of our linguistic knowledge?

[2] Is he right to claim that our knowledge is of the sort he says it is – knowledge to which, as a matter of fact, he has given the label 'innate'?

The point is that even if Chomsky is unwise to employ the term 'innate', it in no way follows that he is incorrect in the substance of his account of language acquisition. Some critics, I fear, confuse Chomsky's thesis with earlier innateness theories with which they have been unimpressed.

Chomsky himself, however, is guilty of considerably exaggerating the affinity between his thesis and older rationalists' doctrines on innateness.[45] First his interpretations of writers such as Descartes, Leibniz, or Cudworth, are shaky. He supposes there to be a uniformity in their thought which was simply not there. Nor indeed can one discover a single, coherent doctrine of innateness in the writings of any one Rationalist. Chomsky confidently ascribes to Leibniz and Descartes the view that innate knowledge is merely a dispositional capacity for acquiring actual knowledge once experience of certain sorts is had. But there are many passages in both philosophers which are recalcitrant to this unequivocal interpretation of their views. Second, Chomsky fails to see that on many issues there is purely a verbal similarity between his and their theses. He and Leibniz might agree that knowledge of what is *universal* is innate; but for Chomsky this means that knowledge of general, widespread features of languages is innate, while for Leibniz it means that knowledge of universal, non-particular truths – such as $2+2=4$ – is innate. Since older innateness doctrines are desperately unclear, and since Chomsky's affinity with these is highly dubious, it is surely unwise of Chomsky to place himself in this Rationalist tradition. The reader will not be helped, and may be hindered, by relating Chomsky to this tradition.[46]

At any rate, the essential point is this: Chomsky makes it reasonably plain what *he* means by 'innate' in his theory. So even if the past history of the term were murky and unrespectable, this would not affect the value of Chomsky's thesis. After all, the term 'innate' is not essential to his thesis. When he says there is innate knowledge he is denying that induction alone can be responsible for our internalization of rules, and saying that speakers must be acquainted with categories and forms which have no representation at the observable level. These claims are not obviously false or unintelligible; so debate over the sense or nonsense of earlier uses of 'innate' is not going to affect the issue.

Let us turn to induction. Chomsky, recall, denies that language can be acquired on the basis of inductive generalization from observed data. According to one critic, this is only so in a special sense of 'induction'.[47] Only if it is used in a restricted way will the Empiricist be unable to account for linguistic competence in terms of induction.

> A resourceful empiricist . . . will deny that information from linguistics refutes his theory; instead he will take this information to reveal something about the correct set of inductive procedures.[48]

The author, though, does not go on to explain what such a 'resourceful empiricist' might be like, or what the 'correct set of inductive procedures' are.

Once more it is essential to distinguish between a substantial question and a verbal one. The substantial question is: is Chomsky correct in his criticism of the Empiricist learning theories sketched in the last section? The verbal question, an interesting one nevertheless, is: is Chomsky correct to restrict the term 'inductive' to those Empiricist learning procedures described? Certainly it is no easy matter to decide what is to count as induction, and what is involved in it. In recent years it has been made plain that inductive inference involves more than the mere passive generalization spoken of by Hume and classical Empiricists. Some ability to formulate hypotheses must be granted if we are to explain how people can engage in inductive inference from observed data at all.[49] We might extend the term 'induction' in a wider way than Chomsky. We might even extend it to such a degree that, in this sense of 'inductive', we can explain language acquisition on the basis of induction. But that would be no criticism of the substance of Chomsky's thesis. His quarrel is not with the word 'inductive', but with the sorts of learning theories – which can be found in works by Skinner, Morris, Quine, and Osgood – that have been sketched. If we decide that he was not justified in restricting the term 'induction' to the processes of learning mentioned by such writers, that in no way affects the substance of his criticisms of them. 'One thing is certain', says Chomsky

> pointless terminological proposals – such as the proposal to define 'empiricism' so as to accommodate all possible views – will not help in resolving the very interesting and serious questions that remain, no matter what terminologies people may devise.[50]

Let us, finally, turn to the term 'knowledge'. Before we can say that some of our linguistic knowledge is innate, it must be established that it is knowledge of a sort that it would make sense to describe as innate. Some philosophers have argued that Chomsky has failed to understand the sense of 'knowledge' in which we can be spoken of as having knowledge of language. Had he properly understood this sense, he would have realized that it could not in principle be regarded as unconscious, tacit, or innate.

For Chomsky there are two interesting areas of linguistic knowledge: [1] unconscious, tacit knowledge of the rules of our language which we have internalized, and [2] unconscious, tacit, and also innate knowledge of those categories and forms which help explain our internalization of the rules of language. Chomsky's critics argue that this view is vitiated by the failure to distinguish between two different kinds of knowledge – knowledge *that* something is the case, and knowing *how* to do something.

When I know the date of Napoleon's death, I know that something is the case. Distinct from this is my knowledge of how to ride a bicycle. To say that I know how to ride a bicycle is to say no more than that I successfully do certain things. There are at least three things to note about knowing how. First, there is nothing especially mental about it. It is not what goes on in my mind, but what goes on in the road, that establishes my knowing how to ride a bicycle. Second, we cannot therefore talk of knowing how as being unconscious, innate, or tacit. If I know that something is the case, there are many times, say while I am asleep, when I am not conscious of this piece of knowledge. But a person's ability to ride a bicycle is not the sort of thing that can be regarded as conscious or unconscious – and knowing how to ride it is no more than this ability. Third, while knowing how to do something will typically involve following certain rules, laws, or principles, we are not tempted to ascribe knowledge of these rules, laws, or principles to people. If I know how to ride a bicycle, I must be obeying certain laws of mechanics – but no one wants to say that I know these laws of mechanics. Nor does the good tennis player have to know of the laws of velocity and friction which play a role in his getting the ball past his opponent.

The point that is emerging is this: if knowledge of grammar is simply knowing how to do certain things – eg reject certain sentences, mark the ambiguity of others, etc – then many of Chomsky's claims about this knowledge become incoherent. For if this knowledge is mere ability then, by analogy with the knowing how to ride a bicycle, [1] there is no reason to say such knowledge is a feature of the mind, [2] it will make no sense to describe it as tacit, unconscious, or innate, and [3] there will be no reason to say that the rules and principles involved in grammatical ability are in any way known to the speaker – as opposed to the professional linguist whose job it is to reveal these.[51] It has been said that there is no more reason to ascribe knowledge of the rules of grammar to speakers than there is to ascribe knowledge of the laws of gravity to stones and apples.

So, if knowledge of grammar is mere knowing how, it seems Chomsky's thesis falls down. Further, it seems that knowledge of grammar can only be knowing how. For it would be false to say that speakers know *that* the rules of grammar are such-and-such, or *that* they are employing certain categories and forms. This knowledge may be possessed by the linguist, but not by the speaker who is probably quite unaware of what the rules, principles, and forms are.

Let us admit that grammatical knowledge is not knowing *that*, in the above sense. However, the criticism of Chomsky only works if we assume that the sole alternative is to describe this knowledge as mere knowing how. Is grammatical knowledge merely an ability or skill? It seems plain to me that there is an extreme lack of analogy between the knowledge of grammar and the man's knowing how to ride a bicycle, which can be regarded as a paradigm of knowing how. A person knows how to ride a bicycle because he has been shown how, and has observed others doing it. To explain his ability we need do no more than cite the instructions he has received, the observations he has made, and certain physical preconditions required for success. We do not have to ascribe to him knowledge of the laws of mechanics, since this would in no way advance our explanation of his ability. But we can see how very different is the case of linguistic competence. In the first place, the child was not shown how to produce and interpret sentences; or rather, what he was shown is a minute, and not especially representative, sample of what he later becomes adept at. Second, we have seen, the child is quite competent to deal with sentences that do not resemble those he has already encountered in observable respects. For these reasons we cannot regard linguistic competence as a mere ability or skill attained through instruction and observation. Consequently we have a reason in the case of linguistic competence, which we do not in the case of the ability to ride bicycles, for attributing to persons acquaintance with rules and principles. Chomsky says

> We do not attribute knowledge of mechanics to a bicycle rider if in fact this assumption does not help explain his ability to ride a bicycle: we do attribute knowledge of the rules of grammar to the speaker-hearer if this assumption does contribute to an explanation of his ability to use a language.[52]

If a person's linguistic knowledge is neither knowledge *that*, nor mere knowing how, what is it? Let's call it knowledge *of*. To say that a child has knowledge of the rules of grammar is to say neither that he knows that the rules are such-and-such, if that implies his consciousness of them, nor that he simply does certain things properly. The doing of certain things properly cannot constitute the knowledge, since the knowledge explains the doing of these things. This theoretically inferred knowledge seems no worse off in status than theoretically inferred unconscious motives. Suppose a man displays irrational fearful behaviour in front of women, and we ascribe to him the unconscious fear of castration. This is not simply to say that he displays the fearful behaviour, but serves to explain this behaviour, which would otherwise be unintelligible. What is this unconscious fear like? Well, we can say no more than that it is like conscious fear of castration, only it is not conscious. It is like it, in the sense that the man behaves just as he would if he was actually conscious of his fear. Equally, we can speak of people having unconscious knowledge of language, since they behave just as they would if they were actually conscious of the rules of language. Or, if you like, they behave like a 'talking' computer which had been explicitly programmed with these rules.

I would not pretend that my discussion of our knowledge of language has got us very far. How to use and apply the term 'knowledge' are hotly debated questions among philosophers today.[53] It is arguable that answers to these questions have little bearing on the substance of Chomsky's thesis concerning language acquisition. Indeed Chomsky himself has suggested that little may be at stake in what appears to be a terminological debate.[54] If we agree that some innate component is at work in language learning, does it matter if we describe this component as 'knowledge'? It depends on what our interests are. As philosophers, concerned with traditional questions about the concept of knowledge, we must be interested in such questions as 'Can there be unconscious knowledge?', 'Is there knowledge *of*, as well as knowledge *that*, and knowing *how*?' etc. But as linguists concerned with the description of learning procedures, perhaps we may safely ignore these questions. If this is so, Chomsky might be accused of tossing out a shoal of red herrings in his exposition of his thesis, for at times he certainly does seem to think that this thesis has radical philosophical implications. Perhaps it is too soon to judge on this issue, for it is never easy to distinguish between substantial, empirical theses, and conceptual claims concerning the formulation of these theses. I stated at the beginning of this chapter that Chomsky's theories do have philosophical implications – perhaps that was too bold. But – and this is an irony of philosophy – it is a philosophical question to decide if another question is philosophical or not. What we require is a clearer account of linguistic universals and other features of language which allegedly enter into the innate component, and a clearer account of the concept of knowledge. Only then will we be in a position to judge if there is innate *knowledge* of these features of language.

Notes

1 Though one of the more pleasant aspects of the 'generation gap' is that today's children do seem to absorb the complex types of grammar to be discussed in this chapter. Most parents, no doubt, will take the same equivocal attitude towards this 'new grammar' as they take towards the 'new maths'.

2 Wittgenstein's notion of 'depth grammar' should not be confused with that of 'deep grammatical structure' to be discussed later in this chapter.

3 R. Lees, 'Review of *Syntactic Structures*', *Language, 33*, 1957, *p* 378.

4 Often Chomsky uses 'grammatical' in an all-encompassing sense to embrace all components of a theory of language. In this sense, syntax becomes just one part of grammar. I shall generally employ 'grammar' in the narrower, and more normal, sense.

5 This is not to say that it is easy, desirable, or even possible to draw sharp boundaries between syntactic and semantic questions. See G. Lakoff, on

'Generative Semantics', in *Semantics: An Interdisciplinary Reader*, ed D. Steinberg and L. Jakobovits. Cambridge University Press, 1971.

6 Such grammars sometimes go by other names; for example, 'Immediate Constituent' grammar.

7 P. Postal, 'The limitations of phrase-structure grammars', in *The Structure of Language*, ed J. Fodor and J. J. Katz. Prentice-Hall, 1964. *p* 140.

8 *Syntactic Structures*. Mouton, 1966. *p* 29.

9 *The Philosophy of Language*. Harper & Row, 1966. *p* 144.

10 'Review of *Syntactic Structures*', *Language*, *33*, 1957. *p* 402.

11 *Syntactic Structures*. Mouton, 1966. *p* 34.

12 'On the notion "Rule of Grammar"', in *The Structure of Language*, ed J. Fodor and J. J. Katz. Prentice-Hall, 1964. *p* 129.

13 *Language and Mind*. Harcourt, Brace, & World, 1968. *p* 87.

14 J. J. Katz, *The Philosophy of Language*. Harper & Row, 1966. *p* 131.

15 'On the notion "Rule of Grammar"', in *The Structure of Language*, ed J. Fodor and J. J. Katz. Prentice-Hall, 1964. *p* 133.

16 *Language and Mind*. Harcourt, Brace, & World, 1968. *p* 27.

17 *Introduction to Theoretical Linguistics*. Cambridge University Press, 1968. *p* 257. For a similar explanation, see J. Fodor et al, 'On the acquisition of syntax: a critique of "Contextual Generalization"', in *Readings in the Psychology of Language*, ed L. Jakobovits and M. Miron. Prentice-Hall, 1967.

18 See, for example, J. J. Katz and P. Postal, *An Integrated Theory of Linguistic Descriptions*. M.I.T. Press, 1964, and N. Chomsky, 'Deep structure, surface structure and semantic interpretation', in *Semantics: An Interdisciplinary Reader*, ed D. Steinberg and L. Jakobovits. Cambridge University Press, 1971.

19 See, for example, G. Lakoff, 'On Generative Semantics', in *Semantics: An Interdisciplinary Reader*, ed D. Steinberg and L. Jakobovits. Cambridge University Press, 1971, and 'Instrumental adverbs and the concept of deep structure', *Foundations of Language*, *4*, 1968, 4–29; J. D. McCawley, 'The role of semantics in a grammar', in *Universals in Linguistic Theory*, ed E. Bach and R. Harms. Holt, Rhinehart, & Winston, 1968.

20 'Interpretative Semantics versus Generative Semantics', *Foundations of Language*, *6*, 1970, *p* 220.

21 *Language and Mind*. Harcourt, Brace, & World, 1968. *p* 24.

22 *ibid*, *p* 23.

23 'Review of *Syntactic Structures*', *Language*, *33*, 1957, *p* 407.

24 *New Essays Concerning Human Understanding*. Preface.

25 *Aspects of the Theory of Syntax*. M.I.T. Press, 1965. *p* 4.

26 J. J. Katz, *The Philosophy of Language*. Harper & Row, 1966. *p* 247.

27 'Recent contributions to the theory of innate ideas', *Synthèse*, *17*, 1967, *p* 11.

28 See, for example, J. Lyons, *Chomsky*. Fontana/Collins, 1970. *p* 111.

29 'Recent contributions to the theory of innate ideas', *p* 4. My italics.

30 N. Chomsky. *ibid*, *pp* 3–4.

31 *The Philosophy of Language*. Harper & Row, 1966. *pp* 272–73.

32 See H. Putnam, 'The Innateness Hypothesis and explanatory models in linguistics', *Synthèse*, *17*, 1967, 12–22.

33 This point is made by E. Lenneberg, 'The capacity for language acquisition', in *The Structure of Language*, ed J. Fodor and J. J. Katz. Prentice-Hall, 1964. This paper discusses in detail much of the empirical evidence which I have sketched in this section.

34 *Language and Mind*. Harcourt, Brace, & World, 1968. *p* 27.

35 *ibid*, *pp* 52–3.

36 *ibid*, *p* 30.

37 There is a danger of terminological confusion here. Chomsky at one point
    denies that subject and object can be regarded as 'categories'. These, he says,
    are 'functional', not 'categorial', notions. The categorial notions are
    NP, VP, etc. (See his *Aspects of the Theory of Syntax*. M.I.T. Press, 1965.
    p 70.) He does, however, claim that the functional notions can be defined in
    terms of the categorial ones. Thus we can define 'subject' as follows:
                        Subject-of: [NP, S].
    In other words, the subject of a sentence is the leftmost NP in deep structure.
    For this reason, and because there is a perfectly good ordinary sense of
    'category' in which subject and object are categories, I shall continue to speak
    of them as categories.
38 *Aspects of the Theory of Syntax*. *p* 28.
39 *ibid, p* 29.
40 See, for example, Chomsky's discussion of the 'A-over-A' principle as a
    possible formal universal, in *Language and Mind*. Harcourt, Brace, & World,
    1968. *pp* 42–8.
41 *The Philosophy of Language*. Harper & Row, 1966. *pp* 276 & 278.
42 N. Goodman, 'The Epistemological Argument', *Synthèse, 17*, 1967, 23–8.
43 See, for example, the arguments of M. D. S. Braine, 'On learning the gram-
    matical order of words', *Psychological Review, 70*, 1963, 323–48.
44 N. Goodman, *op cit.*
45 See the last chapter of his *Cartesian Linguistics*. Harper & Row, 1966.
46 For a detailed account of the relationship, or lack of it, between Chomsky's
    views and those of older Rationalists, see my 'Innateness: Old and New',
    Philosophical Review, 81, 1972, 465–83.
47 G. Harman, 'Psychological aspects of the theory of syntax', *Journal of
    Philosophy, 65*, 1967, 75–87.
48 G. Harman, *ibid, p* 85.
49 See, for example, N. Goodman, *Fact, Fiction, and Forecast*. Bobbs-Merrill,
    1965, on the 'new riddle of induction'.
50 'Comments on Harman's reply', in *Language and Philosophy*, ed S. Hook.
    New York University Press, 1969. *p* 159.
51 This argument can be found in G. Harman, 'Linguistic competence and
    Empiricism', in *Language and Philosophy*, ed S. Hook. New York University
    Press, 1969. See also S. Stich, 'What every speaker knows', *Philosophical
    Review, 80*, 1971, 476–96.
52 'Comments on Harman's reply', *pp* 154–55. For an interesting account of
    how the postulation of unconscious knowledge of grammar might explain
    various diverse phenomena, such as our perception of pauses in speech, see
    J. Fodor, *Psychological Explanation*. Random House, 1968. *pp* 74–86.
53 See, for example, E. Gettier, 'Is justified true belief knowledge?', *Analysis,
    23*, 1963, 121–23.
54 In correspondence with J. Lyons. See *Chomsky*. Fontana/Collins, 1970.
    pp 113–14.

Chapter 7

Truth, the *a priori,* and synonymy

Of all the roles that sentences of various kinds can play, perhaps the most essential is the role of those which serve to state facts. There is little we can do that does not involve knowing what is, and what is not, the case. Given the limitations on his powers, each man must rely upon what others tell him to know what is the case. He must, that is, be fed with true sentences. Now what is truth? What makes a sentence true? This wide question will concern us in the last section of this chapter. Before that I want to consider a particularly important, and difficult class of truths, which we must understand in order to give a general, adequate account of truth. I refer to so-called *a priori* truths. An understanding of these will once again involve us in the question of synonymy; so in the second section I shall try to fill one of the gaps left in Chapter 2.

1 The *a priori* and the analytic

Philosophers from Plato on have sought, and tried to explain, a realm of knowledge that is somehow divorced from the fluctuating contingencies of the world around us; a form of knowledge, therefore, uninfected by the reliance upon our fallible senses. They have, moreover, been concerned to discover forms of knowledge that are beyond any conceivable doubt; knowledge which is superior, as it were, to the more chancy beliefs about the world founded on the testimony of our senses. They have, that is, tried to understand the realm of *a priori* or necessary truths. The most famous attempt in this direction is Immanuel Kant's, in his *Critique of Pure Reason,* which is one long attempt to answer the question 'How is *a priori* knowledge possible?' In recent years the study of *a priori* truth has very much turned to the study of various linguistic phenomena which, supposedly, can help to explain it. How this is so will emerge as we go along.

If we are asked what makes sentences like 'Most dogs have four legs' or 'Napoleon lost at Waterloo' true, it is not too hard to provide a rough answer. They are true in virtue of certain observable features of the universe. Asked how we know such sentences to be true, the reply would be, roughly: through observation by the senses. Of course, *I* did not observe Napoleon lose at Waterloo, but someone did, and that is, ultimately, how we know the sentence to be true. Or, at any rate, someone must have observed something from which it is reasonable to infer that Napoleon lost. Such truths as these are usually called 'empirical' or '*a posteriori*'.

There are many sentences whose truth cannot be explained in the above way. Take the sentences 'All bachelors are unmarried', and 'Two plus two equal four'. These are not true *in virtue of* of observable facts about the world. For, whatever happened in the world, it would still remain true that any bachelor is unmarried and that two plus two equal four. Nor is our knowledge of these derived from sense-experience. A man would be mad who went out observing each bachelor to check, with his own eyes, that the bachelor was unmarried. This is not to deny that sense-experience plays a role in our learning such truths. Plainly it helps a child to learn mathematics if he watches coloured bricks. But, once understood, continued acceptance of these truths does not rest upon our making observations. I do not need to keep my eyes peeled to retain my belief that two plus two equal four, in the way that I do to retain my belief that there are twenty red-headed men in the restaurant. Here are other examples of similar sorts of truths: 'Whatever is, is', 'All triangles are three-sided', 'Whatever is red is coloured', 'If "S" is true, then "S" is not false', and 'All bodies are extended'. Let us call them all *a priori* truths.

How do we know such truths? Not by sense-experience, we have seen. In the past, some pretty bizarre answers have been suggested. Some, for example, have claimed that they are imprinted in our minds at birth by God. God, as it were, acts as an instant learning-device saving us the trouble of learning such truths by the more laborious method of observation. Others have suggested that, in addition to the five normal senses, we possess another whose special role it is to inform us about *a priori* truths.[1] This sense stands to the *a priori* as the eyes stand to colour. That this is no answer at all seems apparent – for if we were asked to describe this special sense we could say no more than that it is the sense which informs us about *a priori* truths.

Any explanation of *a priori* truth must take a further consideration into account. These truths seem to be *necessary* truths. Not only is it true *a priori* that two plus two equal four, it is necessarily true; it could not be otherwise in the way that it could have been otherwise that I have fair hair. Again, while it is possible for any man to get married, it is not possible that a bachelor should be married and also remain a bachelor. In the everyday sense of 'necessary' there are plenty of necessary truths which are not *a priori*. Thus we might speak of it being necessary that an unsuspended apple should fall; or of its being impossible for a man to grow to fifty feet. In philosophical jargon, though, it is customary to restrict the term 'necessary' to *a priori* truths. Either this, or to apply some longer term like 'natural necessity' to truths which are true in virtue of scientific laws like those above. For, since David Hume's time, it has generally been accepted that the laws of science are empirical and contingent, and that we could at least imagine them breaking down, and so imagine a lot of what is in fact true being false. I can tell a good sci-fi story about how the usual laws of nature cease to operate; but I can tell no story about a world of married bachelors or four-sided triangles.

Whether or not there are other necessary truths, it is fairly plain why *a priori* ones should be necessary. For it makes no difference to an *a priori* truth what happens in the world; so, if whatever *could* change in the universe would make no difference, it is difficult to see how our *a priori* truths could have been false. I can describe no occurrences such that, *if* they were to take place, they would falsify 'All bachelors are unmarried'. So any account of *a priori* truth must take into consideration the peculiarly necessary status of such truth.

What, then, is an *a priori* or necessary truth? Many definitions have been provided, but it is doubtful if any has been fully satisfactory. Mainly they have failed through being circular, or through failing to explain its necessity. Consider, for example, Leibniz's definition of an *a priori* truth as one whose denial would be self-contradictory. This will account for the *a priori* nature of a sentence like 'John is John'. But what about the sentence 'All bachelors are unmarried'? The denial of this does not have the explicit form of a self-contradiction; *ie*, it is not of the form 'It is the case that X, and it is not the case that X'. So Leibniz must be using 'self-contradictory' in a wider sense. But what sense? Can we say more than that a sentence is self-contradictory in this sense if it is the denial of an *a priori* truth? If not we have explained nothing. Or consider Hume's view that a necessary truth is one whose falsity is *unimaginable*. Apart from the problem that people's powers of imagination vary widely, and are anyway largely untapped, there is a further difficulty. Let us admit that an *a priori* truth cannot be imagined to be false. Surely, though, we have not been given the reason why it is necessary. The cart has been put before the horse. The reason why we cannot imagine certain sentences to be false is *because* they are necessarily true. So Hume's account would fail to explain the necessity of *a priori* truths even if it was the case that all *a priori* truths are those whose falsity we cannot imagine, and vice versa.

Given the difficulties in finding an adequate account of necessary truth, it is small wonder that some philosophers have given up the chase, and denied that there is such a thing. J. S. Mill in his *System of Logic*, for instance, regards it as an illusion to suppose that mathematical and other supposedly *a priori* truths are necessary. For him, they are no more than especially well-confirmed empirical generalizations. And a more recent philosopher, Quine, says 'In principle . . . I see no higher or more austere necessity than natural necessity'.[2] They may be right. Perhaps the *a priori* is a white elephant. But it is too early for us to admit this. Let us search for more adequate definitions of the *a priori*.

Since the eighteenth century, discussion of *a priori* truth has usually been conducted within the framework set up by Kant. Indeed, the division into *a priori* and *a posteriori*, in those terms, is Kant's. In addition to this division, Kant made another. All truths, he says, are either *analytic* or *synthetic*.

> In all judgments in which the relation of a subject to the predicate is thought . . . this relation is possible in two different ways. Either the predicate B belongs to the subject A, as something which is (covertly) contained in this concept A; or B lies outside the concept A, although it does indeed stand in connection with it. In the one case I entitle the judgment analytic, in the other synthetic.[3]

As an example of an analytic truth he gives 'All bodies are extended'. He seems to mean that the idea of extension is included in the very concept of a body; that in thinking of a body one is already thinking of extension. This is to be distinguished from a synthetic truth such as 'All bodies have weight'; for the idea of heaviness is not actually contained in the concept of a body.

While Kant is getting at something important here, his description of the analytic/synthetic distinction is unsatisfactory. For it is not at all clear what this psychological talk of ideas containing one another, or of our thinking the predicate in the subject, means. Recent philosophers, consequently, have given different accounts of the distinction, though they have remained, supposedly, true to the spirit of Kant's. According to these philosophers, saying that one idea is contained in another is a misleading way of saying that one term is part of the meaning of another. On this account, 'All bodies are extended' is analytic because the word 'body' *means, inter alia*, something that has extension. A synthetic truth, on the other hand, is one that is not similarly true in virtue of the meanings of the component expressions.

We can now see the relevance of linguistic considerations to the *a priori*. For all analytic truths are *a priori* truths; and analytic truths, we have just seen, are those which supposedly are true in virtue of meanings alone. So far, though, what we are saying is very vague, because of the extreme vagueness of 'meaning'. Nor would it help matters to employ

A. J. Ayer's account, that 'a proposition is analytic when its validity depends solely on the *definitions* of the symbols it contains'.[4] For the notion of definition is scarcely clearer than the notion of meaning. It has been said that there are at least fourteen distinct kinds of definition; and not all of these – ostensive definition, for example – could be involved in analytic truth.[5] Nor is it much use to say with Carnap that analytic truths are those which are true in virtue of the 'semantical rules' of language.[6] Unlike an artificial logician's language, which contains explicit instructions for the use of symbols, a natural language – despite the attempts of the French Académie and Fowler to impose them – does not contain explicit rules of the form 'Always use "body" so that it means something extended'. The semantic rules, if there be any, are implicit. But then how do we know what they are? Not by looking in the dictionary, for the lexicographer is only describing how we use words; he is not a legislator. It seems we can say little about such rules except they are the rules which, if we infringe them, result in the denial of analytic truths. If so, we must first recognize *a priori* truths before we can extract the semantic rules, and so we cannot explain the *a priori* in terms of these rules.

The definition of analytic truth which has, I believe, the most chance of success is one in terms of *synonymy*. It has been suggested that an analytic truth is one which can be transformed into a logical truth once synonyms are replaced by synonyms. For example, since 'bachelor' is synonymous with 'unmarried man' then we can transform the sentence 'All bachelors are unmarried men' into 'All bachelors are bachelors' when we replace one expression by its synonym. Now the latter sentence is a truth of logic; that is, it has the form 'All A's are A's'. This view of analytic truth depends upon our being able to give an adequate account of synonymy. This is something we should want to do anyway, since it constitutes one of the two major problems about meaning (see Chapter 2). But the role that synonymy plays in answering the question 'What is *a priori* truth?' provides an added spur to studying it.

We are now in a position to state what is normally called the 'linguistic theory of *a priori* (necessary) truth'. We have already noted that analytic truths are *a priori*, and we are assuming that analytic truths depend upon synonymy relations. If it could be shown, further, that all *a priori* truths are analytic, it would then follow that all *a priori* truths are true in virtue of synonymy relations. So what the linguistic theory asserts is:

[1] All *a priori* truths are analytic.
[2] All analytic truths are true in virtue of purely linguistic data (*eg* synonymy relations).

The purpose of section 2 is to defend the second assertion, by giving an adequate account of synonymy. But what about the first claim? Kant, famously, denied this, and insisted that there existed a class of synthetic *a priori* truths. These are truths which are [1] necessarily true, but [2] not true simply in virtue of meanings or synonymy relations. Many reasons have been given against the claim that all *a priori* truths are analytic. Some of these are of an especially linguistic nature, and will be discussed and, I hope, rebutted, in section 3. However, it is only fair to mention that there are other objections which it is not in the scope of this book to consider. I believe these objections fail – but I can do no more than state just that.[7]

It should be stressed that the acceptability of the linguistic theory would be of vital importance in philosophy. Traditionally, two great schools have opposed one another – rationalism and empiricism. One of the crucial issues between them was discussed in the last chapter – but another crucial issue has been the status of necessary truths. It can hardly be claimed that a necessary truth depends upon sense-experience, so how can one avoid the rationalist conclusion that men possess some special faculty of mind whereby they divine non-empirical truths? This has always been the problem for the empiricist – but the answer he can give is the 'linguistic theory of necessary truth'. For, if necessary truths are simply generated by our happening to use symbols in certain ways, then we do not have to postulate any rational faculty in order to account for necessary truth. Contemporary empiricists, like Ayer and Carnap, typically insist, therefore, that there are just two kinds of truths – empirical ones, which are tested by observation, and analytic ones, which are tested by seeing how words are employed. The rationalist, to save the day, would have to establish the existence of *synthetic a priori* truths, it appears.

2 Synonymy

I discussed and rejected three accounts of synonymy in Chapter 2. In this section I hope to present a more satisfactory one. This account will not be entirely complete, since a complete one will have to await a discussion of speech acts in the next chapter. However, the amendment or addition that will be made in the next chapter is a simple and minor one – so what follows now is the meat of the matter.

First, though, a preliminary point. According to Fowler's *Modern English Usage*

> Synonyms, in the narrowest sense, are separate words whose meaning, both denotation and connotation, is identical, so that one can always be substituted for the other without change in the effect of the sentence in which it is done.[8]

It is not clear what is meant by 'effect' here, but I take it that Fowler means to include the various psychological and emotional effects a sentence can have upon hearers. What needs to be noted is that when philosophers talk of synonymy, they are not normally concerned with such effects. I have argued already that these psychological and emotional effects should not be brought under the heading of 'meaning' at all. The theory of synonymy I want to consider is concerned with the substitution of one word for another only insofar as this might change the *truth-value* of sentences – not with how it might alter the psychological or emotive force of the sentences. So it may well be that philosophers use 'synonymy' in a different sense from Fowler's. This can be defended on various grounds. First, given the purposes for which philosophers discuss synonymy – *eg* to study *a priori* truth – the question of psychological effects is unimportant (see *p* 19). Second, many people surely do not use 'synonymy' in such a narrow sense as Fowler – indeed if they did it would follow pretty immediately that there are no such things as synonyms, since it is doubtful that any two words have exactly identical psychological effects. Third, the philosopher is at least picking upon what is the most essential factor in anyone's concept of synonymy – namely, that if two terms are synonymous it cannot make any difference to the truth of sentences which one we employ; though this remark needs qualification in what follows.

The theory of synonymy I want to discuss and amend is often called the 'interchangeability theory'. Put loosely, the claim is that synonymy is a function of words being interchangeable in sentences without altering the truth-values of those sentences. The extreme version of the theory is well stated by Benson Mates as follows:

> Two expressions are synonymous in a language L if and only if they may be interchanged in *each sentence* of L without altering the truth value of that sentence.[9]

So, for example, 'bachelor' and 'unmarried man' are synonyms if any true sentence containing 'bachelor' remains true when 'unmarried man' replaces 'bachelor' – and similarly for false sentences.

There seems to be an immediate problem for this extreme version – for there are sentences in which it would be quite hopeless to expect any two words to be generally interchangeable *salva veritate* (*ie* without altering truth-values). If so, then by the extreme theory, it is quite hopeless to suppose that there are any synonyms. Let us call any sentence in which it would be hopeless to expect interchangeability a 'recalcitrant' sentence. I shall now mention some types of recalcitrant sentences.

[1] '"Bachelor" has eight letters.' Obviously this becomes false if we replace 'bachelor' by 'unmarried man'. So these two putative synonyms fail to interchange here – and, of course, no two words that are not

orthographically identical will be interchangeable in all sentences of this sort.

[2] '[di'said] (*ie* decide) has less phonemes than [di'laitid] (*ie* delighted).' This would become false if we replaced 'decide' by the putative synonym 'make a decision' – and again we could not expect any two words which are phonetically distinct to be interchangeable in all such sentences.

[3] 'He'll get over her; it's only puppy-love', or 'John, Mary, and Susan form a passionate love-triangle'. The first becomes absurd if we try to replace 'puppy' by 'young dog'. The second becomes absurd if we replace 'triangle' by 'plane, trilateral figure'. When a word forms part of some longer compound expression, it will, in general, be hopeless to expect any other word to be interchangeable with it *salva veritate*.

[4] 'Too many cooks spoil the broth', or 'Life is just a cherry-cream pie'. Try replacing 'cooks' by some putative synonym like 'culinary workers' in the first. And try replacing 'cherry' by 'pulpy drupe from a species of prunus' in the second. Both the proverb and the metaphor become absurd as a result. To the extent to which, *qua* proverb and metaphor, they are true, they cease to be true once 'cooks' and 'cherry' are replaced by their putative synonyms.

[5] 'Whoever believes all the men in the room are bachelors, believes all the men in the room are bachelors.' This is certainly true. But suppose we replace the second occurrence of 'bachelors' by 'unmarried men', and derive 'Whoever believes all the men in the room are bachelors, believes all the men in the room are unmarried men'. This is almost certainly false – for there is almost certainly someone who does not believe that all bachelors are unmarried. And in general one should not begin to expect any two words to be universally interchangeable in all so-called 'intensional' sentences – ones of such forms as 'He believes that X is Y', or 'She hopes that X will be Y', or 'They want X to be Y', or 'He wondered if X was Y', etc.

So we have at least five types of recalcitrant sentences – ones in which it would be absurd to expect any two words to be, in general, interchangeable *salva veritate*. Faced by the existence of such sentences, there are two reactions we might have. We might conclude with Mates that, since the extreme version of the interchangeability theory provides an adequate definition of 'synonymy', therefore no two words ever are synonyms – for no two words ever are interchangeable in *all* sentences. Or we might insist that since there are, or might be, expressions which are synonymous, therefore the interchangeability theory needs to be mellowed to some less extreme form. The latter path is surely the more sensible to follow. For the extreme version of the theory does not set up a severe test that words could, but as a matter of fact do not, meet. Rather it sets up a test which immediately and trivially rules out the possibility of two expressions ever being synonymous. And surely one should be suspicious of a criterion which immediately and trivially rules out the very possibility of an ancient and oft-used concept, in this case synonymy, ever being applicable. So it will be wiser to search for a more mellow version of the theory. It may still turn out that no two terms are synonyms; but any acceptable test should at least allow for the possibility of there being synonyms.

What could this more mellow version be? The following might be suggested: two expressions are synonymous if and only if they are interchangeable *salva veritate* in all sentences *except* ones of type [1–5] above. By doing this, we state the theory so that it becomes irrelevant to the synonymy of words whether they interchange in recalcitrant sentences or not. However, there are two insuperable objections to this suggestion. First, I mentioned five types of recalcitrant sentences, but I could have mentioned more. And however many I mention, how can I be sure that I have completed the list?[10] But if I do not know when the list is finished, I can never know whether two expressions are synonymous or not. For it is always possible that someone will produce a sentence in which two putative synonyms are not interchangeable. If that sentence is not included in our list of recalcitrant ones, we shall have to conclude that the expressions are not synonymous – or, by an *ad hoc* procedure, simply add that sentence to our list. At present, then, we can say no more than that two expressions are synonymous if and only if they are interchangeable in all sentences except [1–5] *and* any other recalcitrant sentences. Lacking a general notion of recalcitrance, this definition is not much help. The second problem is this: our mellowed version provides no explanation of why certain sentences are recalcitrant; of why, that is, synonyms need not be interchangeable in them. The theory, therefore, appears to be trivial. We are being told that two expressions are synonymous if and only if they are interchangeable, except where they are not interchangeable. This is like being told that all objects are composed of electrons apart from the ones which are not.

What we require is a general criterion and explanation of recalcitrance. We want to know when and why expressions can be synonymous despite not being interchangeable in all sentences. Our theory must take the form: two expressions are synonymous if and only if they are interchangeable in all sentences except those of the following recalcitrant type . . . , for the following reason . . .

I now want to sketch just such a theory. Here is a consideration which gives the clue to the theory. Synonymy, trivially, is a matter of meaning. The synonymy of two expressions is a function of their semantic, as opposed to, say, their phonetic, aspect. Now sometimes a word can appear in a sentence in such a way that its meaning, so to speak, is irrelevant.

This is the case with '"bachelor" has eight letters'. No matter what 'bachelor' means, even if it meant nothing, the sentence would still be true. So in such a case it would seem to be irrelevant whether some putative synonym of 'bachelor' interchanges with it or not. For since the meaning of 'bachelor' is immaterial in the sentence, and since the meaning of any putative synonym that replaces it would be equally immaterial, we can discover nothing about the meanings of these words by discovering that they are, or are not, interchangeable in that sentence. To take an analogy: two tools may be of different colours, and so are not interchangeable on colour charts. But that tells us nothing about whether the tools are the same in the sense of having the same function. Colour and function are different aspects of a tool; and meaning and spelling are two different aspects of a word.

Using the above as a clue, I now want to suggest the following criterion of synonymy: two expressions are synonymous if and only if they are interchangeable *salva veritate* in all those sentences *attempted confirmation of which presupposes giving a semantic interpretation of the expressions*. This is meant to lend formality to the point made in the previous paragraph; that it is only of relevance to the synonymy of words if they are interchangeable in sentences where their meanings are material. To say that their meanings are material is to say that we should have to have some idea of what the expressions mean in order to judge the truth or falsity of the sentences. As we saw in the case of '"bachelor" has eight letters', the meaning of 'bachelor' is immaterial since, we can now say, the truth of the sentence can be established without our having the least idea of what 'bachelor' means.

Let me first expand on two terms used in my definition – 'attempted confirmation' and 'semantic interpretation'. By an attempted confirmation of a sentence, I mean anything that would count as an attempt to find out if the sentence was true or false. This might range from a full-blooded laboratory test to establish the truth of a sentence, to groping, uncertain, indirect ways of finding out if it was true or false. The confirmation might be empirical – as when one looks and listens – or of a quite different type, as when one tries to find out if a statement in mathematics is true by employing the deductive techniques of that discipline. The point is that one can sometimes set about confirming a sentence in these ways without having the least idea what one of the words means, as in the 'bachelor' case. Usually, of course, one does have to have some idea of what each word in the sentence means to do this.

By a semantic interpretation of an expression, I mean just about anything that would count as an attempt to explain what an expression means, what is to be understood by it, or what is implied by it. Thus a man's saying '"bachelor" means *unmarried man*', or a person's pointing to Russian flags and pools of blood in answer to the question 'What does "red" mean?', could both be counted as semantic interpretations. Again the point is that we need not always be able to provide such a semantic interpretation of each word in a sentence in order to set about confirming it.

The test of my criterion is this: does it succeed in showing that interchangeability in recalcitrant sentences like [1–5], and any others that can be thought up, is indeed irrelevant to the synonymy of expressions? Is it the case that these sentences are all such that attempted confirmation of them does not presuppose providing a semantic interpretation of the relevant words? Let us take them one by one.

[1a] I have already dealt with these cases. It is surely clear that where an expression occurs inside quotes, and where the truth or falsity of the sentence depends on the written form of the word, there is no need to understand what the word means in order to judge the truth or falsity of the sentence.

[2a] Just as the truth of sentences in which an expression occurs in quotes can be tested without knowing what it means, so clearly the truth of a sentence in which the word occurs in phonetic transcription can be tested without knowing what it means. If its truth depends upon the sound of the word in question, it does not depend upon its meaning.

[3a] Surely, too, one could attempt to confirm 'John, Mary, and Susan form a passionate love-triangle' without having any idea what 'triangle' by itself means. For in a compound expression like 'love-triangle', 'triangle' does not retain its normal, literal meaning. The paraphrase of our sentence is 'John etc form a relationship such that the one is in love with the second, the second with the third, and the third with the first'. Provided a person knew that was the paraphrase, he could set about confirming the sentence even if he had no idea what 'triangle' normally means. So, by my test for synonymy, it will be immaterial whether or not some putative synonym of 'triangle' interchanges with it in such a sentence.

[4a] One could also set about confirming a proverb like 'Too many cooks spoil the broth' without having any idea what 'cook' means. For in the context of a proverb, the normal meaning of 'cook' is irrelevant. One understands the proverb if one can provide some paraphrase such as 'If lots of people engage on a task, they will probably bungle it'. So, again, it is irrelevant to the synonymy of 'cook' with some expression, say 'culinary worker', that the latter cannot replace 'cook' in the proverb. (At one time I knew what 'Que sera sera' meant, but had no idea what 'sera' or 'que' meant. On the contrary, I thought the spelling of the saying was 'Queserraserra'.)

[5a] It seems to me that one can attempt to confirm a sentence like 'John

believes Harry is a bachelor' without having any idea what 'bachelor' means. For we can ask John 'Do you believe that Harry is a bachelor?'; and we can ask this without knowing what 'bachelor' means. A journalist, covering a science conference, could come away knowing that the physicists believe that positrons are given off when alpha particles strike aluminium, without having the slightest idea what 'positron' means. He may simply have heard the scientists say that positrons are like this, and on the assumption that they are being sincere, this counts as confirmation of the sentence 'They believe that positrons are given off when . . . etc'. So, again, it seems irrelevant whether putative synonyms, 'X' and 'Y', interchange in such sentences as 'He believes they are X', or 'She wants it to be Y', etc.

As far as I can see, then, my test for synonymy succeeds in showing why we can regard two expressions as synonymous despite the fact that there are sentences in which they are not interchangeable. These sentences will be ones whose truth or falsity does not depend upon the meanings of the relevant expressions, in the manner described. Suppose we have two putative synonyms. To establish that they are really synonymous, we see whether or not they are interchangeable *salva veritate* in all non-recalcitrant sentences – all sentences, that is, whose attempted confirmation does presuppose giving a semantic interpretation of the expressions. We have thus provided a general criterion for synonymy, and have explained *why* failure of synonyms to interchange in certain sentences is immaterial. (I should add that my criterion would have to be defended against certain objections before we could rest content with it.)

Now I must face one problem which confronts an interchangeability theory of synonymy like mine. To show that two expressions are synonymous, it is not enough to show that they apply to all and only the same things. 'Creature with a heart' and 'creature with a kidney' may apply to all and only the same things, but are plainly non-synonymous. For expressions to be synonymous they must *necessarily* apply to all and only the same things. Or we may put it like this: not only must the sentence 'All X's are X's' remain true when the second occurrence of 'X' is replaced by 'Y', in order for 'X' and 'Y' to be synonyms, but also the sentence 'All X's are necessarily X's'. That is, the sentence 'All X's are necessarily Y's' must be true if 'X' and 'Y' are to be synonyms.

But now we have a problem. For how do we know that the sentence 'All bachelors are necessarily unmarried men' is true unless we already know that 'bachelor' and 'unmarried man' are synonymous. If we do not, our test for synonymy is circular. For in order to know that two expressions are interchangeable in all non-recalcitrant sentences, one would already have to know that they are synonymous – in which case one cannot use interchangeability as a test for synonymy.

I think this problem can be resolved in the manner sketched by Nelson Goodman in a number of articles.[11] Goodman stresses that two expressions are not synonymous just because they apply to all and only the same things. 'Centaur' and 'unicorn' are not even alike in meaning, yet they apply to all and only the same – namely nothing at all. However, Goodman argues, it is not required that we interchange expressions in sentences like 'All X's are necessarily Y's' in order to know that they are synonymous. Corresponding to any expression, there are various compound expressions we can devise containing the original one. For example, corresponding to the word 'centaur' we can devise the compound expressions 'centaur-picture', 'centaur-statue', 'centaur-description', etc. Let us call what the word 'centaur' applies to the *primary extension* of the word; and let us call what the compound expressions apply to the *secondary extension* of the word. Then, according to Goodman, two words are synonymous if both their primary and secondary extensions are identical. Thus, although 'centaur' and 'unicorn' have the same primary extension, they do not have the same secondary extension, since 'centaur-picture' refers to things which 'unicorn-picture' does not. Consequently, 'centaur' and 'unicorn' are not synonyms. 'Bachelor' and 'unmarried man', on the other hand, have the same primary extension, and the same secondary extension, since expressions like 'bachelor-picture' refer to the same as 'unmarried man-picture'.[12]

The point is that we do not have to *test* for synonymy by interchanging expressions in sentences like 'All X's are necessarily X's'. The expressions are synonymous provided that they and their compounds derived from them are interchangeable in all other (non-recalcitrant) sentences. If they are interchangeable in this manner then we infer that they will also be interchangeable in sentences like 'All X's are necessarily Y's'.

So let me restate my definition of synonymy: two expressions are synonymous if and only if they, and various compound expressions derived from them, are interchangeable *salva veritate* in all sentences attempted confirmation of which presupposes giving a semantic interpretation of the expressions.

It seems to me that we have nearly reached an adequate account of synonymy. It is not fully adequate, because it is too limited. I have discussed interchangeability only in true or false sentences, whereas we must widen the account to cover interchangeability in other types of sentences. This can be quickly done when we consider these other types of sentences in the next chapter. However, to the extent to which our account is adequate, we have an adequate account of analytic truths; for I suggested that an analytic truth is precisely one which can be reduced to a truth of logic once synonyms replace synonyms.[13] Since analytic truths are co-extensive with, or a subclass of, *a priori* truths, we have either fully or partially explicated *a priori* truth.

3 Sentences and propositions

I have twice said that there are certain necessary truths, perhaps the only ones, which are true simply in virtue of certain linguistic data – namely synonymy relations. These are analytic truths. Some philosophers, however, have insisted that this account of necessary truths is based upon an extreme confusion, and that once the confusion is revealed it will be seen that *no* truths depend upon linguistic data, so that no truths are analytic in the sense defined. The alleged confusion is between *sentences*, which are linguistic entities, and certain non-linguistic entities which sentences are used to express. These latter are usually called 'propositions', in a somewhat technical sense of that word. The claim is that truth and falsity belong not to sentences, as I have been assuming throughout this book, but to these different things, propositions. If this is so, it is difficult to see how a necessary truth can depend upon linguistic data, since what is necessarily true, a proposition, is not something linguistic at all. Allegedly, to suppose that sentences are true or false is like supposing that it is the written score of a symphony that is beautiful rather than the symphony itself. Just as the beauty of the symphony does not depend upon the nature of the symbols used in writing the score, so the truth of a proposition does not depend upon the nature of the symbols used in a sentence which expresses it. As one writer puts it, the idea that necessary truths depend upon linguistic data

> rests on . . . confusion between sentences and propositions . . . What makes the *sentence* 'All bodies are extended' express the proposition which it does express . . . is the fact that the word 'body' means 'extended substance'. It is not the case that the proposition in question is true because of the meaning and definition of 'body' . . . but that the sentence used expresses the proposition in question because of the meaning or definition of 'body'. A little reflection will reveal that every alleged instance of 'truth by definition' is to be explained (or explained away) in the same way.[14]

So, because words have the meanings they do, sentences containing them will express the propositions they do. But the truth or falsity of the propositions so expressed in no way depends upon the meanings of the words. Analogously, because various musical symbols have the functions they do, a score containing them will represent the symphony that it does; however, the beauty or repulsiveness of the symphony so represented does not similarly depend upon the nature of the symbols. If this argument is correct, it would count as a sufficient refutation of the linguistic theory of necessary truth mentioned in section 1.

What motivates the distinction between sentences and propositions? I shall consider three arguments designed to show that there must be propositions distinct from sentences, and that truth and falsity belong to the former. I shall also try to show that each of these arguments fails, and that we can rest content with the view that it is sentences which are true or false. The first argument is a general one, having no particular connection with necessary truths, whereas the other two do have this connection.

[1] Suppose you come across a tree upon which are carved the words 'I love you'. Is this sentence true or false? Of course one cannot say, since one does not know to whom 'I' and 'you' refer, and one does not know when it was written. If carved at the height of his passion by Romeo to Juliet, what is carved would be true. If carved by Lee to Grant at the height of the American Civil War, it would be false. So, supposedly, one cannot say of the sentence that it is true or false; for one and the same sentence may be used on one occasion to say something true, and on another something false. The conclusion should be, allegedly, that what is true is the proposition expressed by that sentence when written by Romeo, and what is false is the proposition expressed by it when written by Lee. Unless we said it was these different propositions that were respectively true and false, we should have to say that one and the same sentence could be both true and false.[15]

This argument fails. As E. J. Lemmon points out, to say that a sentence cannot have a truth value because on one occasion it says something true and on another something false, is like arguing that a gate cannot have a definite colour because the same gate may have been different colours, at different times.[16] That is: the reason why we cannot judge of a sentence like 'I love you', that it is true or false is that we do not know the context in which it was produced. But once we do know the context, why can we not say that it is the sentence which is true or false? Admittedly a sentence taken in abstraction from context cannot be judged true or false; but the reply is that it is sentences *taken in context* that are true or false. It is worth noting that some sentences are context-free, unlike 'I love you'. For example, 'All triangles are trilateral'; and in such a case we can say straightforwardly that the sentence is true. So this argument fails to show a need for introducing any non-linguistic entities as the bearers of truth-values.

[2] Take the sentence 'All bachelors are unmarried'. In 1972 someone who uttered this would be uttering something true. But suppose that, over the course of the next ten years, the meaning of 'bachelor' alters and becomes synonymous with 'chemist'. If so, someone who uttered 'All bachelors are unmarried' in 1982 would be taken to be saying something false. But if so, the argument runs, we cannot say that the sentence 'All bachelors are unmarried' is necessarily true. For if something is necessarily true, it cannot cease to be true; for a necessary truth is one

that could not possibly be false. As Arthur Pap says '"necessary" as predicated of propositions is . . . clearly time-independent'.[17] Since the sentence does cease to say something true, then it cannot be that which is itself ever true. The problem vanishes, supposedly, once we distinguish between sentences and propositions. It is the proposition expressed by 'All bachelors are unmarried' in 1972 that is necessarily true. And that proposition is just as necessarily true in 1982 or in any other year. All that happens as a result of the change in the meaning of 'bachelor' is that the sentence is no longer capable of expressing the same proposition in 1982. Briefly, then: if necessary truths were sentences they could cease to be true – but that is absurd, so it is certain non-temporal entities, propositions, that are necessarily true. This shows, allegedly, the irrelevance of definitions and synonymy to truth. A definition or a synonymy relation may determine that a given sentence expresses the proposition that it does, but cannot determine the truth or falsity of what is expressed; for that would remain true whatever changes might take place in the definitions of the words.

This argument fails. It is possible, in fact, to reconcile the claims that

[1] necessary truths are eternally true, and

[2] necessary truth belongs to sentences, despite changes in meanings of sentences.

I noted on *p* 175 that the production of a sentence typically presupposes a context – *eg* that 'I' refers to Romeo – which must be revealed before we can judge the truth of it. Now there is a different sort of presupposition that is always involved whenever anyone seriously utters anything; and this is that his words are being used with certain meanings rather than others. Sometimes such presuppositions have to be made explicit. A person may say 'East Germany is a democracy'. Another replies 'Surely not'. The first man says 'Well it is in the sense of "democracy" I am using – Lenin's sense rather than De Tocqueville's'. Here the first speaker is laying bare the semantic presupposition of his utterance. This often has to be done where words are vague or ambiguous, or where the person is using a word in an unusual sense. Normally we do not have to lay bare these presuppositions, since the speaker and the audience will normally be agreed on what they are. However, unless such presuppositions are being assumed it is impossible to judge on the truth or falsity of what is said. If a person said 'I have just been to the bank' when in fact he had been to his local bar, we might assume he is saying something false. But he only has to point out that he means by 'bank' what we mean by 'bar' in order to keep his drinking habits secret from his wife, and we are forced to say that he uttered something true.

I am suggesting this: it is the sentence, taken together with its semantic presuppositions, that is true or false. A sentence taken in abstraction from these is neither true nor false; for it is a mere string of noises. Once this is realized, we can retain the view that it is sentences that are necessarily true. For if we take a sentence together with its semantic presuppositions then that sentence, if necessarily true, will always be necessarily true *given just those semantic presuppositions*. The sentence 'All bachelors are unmarried', given its normal 1972 semantic presuppositions, is necessarily true. Now however much the word 'bachelor' may alter meaning over the next ten years, that sentence will be true in 1982 provided that it is used with its 1972 presuppositions. If someone were charged with saying something false in 1982 when he says 'All bachelors are unmarried', he could quickly defend himself by pointing out that he is using 'bachelor' in its 1972 sense.

So, it is only if we take sentences in abstraction from their semantic presuppositions that we are forced to introduce propositions as the bearers of timeless necessary truth. This becomes quite unnecessary once we regard sentences together with these presuppositions as the bearers of necessary truth.

[3] A simple, but interesting, argument against the view that sentences are necessarily true has been urged by Professor Aune.[18] The existence of the English language is a contingent matter of fact. English might well never have developed. If so, how can a necessary truth depend upon facts about the English language – such as synonymy relations? This would mean that a necessary truth depends upon a contingent fact – and surely that is absurd. For this implies that had the contingent fact been otherwise, which it might have been, then the necessary truth would not have been a truth – which contradicts the very idea that it is a necessary one, since a necessary truth is precisely one that could not have been not true. According to Aune the puzzle disappears once we distinguish between sentences and propositions. It is indeed a contingent fact that the English sentence 'All bachelors are unmarried' expresses the necessary truth it does. But the truth so expressed is quite independent of the fact that this sentence expresses it, and more generally of the English language itself. Had there not been English, there would still have been the truth.

This argument fails. There is a sense in which we can admit that a necessary truth is independent of the sentence used to express it – but this admission does not commit us to denying that it is sentences which are necessarily true. First, let me give an analogy. Suppose I trump you with my King of Hearts. Does my trumping you depend upon my laying the King? Well, in a sense, no; not if I also have the Ace and could have laid that instead. Now it would be absurd to explain the sense in which my trumping is independent of my laying the King by saying that trumping is a non-card-playing activity which might or might not be 'expressed' by laying a King. We explain the sense by saying, simply, that I could have laid a card other than the King, and still have trumped you. Similarly, there is a sense in which the necessary truth of 'All bachelors are unmarried' is independent of my producing just that sentence – namely, I could have produced a sentence synonymous with it. There are a number of sentences, in different languages, which are available for saying the same thing, in that they are synonymous. To that extent, a necessary truth does not depend upon any particular one of these being produced – for any other one could have been produced in its stead. We do not have to appeal to non-linguistic propositions to explain the sense in which a necessary truth is independent of a particular sentence in a language, and so of the language in question – any more than we have to explain the sense in which my trumping you was independent of my laying the King in terms of a non-card-playing activity called 'trumping'.

Someone might reply: if the existence of English is contingent, then surely the existence of any language is contingent. No language at all might have existed – but there would still have been necessary truths. So it cannot be sentences that are necessarily true, for these belong to language; therefore it must be non-linguistic propositions that are necessarily true, and were necessarily true before the dawn of language. The first problem here is that it is not at all clear what is meant by talking of propositions existing independently of languages. Trees could exist without there being a language in which to refer to them or describe them, for there are plenty of non-linguistic means of identifying trees, and of encountering them. We can point at them, and bump into them. But it seems that with propositions the only way of identifying them, or of recognizing them, is by using sentences to describe them.

> A good case can be made for the contention that the only way in which we can refer to statements [*ie* propositions, D.E.C.] is by definite description.[19]

If we want to mention a proposition we can only do so by talking of the proposition expressed by the sentence '. . .'. This is not to make the trivial point that we cannot talk about something except by talking about it. It is to say that propositions, if they exist at all, can, unlike trees, only be identified by linguistic means. If so, to suggest that there might be propositions in the absence of any language is incoherent. It would be like saying that there might be trees in the absence of colours, shapes, or smells. There could, in fact, be only one reason for postulating the existence of propositions – that postulating them helps explain things we could not explain otherwise. This is what was claimed by the first two arguments for them which I have considered. I rebutted those arguments; so to that extent there is no reason as yet for supposing that there are such things as propositions. And even if there are, there is an incoherence in suggesting that they could exist in isolation from any language.[20]

What of the claim that there were necessary truths, but no sentences, prior to language? We can accept this, given its correct interpretation. There is a sense in which we can say there were gardening jobs to be done before there were any humans to do them. This just means that *if* there had been any humans around at the time, some of them could have been usefully employed on gardening. Equally it seems to me, to say that there were truths before there were men and languages is to say that *if* there had been men, and if they had uttered the appropriate sentences, these sentences would have been true. There is no need to suppose there were truths floating around, waiting to be incarnated into sentences; just as there is no need to suppose there were literally gardening jobs floating around waiting for men to embody them. Alternatively, we might explain the sense in which it was true that bachelors were unmarried before there were any sentences, by saying that the sentence 'All bachelors are unmarried' is true, and that it has no temporal reference, and so applies to bachelors of the Stone Age as much as to bachelors of the twentieth century.

I claim, then, that none of the three arguments designed to show that it is not sentences but non-linguistic entities which are true succeeds. So the attempt to show that necessary truths must, all of them, be independent of linguistic data fails. I should point out that these are not the only attempts to demonstrate the existence of propositions. The matter is a very tricky one. It seems I have rejected some of the most powerful reasons for introducing propositions, and I believe I could reject the others.[21] If so, we can rest content that certain sentences, analytic ones, are necessarily true in virtue of linguistic data, *ie* synonymy relations.

A final point. The arguments against the view that necessary truths are analytic which I have considered have all tried to show that *no* necessary truths are analytic. There exists a set of claims with a more modest aim, however. This is to show that while many necessary, *a priori* truths are analytic, there are others which are not. Thus, according to Kant, there are certain synthetic *a priori* truths, which are necessary but not in virtue of linguistic data. For him the sentence 'Every event has a cause', as well as all the truths of mathematics, have this status. I have no space to assess such claims, and anyway, they tend to rely upon deep metaphysical and epistemological grounds rather than purely linguistic ones. I think such claims fail – but that is all I can say.

I would conclude then that all necessary, *a priori* truths are analytic, and that all analytic truths, with the exception of certain truths of logic which require special treatment, are true in virtue of synonymy relations.

If correct, this view is satisfyingly simple, and takes the mystery out of the *a priori*. We need not appeal to special faculties of the mind capable of intuiting necessary connections, even less to God implanting such truths in our minds. It is men's manipulations of symbols that give rise to *a priori* truth, and their ability to reflect upon how they have manipulated their symbols that allows them to recognize *a priori* truth.

4 '... is true'

Throughout this book, and especially in this chapter, I have been using the terms 'true' and 'false' without explaining these terms. This procedure is justifiable enough, for even if the normal person would be hard pressed to give definitions of them, he certainly has a working grasp of them, and to that extent knows what they mean. In this section, though, I do want to give some account of these crucial little words.

There are many questions that can be asked about truth, which would all fall under the question 'What is truth?' The question could mean 'What things are true?', which would be a request presumably for the list of all true sentences. This list could never be completed, since the number of truths is infinite. For example, there are an infinite number of true values for the function 'There was a point in time n minutes before now'. The question could mean 'How do we establish what is true and what is false?' And this question, in turn, could be interpreted either as a scientific question about how, in practice, we set about verifying sentences, or a conceptual question about the nature of knowledge and belief. Some have even interpreted 'What is truth?' to mean 'What sort of entity is referred to by the word "truth"?' – which, if taken literally, seems a pretty silly question.

The question I want to ask is a more modest one, and not at all like the ones people ask their Indian gurus. The question is: What do the words 'is true' mean, when we say of a sentence that it is true? (One presumes the answer can be carried over to answer a similar question about 'is false'.) Traditionally, there have been two favourite theories which have tried to provide the answer – the 'coherence theory', and the 'correspondence theory'. Both regard truth as a relation holding between a sentence and something else; but they differ as to what the something else is. For a coherence theorist a sentence is true if and only if it is related in a special way to other sentences; if it coheres with these in some manner. For a correspondence theorist a sentence is true if and only if it is related in a special way to the world; if it corresponds to something in the world. I shall not discuss the coherence theory, since I believe it has been sufficiently discredited in recent years.[22] I shall say only this: it is no doubt true that, often, I will only accept a sentence as true if it fits in with what I already accept as true. I would not accept your claim to have been in India last month if I also accepted your wife's claim that you were in prison at Alcatraz. However, it is implausible to suggest that what I mean when I call a sentence 'true' is that it fits in with what I already accept. The coherence theory is best regarded not as an explanation of what 'true' means, but of why it is that we accept sentences as true in many instances.

Turning to the correspondence theory, I shall distinguish between an old-style, and a new-style version. The former is much less plausible, but its mistakes will be instructive.

[1] *The old-style theory.* We can think of this theory as claiming that the relation between a true sentence and some aspect of the world is analogous to the relation between a photograph of a face and the face. For the photo to be accurate it is necessary that, corresponding to each area on the cellulose, there is an area on the surface of the face. In addition, the areas on the cellulose must be ordered or structured in a way corresponding to the structuring and ordering of the areas on the face. This second condition is required; it is not enough that bits of the photo should correspond to bits of the face, since the photo might be cut up into little pieces and stuck back together again so that it does not resemble the subject.

Analogously, it has been suggested, for the sentence 'The cat is on the mat' to be true, it is necessary (*a*) that there corresponds to each part of the sentence something in the world, and (*b*) that the components of the sentences be ordered or structured in a way corresponding to the order or structure of the features in the world. So, not only must there be a cat corresponding to 'cat', and a mat to 'mat', but the cat and the mat must be related to one another in a way which corresponds to the way in which 'cat' and 'mat' are related.[23]

This suggestion raises a host of challenging questions. How, quite, do words like 'if', 'of', 'an', etc correspond to components in the world? What is it for the structure of a sentence to correspond to the structure of things in the world? After all, the word 'cat' is not on top of the word 'mat' as the cat is on top of the mat. Luckily we need not bother to answer these heady questions, since there are sufficient reasons for rejecting the theory. For it to be acceptable, it is essential that we can separately identify the components in a sentence from the components in the world. For only then could it make sense to speak of comparing the sentence with the world to make sure that the sentence fits or matches. By analogy, we could only say that a photo is accurate if we can identify the photo, identify the subject, and see whether they are similar in look. Now it can be shown that it is not possible separately to identify the components in a sentence from the components in the world.

First, suppose there is a language in which the one-word sentence

'Catamat' is used when and only when we would use the sentence 'The cat is on the mat'; and that speakers of this language hold 'Catamat' to be true when and only when we hold our sentence to be true.[24] We may then say that 'Catamat' means the same as our sentence; they describe the same situation in the world. Yet, it seems, the components of the two sentences are quite different. Theirs has one; ours has several. But if so, how can truth reside in a special correspondence between components in the world and components in sentences? For here we have two sentences differing in their components, but describing the same situation in the world. If 'The cat is on the mat' were true in virtue of a special relation holding between each of its components and components in the world, then 'Catamat' could not be true, since it does not have that relation.

It is tempting to reply: but 'Catamat' must really have several components, and is simply an abbreviated way of saying what we say. This reply is based on linguistic ethnocentrism. For surely a speaker of their language could say with equal justice that our sentence 'The cat is on the mat' really has only one component, and is a long-winded way of expressing what they express. The fact is that until we have decided how many components there are in the situation in the world, there is no way in which we can say how many components, in the relevant sense, there are in true sentences describing that situation. If we regard the cat's being on the mat as a situation comprising n components, then no doubt we shall say that any sentence describing that situation contains just n relevant components. If, on the other hand, we regard the cat's being on the mat as a single feature, like the colour of a wall, we shall regard the corresponding sentences as having just the one component. This means, in effect, that we cannot carry out the required separate identification of components of the sentence from components in the world.

The second argument, which has the same aim, is perhaps more telling. This shows that we cannot decide what the components in the world are without already knowing certain facts about the words we use to describe the world – so that, again, the separate identification required by this old-style correspondence theory cannot be given. Suppose I say, truly, that two pieces of paper have the same colour. What makes them the same colour? The fact that the same predicate, 'red' say, applies to them both. Now as we saw in section 2 of Chapter 5, it is, in a good sense, a matter of convention what we apply the same colour predicate to. We saw that the Zulus, for example, do not apply the same predicate to two patches of colour for which we do have a single predicate. The question, that is, of whether there are two or more colours on a wall cannot be decided except by reference to some system of verbal classification. Independently of some such classificatory convention, it makes no sense to say that two colours are the same or different. Let me give another example. Independently of some convention as to what counts as a separate, single, discrete, physical object, it makes no sense to say that there are two, twenty, or two million physical objects on the table. In our system of classification, a stick stuck into a brush is counted as a single object – a broom; whereas we do not count a football glued onto a brick as a single object. However, things might have been different. If a football stuck onto a brick had a common use, like a broom, then no doubt we should devise a single name for it, and count it as one object. So whether or not a situation in the world contains two, twenty, or two million objects is not a matter that can be decided independent of some background system of classification. If so, it makes no sense to speak of *first* identifying the components in the world, and *then* matching these up with our means of describing them – for what these components are, and how many of them there are, is not something which can be ascertained except in terms of how we describe them. The analogy with the photo breaks down. It is as if the only knowledge we could get of a man's face was from the photo; in which case it would be absurd to speak of matching the photo with the face for a correspondence.

What both of the above arguments show is that the relation between a sentence and something in the world is a conventional relationship. It is a matter of convention which sentences we employ to describe the world; and it is, in a sense, a matter of convention what we count the situations in the world as comprising and being like.

[2] *The new-style theory.* This amended version of the correspondence theory admits all that I have said so far. Indeed, proponents of it stress that the relation between sentence and the world is conventional, and not natural like that between a photo and a face.[25] What is suggested is this: when a person utters a true sentence he must be obeying certain conventions which relate his words to the world. These conventions will include at least the following: (*a*) conventions whereby referring expressions are used to refer to things in the world, and (*b*) conventions whereby predicates can be used to express characteristics of things. Such conventions were discussed in Chapter 3. Let us call them 'demonstrative' and 'descriptive' conventions respectively.[26] So on this view the sentence 'The cat is on the mat' is true if and only if the demonstrative conventions governing the use of the referring expressions (*eg* 'the mat'), and the descriptive conventions governing the use of the predicate (*eg* the cat must be *on* the mat), are both obeyed. To say that a sentence is true is to say just this – that the conventions in question are being obeyed. This is the sense in which 'is true' serves to assert a correspondence of a conventional sort between sentences and the world.

Let us admit that when a person utters a sentence 'S' truly, he is obeying the relevant conventions. It does not follow, however, that

'"S" is true' means the same as '"S" was uttered in accordance with the relevant conventions'. It does not follow that calling a sentence true is the same thing as asserting that the sentence obeyed the conventions. It may be that the theory under discussion informs us of the necessary and sufficient conditions for a sentence's being true, but does not inform us what 'true' means.

The theory does fail to tell us what 'true' means, despite the fact that some objections to the theory themselves fail to disrupt it. For example, it has been argued that if the theory were correct then, whenever we call a sentence true we should be talking simply about the meanings of words and rules for using words.[27] And this, it is alleged, is an unacceptable consequence since, surely, we are at least partly talking about the world when we say a sentence is true. We are in part reasserting that fact about the world which the sentence in question asserted. It seems to me, though, that on the new-style theory we would in part be talking about the world in calling a person's sentence true. The reason is this: a true sentence only obeys the relevant conventions if something in the world is the case. If I call something 'red' when it is not red, I have not obeyed a descriptive convention. I need not have consciously broken the convention, since in the bad light I may have thought the object was red. Still, the convention has been broken, just as a rule in football can be broken without the player's intending to break it. So, in saying that a speaker obeys all the relevant conventions we are saying something about the world; for only if we know something about the world can we know that he has obeyed all the conventions. These conventions are not like those in grammar, which can be obeyed irrespectively of whether what is said is true or false.

There does seem to be a more effective reason for denying that the new-style theory gives us the meaning of 'is true'. There is a good sense in which necessary truths, as discussed earlier in this chapter, are not about the world at all. Certainly they do not need to be established via observation of what is happening in the world. When I say 'If anyone is over seven feet tall, he is over six feet tall', what I say is independent of any observable things in the world, but is true nevertheless. This being so, it is difficult to see how reference to demonstrative conventions can be relevant to explaining what is meant by calling such a sentence true. None of the words in my sentence even purport to refer to anything in the world. No demonstrative conventions are either being obeyed or disobeyed. It would follow that if 'true' means 'obeys certain conventions, including demonstrative ones' when applied to some sentences, it must mean something different when applied to others. It would follow, that is, that 'true' is ambiguous. But this is an odd conclusion. There are many kinds of true sentences, no doubt, but in calling any of them true we seem to mean the same thing. At the very least, an account of 'true' which did not make it ambiguous would appear to have a *prima facie* advantage over one which did.[28]

So let us try again. It is important to note that in a good sense the expressions 'is true' and 'is false' are superfluous. For, whenever one says a sentence is true, one could instead simply reassert that sentence. If you say that it is raining I could agree with you either by saying 'That's true', or by simply reasserting what you said. To this extent 'true' is a bit like 'yes'. If we wish to reply affirmatively to a question, we need not employ 'yes'. We could, like the Romans, utter a whole sentence in the indicative. Or, we might put the point like this: whenever it is the case that P it is also the case that the sentence 'P' is true. In other words the truth conditions of 'P' and '"P" is true' are the same.[29] It might seem that describing 'true' and 'false' as superfluous is to downgrade the importance of truth and falsity. But this is an illusion. It is, of course, important to know if a sentence, say 'The war will end next year' is true or false. But to say this is simply to say that it is important to know if the war will end. Whatever we say with the use of 'true' and 'false' could be said without them – or almost, as we shall see in a moment.

It would be natural to conclude that when a person says '"P" is true' he means no more than when he says simply 'P'. But this would be too hasty. 'True' is not completely superfluous. This can be seen in the following way. It would be quite natural for you to walk into my office and say 'It is raining outside'. But it would be most peculiar for you to start by saying 'It is true that it is raining'. This shows that the uses of 'P' and '"P" is true' are not identical, even though it is the case that whenever the one is true so is the other. We would only say '"P" is true' rather than plain 'P' if certain conditions hold. Most commonly we say '"P" is true' only where someone has already said 'P'. I use 'is true', that is, to endorse, or agree with what you have already said. This is not always so. I may say 'It is true that it is raining' when I anticipate that you are about to say 'It is raining', or when I think that you are contemplating its raining. We may generalize, and say that 'true' is only used when the sentence being called true is somehow provided by the context – by your having uttered it, by my envisioning that you will utter it, by my having already mentioned the sentence on an earlier page, etc. This is what distinguishes the use of '"P" is true' from that of 'P'. Note that if 'is true' simply meant 'obeys certain conventions', no explanation is given of the above differences in the uses of 'P' and '"P" is true'. So this is a further, albeit minor, objection to the new-style correspondence theory.

If asked what 'is true' means then, we must first point out that the information-content of calling a sentence true is precisely the same as that of simply asserting the sentence in question. In addition, we must point out that calling the sentence true differs from merely asserting the sentence, in that the former plays an endorsing role not normally played by the assertion itself. None of this is to deny that, in order for a sentence to be true, the speaker of it must be obeying certain conventions. All that we deny is that reference to such conventions enters into the explanation of the meaning of 'true'. To that extent we reject the new-style correspondence theory without rejecting its explanation of what, in a sense, makes some sentences true.

This account has been rough. More work would have to be done on just what range of roles 'is true' can play. Endorsing is not the only one. Second, it is plain that several expressions other than 'is true' play the role of endorsing what a man has said. For example, 'That's right', 'I agree', 'Ditto', or 'You can say that again'. What, quite, distinguishes 'is true' from these other expressions? I cannot go into this question here. I have, I hope, at least provided the bare bones of an account of the words 'true' and 'false'.

Notes

1 Sometimes remarkable powers were ascribed to such a special sense. Sir Matthew Hale, for example, attributed to this source his knowledge that 'the obscene parts and actions shall not be exposed to the publick view'. For these and other bizarre seventeenth-century views on *a priori* truths, see J. Y. Yolton, *John Locke and The Way of Ideas*. Oxford University Press, 1956.
2 'Necessary truth', in his *Ways of Paradox*. Random House, 1966. *p* 56.
3 *Critique of Pure Reason*, trans N. Kemp-Smith. Macmillan, 1964. *p* 48.
4 *Language, Truth, and Logic*. 2nd edn. Dover Books. *p* 78.
5 See R. Robinson, *Definition*. Oxford University Press, 1950.
6 *Meaning and Necessity*. Chicago University Press, 1947.
7 One objection that leaps to mind is this: I have defined an analytic truth as one that is reducible to a logical truth once synonyms replace synonyms. What then is the status of such a logical truth? (For example, 'either P or not-P'.) (See A. Pap, *Semantics and Necessary Truth*. Yale University Press, 1966. Chapter 1.) I believe this problem can be dealt with, but do not attempt to do so here.
8 Revised version, ed Sir E. Gowers. Oxford University Press, 1965. *p* 611.
9 'Synonymity', in *Semantics and the Philosophy of Language*, ed L. Linsky. Illinois University Press, 1952. *p* 119. (My italics.)
10 For some unexpected recalcitrant sentences, see N. Goodman, 'On likeness of meaning', *Analysis, 10*, 1949, 1–7. If one writer can dig up unexpected cases, so can others. See my 'Synonymy', *Ratio*, forthcoming 1973.
11 'On likeness of meaning', and 'On some differences about meaning', *Analysis, 13*, 1953, 90–6. Both articles are reprinted in *Philosophy and Analysis*, ed M. MacDonald. Blackwell, 1954.
12 Goodman in fact denies that any two expressions can be synonymous, since secondary extensions are never identical. I think he is wrong here. The only sentences in which the compound expressions in question fail to be interchangeable are recalcitrant ones in the above sense. So failure of interchangeability does not affect synonymy in such cases.

13 There may seem a problem in applying this account to those necessary truths whose relevant component expressions do not have synonyms in any obvious way, or are not definable in any obvious way. (See H. Putnam, 'The Analytic and the Synthetic', *Minnesota Studies in the Philosophy of Science*. University of Minnesota Press, 1962. Vol 3.) I believe this problem can be handled by providing *un*obvious synonyms and definitions. See my 'Definition and "clusters"', *Mind, 81*, 1972, 495–503.

14 See D. Mitchell, *Introduction to Logic*. Hutchinson, 1962. *pp* 162–63.

15 For such an argument, see P. F. Strawson, 'On referring', *Mind, 50*, 1950, 320–44. Reprinted in *Essays in Conceptual Analysis*, ed A. Flew. Macmillan, 1963.

16 'Sentences, statements, and propositions', in *British Analytical Philosophy*, ed B. Williams and A. Montefiore. Routledge & Kegan Paul, 1966. *p* 91.

17 *Semantics and Necessary Truth*. Yale University Press, 1966. *p* 120.

18 See B. Aune, 'Is there an analytic A Priori?', *Journal of Philosophy, 60*, 1963, 281–90.

19 B. Skyrms and E. Sosa, 'Necessity, the a priori, and unexpressible statements', *Philosophical Studies*, 1965. *p* 71.

20 There is an everyday sense of 'proposition' in which, of course, there are propositions. But in this everyday sense, as far as I can see, proposition = sentence.

21 For some plausible arguments in favour of propositions, see R. Cartwright, 'Propositions', in *Analytical Philosophy*, ed R. Butler. Blackwell, 1966. 1st Series. And for some arguments against, see H. Pospesel, 'The nonexistence of propositions', *Monist, 53*, 1969, 280–91.

22 For some powerful arguments against the Coherence theory, see A. Woozley, *Theory of Knowledge*. Hutchinson, 1949.

23 For a more sophisticated way of presenting such a theory, see Bertrand Russell, *The Problems of Philosophy*. Oxford University Press, 1967. Chapter 12.

24 For the example and the argument which follows, see G. Pitcher's Introduction to *Truth*, ed G. Pitcher. Prentice-Hall, 1964.

25 See, for example, J. L. Austin, 'Truth', *Proceedings of the Aristotelian Society (Supplementary Volume), 24*, 1950, 111–28. Reprinted in *Truth*, ed G. Pitcher. Prentice-Hall, 1964.

26 These terms are Austin's. Indeed, I regard my sketch of the new-style theory as a simplified version of Austin's.

27 See P. F. Strawson, 'Truth', *Proceedings of the Aristotelian Society (Supplementary Volume), 24*, 1950, 129–56. Reprinted in *Truth*, ed G. Pitchers. Prentice-Hall, 1964.

28 It is not clear how demonstrative conventions could be relevant to the truth of certain other types of sentence; for example, existential ones like 'There is at least one tiger'. See T. Honderich, 'Truth: Austin, Strawson, and Warnock', in *Studies in Logical Theory*, ed N. Rescher. Blackwell, 1968.

29 But for some interesting objections to this over-simple claim, see M. Dummett, 'Truth', in *Truth*, ed G. Pitcher. Prentice-Hall, 1964.

Chapter 8

Speech acts

Traditional grammar divided sentences into a small number of different types, according to their forms. Indicative, imperative, and interrogative would be three such types. While not useless for some purposes, such a classification is quite inadequate for revealing the great variety of functions which sentences can be used to perform. Sentences of the interrogative form, for example, can be used to perform several functions. 'Would you pass the salt?' might be used, depending upon context and intention, to ask a question, make a request, a demand, a plea, or issue a command. An indicative sentence is probably even more versatile; it may be used to warn, state, hypothesize, describe, report, promise, etc. A proper understanding of the functions of sentences would have to go well beyond traditional classifications.

One might wonder of what interest to a philosopher, as opposed to a linguist, a study of these functions might be. One such interest can be mentioned straight away. In Chapter 2 I argued that meaning can be explained in terms of use, but only after a sophisticated theory of uses of language had been developed. And we shall see how this connection with meaning can be made in section 3 of this chapter. But in addition to this, it seems that awareness of the multiplicity of uses and functions has paid, and will pay, philosophical dividends. Some of these will be discussed in section 2. There is one particular way in which it is essential that philosophers should be aware of this multiplicity. Despite their concentration upon language, it is clear that many philosophers, until fairly recently, have focused upon a very narrow sector of language; upon sentences whose essential function it is to state facts. These philosophers have, in other words, concentrated upon the reporting, describing, and stating roles of sentences. This narrow focus, it has been suggested, has been responsible for several errors in philosophy. I have already mentioned how it might be a mistake to assume that the role of a sentence like 'This is good' is to state a fact. Let me give another example. Take the sentence 'I am in pain'. If we treat this as essentially reporting or describing something, we can ask 'What is being described or reported?' It is plain that when a person says this he is not describing his physical state; not reporting upon some bodily characteristics he has noticed. So, some say, he is describing or reporting an inner, private, mental occurrence. It is a short step from here to saying that 'pain' is the name of an essentially private, inner item – and this, in turn, leads on naturally to scepticism about whether other people are ever in pain. For how can I know what inner, private items you have? Now there are many arguments against this view of pain, which I cannot mention here. But let us suppose the view of pain is mistaken. The point is that this view of pain is naturally encouraged by thinking of the sentence 'I am in pain' as a description or a report. Perhaps, though, this is not the way to treat the sentence. Perhaps we should regard it as a sophisticated replacement of 'ouch', or of a groan. Since 'ouch' and a groan do not describe or report anything, but are merely ways of showing one's pain, then perhaps we should treat 'I am in pain' as a method of showing one's pain, as part of pain behaviour, and not as a report or description at all. If so, we shall be less tempted to regard 'pain' as the name of some inner, private item; after all, we are not tempted to think of 'ouch' as such a name.[1] Here, then, might be a case – though it is a very debatable one – where philosophical error has been encouraged by a failure to appreciate the function of a sentence.

A further point is this: if we concern ourselves solely with the fact-stating role of sentences, we shall be obsessed with assessing sentences only in so far as they are true or false. But this would be to ignore the many other, interesting ways in which what people say can be assessed. Some of these ways may be of philosophical interest. For example, it is arguable that moral and aesthetic judgments are neither true nor false. But it does not follow that we cannot assess them. All that would follow is that we must assess them along different lines from, say, scientific hypotheses. Again, the laws of the land cannot be said to be true or false, since they are best considered as rules or commands. Yet obviously one wants to be able to assess laws. In brief, then, one of the major reasons for philosophers taking an interest in the multiplicity of uses of language is to avoid the dangerous myopia involved in concentrating upon the fact-stating, true or false, sentences of our language.

1 How to do things with words

It would be impossible to discuss speech acts except in conjunction with the work of J. L. Austin, the Oxford philosopher who died prematurely in 1960. His influence upon linguistically-orientated philosophers would be hard to exaggerate. As one historian says, Austin 'exercised in postwar Oxford an intellectual authority nothing short of remarkable'.[2] Austin's basic insistence was that philosophers should take as the basic unit of study, not the word or the sentence, but the *act* which a person performs with the aid of words or sentences. The theory of language is to become, as it were, a branch of the theory of action. Just as there are acts performed in a game of cricket, or in warfare, or in building bridges, so there are speech acts, such as stating, swearing, reporting, beseeching, questioning, and so on. There were at least two reasons for this insistence. First, as we have seen, the form of a sentence tells us little about it. To discover what the sentence was being used to say, we must look at the total act performed by the speaker with the aid of the sentence. Second, there is the pragmatic justification that by studying sentences as parts of total speech acts, unsuspected contributions to various philosophical debates may be derived.

Austin's programme, in a series of articles and lectures, was roughly this: first, to exhibit the variety of acts which can be performed with language, and in particular to distinguish many of these from the acts of stating, reporting, or describing. Second, to lay down a framework for the assessment of speech acts; one which will allow us to describe the ways in which speech acts can go right or wrong. Finally, to reveal the different aspects of speech acts; for it should not be supposed that performing a speech act is performing a single, indivisible act rather than a complex of sub-acts. Failure to distinguish between these components of a speech act can only lead to confusion.

In what remains of this section I shall describe how Austin tries to carry out this programme. That not every sentence has the role of stating facts is clear from the existence of interrogatives and imperatives. Austin points out, though, that by no means every sentence of the indicative form plays this role either; and this, not being so obvious, requires to be stressed all the more. His initial distinction is between *constative* and *performative* utterances. A constative one is an utterance which, roughly, serves to state a fact, report that something is the case, or describe what something is. Performative utterances, on the other hand, are those that have the characteristics

A: they do not 'describe' or report or constate anything at all, are not 'true or false'; and
B: the uttering of the sentence is, or is part of, the doing of an action, which again would not *normally* be described as saying something.[3]

Examples of performative utterances will help here. Take the sentences 'I promise to come to dinner', 'I name this ship *SS Abraham Lincoln*', and 'I hereby appoint you Prime Minister'. None of these describe anything. 'I promise . . .' does not describe an act of promising; rather, in context, the uttering of these words *is* the act of making a promise. 'I hereby appoint you . . .' does not report an appointment; in context, it *is* the making of an appointment. For this reason we cannot regard any of the sentences as true or false. A promise, a christening, and an appointment are neither true nor false; so if an utterance *is*, in context, a promise, a christening, or an appointment, then it can be neither true nor false. A promise can be sincere or insincere, wise or stupid, but not true or false. To suppose that 'I promise . . .' is a true or false description leads us into philosophical error, or may do. For if it is a description, we can ask 'What does it describe?', to which we may feel tempted to reply 'An inner, mental act of promising'. If so, how could we ever know whether people really make promises or not, for we do not know what inner, mental acts are going on inside them? Yet, of course, we do often know that men make promises. If a man utters the right words in the right context, he has made a promise; no doubt about it. Inner, mental acts seem to be irrelevant.

Before continuing, two points need to be noticed. First, a performative utterance does not have to be explicit in the way the three so far mentioned were. To make a promise I need not say 'I promise . . .'; it may be enough, given certain circumstances, for me to say 'I will . . .'. Again I can appoint someone to a position without using the explicit formula 'I hereby appoint . . .'. Second, Austin is quite aware that the performative/constative distinction is not completely clear, and is indeed unsatisfactory. For example, once we drop the fiction that performatives are all explicit, it is apparent that some performative utterances can be true or false. I may say 'There is a bull behind you' to perform the act of warning you. Yet the sentence can be true or false. We shall see as we progress that Austin eventually drops the performative/constative dichotomy in favour of a more complex set of distinctions. But, for the moment, in order to appreciate some of the points Austin makes, it is useful to hold on to the dichotomy in the rough-and-ready manner described.

Performatives are neither true nor false, so we are assuming. But this does not mean they cannot come up for all sorts of assessment. There are lots of ways in which a performative utterance can fail to be one hundred per cent acceptable. Austin gives the name 'infelicity' to any defect from which a performative can suffer, and which makes it sub-par. Let us identify some of these.

> First, our performative, like any other ritual or ceremony, may be, as the lawyers say, 'null and void'. If, for example, the speaker is not in the position to perform an act of that kind . . . then he doesn't manage, simply by issuing his utterance, to carry out the purported act.[4]

For example, if I am not the monarch of England, I do not succeed in knighting someone by uttering the words 'I dub thee knight'.

Second, a performative utterance may be, though not void, 'unhappy' in a different way – if, that is, it is issued insincerely.[5]

For example, if I say 'I promise . . .' with my fingers crossed behind my back, then although I can be said to have promised, this is not a straight-forward, paradigmatic, fully felicitous promise. Third, a performative may be 'unhappy' if a person does not follow the correct procedure. Suppose, after too many drinks, the President's wife says 'I name this ship *SS Benedict Arnold*', instead of the intended 'I name this ship *SS Abraham Lincoln*'. We can say she named the ship *SS Benedict Arnold*, but we should have to qualify this. The christening was hardly one hundred per cent 'happy'. A fourth type of infelicity arises if certain subsequent behaviour follows, or fails to follow, the speech act. Suppose John says 'I will' in the church, and thereby marries Mary; but suppose, though, that on the church steps he turns to Mary and says, 'Well, very nice to have met you. I must go now. Perhaps I'll see you again some time'. Did he, or did he not, perform the act of marrying with his words inside the church? His subsequent behaviour is too strange to permit us to reply 'Yes' without any qualification.

We see, then, that there are several ways in which performative utterances can be infelicitous; and Austin mentions several that I have not. Indeed a performative is peculiarly liable to go wrong in many ways, for as Austin says

> Our performative is both an action and an utterance; so that, poor thing, it can't help being liable to be sub-standard in all the ways in which action in general can be, as well as those in which utterances in general can be.[6]

So far we have seen that not all utterances of the indicative form are of the constative, fact-stating type; and that this does not prevent other utterances from being assessed in a variety of ways. Truth and falsity are just two among many ways for utterances to be assessed, favourably or otherwise. The next stage in Austin's account is this: it would be a great mistake to suppose that an utterance is the performance of a single act, rather than a complex of acts. According to him, any speech act comprises at least two, and typically three, sub-acts. These are what he calls the *locutionary*, the *illocutionary*, and the *perlocutionary* acts involved in a total speech act. When we ask what a person is doing when he makes an utterance, there are typically three types of answer we can give. One answer is to describe the noises he makes, the grammatical construction these noises are in, and their meaning. This is to describe the locutionary aspect of the utterance. This

> includes the utterance of certain noises, the utterance of certain words

in a certain construction, and the utterance of them with a certain 'meaning'.[7]

A second sort of answer to the question 'What was he doing when he uttered "..."?' would be 'He was making a promise', or 'He was issuing a warning'. This is to describe the illocutionary aspect of the utterance. Roughly, the illocutionary act is the act, like promising, which we perform *in* uttering certain words in context. Or, as Austin also puts it, the illocutionary act can be regarded as the force with which the sentence was employed. A final sort of answer to the question 'What was he doing when he uttered "..."?' could be 'He was frightening someone', or 'He was persuading them to do something'. Here we describe the perlocutionary act he was performing.

> Saying something will often, or even normally, produce certain consequential effects upon the feelings, thoughts, or actions of the audience, or of the speaker, or of other persons: ... we shall call the performance of an act of this kind the performance of a perlocutionary act or perlocution.[8]

Crudely put, the perlocutionary act is what is performed *by* uttering certain words. So, then, 'I promise to come to dinner' will be the performance [1] of a locution – *eg* employing a certain grammatical construction, [2] of an illocution – that of making a promise, and [3] of a perlocution – *eg* cheering you up.

Austin is aware that the locution/illocution/perlocution trichotomy is not crystal-clear. There are marginal cases of acts which we would not be happy to assign, immediately, to one rather than another category. And, further, it is no easy matter to state any general formulae for precisely defining the categories. The locution/illocution distinction I shall leave until section 3, since it is of peculiar interest for the problem of meaning. But I shall say a few words now about the illocution/perlocution distinction.

It is important to distinguish and isolate perlocutions, for they are unlikely to be of great interest in understanding the nature of sentences. The reason is that just about any sentence can, given the right background, produce just about any perlocutionary effect. So the perlocutionary effects are not, as it were, due to the intrinsic nature of sentences. To return to an example used earlier in this book, the words 'Good evening' said in a Boris Karloff voice on a lonely forest path would perform the perlocutionary act of terrifying the wits out of someone. But this tells us nothing about the sentence itself; about, say, the conventions governing its use. In addition it is difficult to see how studying perlocutions would help philosophers examine concepts. It tells me nothing about the concept of knowledge if I am told that the sentence 'I know that the sun will rise tomorrow' could be used to startle a sleeping man if yelled out very loudly.

While it is important to distinguish illocutions from perlocutions, this is no easy matter. It is clear, for example, that the *in/by* test is most slippery. Surely it is not *wrong* to say that a person made a promise *by* uttering the words 'I promise . . .'. Nor is it wrong to say that I terrified a person *in* uttering 'Good evening' in a horrible voice. It may not be how Fowler or Austin would talk, but it is quite intelligible. Yet the first mentions an illocutionary act, and the second a perlocutionary one. A second difficulty is that there seem to be some acts which it is not simple to ascribe to one category rather than the other. Take the act of insinuating. This does not seem to be the perlocutionary effect of what I say; on the other hand it differs from such illocutionary acts as promising and warning, since while I can say 'I promise . . .' and 'I warn . . .', it would be absurd to say 'I insinuate . . .'. Insinuation is necessarily not something that can be made explicit.

Admitting these difficulties should not, however, make us conclude that there is not an important, and often obvious, distinction between an illocution and a perlocution. There seems to be at least the following essential difference. An uttered sentence can easily produce a perlocutionary effect without its being the case that the speaker intended that effect, and without its being the case that any linguistic or social conventions determine that the utterance should typically have that effect. Thus I might say 'Good evening' in a horrible tone of voice while believing myself to be alone. Someone hears me and is terrified. But I neither intended to frighten him, nor is there any convention governing 'Good evening' that makes it an appropriate vehicle for terror.

> We can achieve some sequels of perlocutionary acts by entirely non-conventional means . . . by acts which are not conventional at all, or not for that purpose: thus I may persuade someone by gently swinging a big stick or gently mentioning that his aged parents are still in the Third Reich. Strictly speaking there cannot be an illocutionary act unless the means employed are conventional.[9]

Austin seems to be wrong in his final comment here. It is true that many utterances perform the illocutions they do in virtue of certain conventions governing them. But this is not so in all cases. Sometimes, it seems, it is the intention of the speaker, rather than some convention governing his words, which determines that he is performing a particular illocutionary act. Thus 'It is red' might perform the act of objecting to you; but there is no convention which determines that 'It is red' is typically an objection, in the way that there is a convention governing the use of 'I promise . . .' to make a promise.[10] So we might say that an utterance only performs an illocutionary act, A, if a convention determines that the utterance is a performance of A, *and/or* it is the speaker's intention to perform A with the utterance. Since this is not the case, as we have seen, with perlocutions, which may be neither intentional nor conventional, we have a rough test for distinguishing between illocutions and perlocutions.

Let us now see how the original constative/performative dichotomy appears in the light of what has been since discussed. It is becoming plain that a great deal that can be said about performatives can also be said about constatives. In the first place, a constative utterance is liable to just as many types of infelicity as performatives are. Just as I can promise insincerely, I can report insincerely. Just as I may be in an inappropriate position to make an appointment, so I may be in no position to provide a description. Second, a constative utterance can also be analysed into locutionary, illocutionary, and perlocutionary aspects. When I say 'My nose is red', I perform the locution of uttering certain words, in a certain construction, with a certain meaning. In addition, I perform the illocutionary act of telling someone that something is the case. And finally, I may perform the perlocutionary act of convincing you, as you had suspected all along, that I am a drunkard. Thus the original idea, that in constating I am merely saying something, whereas in making a performative utterance I am *doing* something, falls apart.

It might still be insisted that there is this crucial distinction between constatives and other utterances: only constatives can be true or false. But even this distinction is not as solid as it seems. First, although an explicit performative is not, strictly speaking, true or false, nevertheless its happy functioning may depend upon something's being true. If I say 'I warn you not to eat those toadstools', I am warning and not stating. Still, my utterance is plainly infelicitous if it is not true that the items are toadstools. So a performative utterance like warning is not divorced from questions of truth and falsity. Second, as we saw earlier, a performative utterance of, say, warning can be put in a form which does permit it to be true or false. 'There is a bull behind you' may be true, even though I am warning rather than idly describing the landscape. Finally, constative utterances can be put into a form where they cannot, strictly speaking, be called true or false. Instead of saying 'My nose is red', I could say 'I state that my nose is red.' Since this describes nothing, but *is* to state, it cannot be true or false. Yet since it is, in information value, equivalent to the true or false utterance 'My nose is red', it is surely a constative utterance.

For these, and other reasons, Austin concludes that 'to state is surely every bit as much to perform an illocutionary act as, say, to warn or to promise'.[11] This is not to deny that there are important differences between constatives and other utterances. But the difference is no longer one between performative utterances *and* something else. Rather it is the difference between kinds of performative utterance. As Austin puts it

> The doctrine of the performative/constative distinction stands to the
> doctrine of locutionary and illocutionary acts in the total speech act
> as the *special* theory to the *general* theory.[12]

In other words, every utterance can be regarded as a performative
utterance that comprises locutionary, illocutionary, and (typically)
perlocutionary aspects. Among the illocutionary acts that can be performed are the constative ones, which are important in themselves, and
important to distinguish from other illocutionary acts.

To summarize: first, we should concentrate not upon items of language,
but upon the acts people perform with the help of items of language.
Second, any such act is liable to go wrong in all sorts of ways – including
those of being false, null and void, insincere, and inappropriate. Finally,
any such act is to be regarded as a complex of sub-acts; and among those
sub-acts called illocutions, it is particularly important to distinguish
constative ones.

2 Some philosophical applications

It is one of the aims of this book to show how views about language
influence approaches to traditional philosophical problems. So, in this
section, I want to see how two problems can be approached in terms of
the theory of speech acts described in the last section. The problems –
those of knowledge and reality – were discussed by Austin himself. But
two points should be made here. First, Austin's published discussions of
these problems preceded the development of his speech act theory. It is
clear, though, that his approach to them is very much within the spirit
of that theory, even if it does not accord with it in terminology. Second,
I shall not be concerned with the correctness of Austin's solutions of the
problems. The point is that they represent interesting attempts which
any subsequent philosophers must take due note of.

A: KNOWLEDGE AND BELIEF

The basic question in epistemology is 'What is knowledge?'; or, if you
prefer, 'What is it to know that something is the case, as opposed to
merely believing that it is?' It is tempting, no doubt, to suppose that the
difference between knowing and believing is merely one of degree; that
knowing is like believing, only rather better – in the way that loving is
similar to, only more intense than, liking. The simple view at once faces
an obvious difficulty. You can believe that Paris is in the south of France,
albeit falsely; but you cannot know that Paris is in the south of France.
Whereas beliefs can be false, knowledge cannot. Or we may put it
like this: if a person knows something, he cannot be mistaken. This

consideration causes trouble for the simplistic assumption that knowledge is on the same scale as belief, only higher up.

Noticing this, philosophers in the past have tended to take off in one of
two directions. Some, insisting that there is such a thing as knowledge,
but also realizing that if a person knows then he must be right, have concluded that knowledge is a peculiarly self-guaranteeing state of mind.
When you know something, then merely by being in that state of mind
the truth of what you say you know is somehow guaranteed.[13] Knowledge
is, as it were, an infallible searchlight that illuminates facts for us. Other
philosophers, sceptics, have insisted that since there is nothing that has
to be the case, then we never really know anything. For if when a person
knows something he cannot be mistaken, and if further there is nothing
about which a person cannot be mistaken, it follows that he never knows
anything.

Both these views seem plainly unsatisfactory. The objection to the
first view is, simply, that there do not exist these self-guaranteeing states
of mind called 'knowledge'. Or, to put it more soberly, it can never
follow from the fact that I am in a certain state of mind with respect to
X, that X is actually the case. Nothing about my state of mind, for
example, could guarantee that Paris is in the north of France. The objection to the sceptic is that there are any number of things we know to be
true, and that only some perverse definition of 'knowledge' could make
us want to deny this.

Both views typically share two characteristics. Both assume that
knowledge, if there is such a thing, is a special state of mind; that 'I
know' like 'I believe' describes such a state. The difference between the
views is that, according to the sceptic there are no such states of mind in
actual fact, whereas there are according to his opponent. Second, it is
being assumed on both views that a certain interpretation must be given
to the truth that if a person knows, he cannot be mistaken. Both interpret
this as meaning that knowledge is incompatible with the possibility of
being mistaken. Both these assumptions seem to be false. And once we
reflect upon how 'I know' is used, this can be seen.

Suppose we cease to compare 'I know' to 'I like', 'I believe', 'I feel',
etc, and compare it instead to 'I promise', 'I swear', 'I guarantee', etc.
Let us, that is, compare 'I know' not to expressions which describe mental
states, but to performative utterances of the type discussed in the last
section. There is, clearly, a difference between saying 'I promise to do X'
and saying, merely, 'I will do X'. There is a difference, too, between
saying 'I know that P', and saying merely 'P'. And perhaps the differences are not too different in these cases. Austin says the following:

> ... when I say 'I promise', a new plunge is taken: I have not merely
> announced my intention, but, by using this formula (performing this

ritual), I have bound myself to others, and staked my reputation, in a new way. Similarly, saying 'I know' is taking a new plunge. But it is *not* saying 'I have performed a specially striking feat of cognition, superior, in the same scale as believing and being sure, even to being merely quite sure': for there is nothing in that scale superior to being quite sure. Just as promising is not something superior, in the same scale as hoping and intending, even to merely fully intending. When I say 'I know', I *give others my word: I give others my authority for saying* that 'S is P' . . . When I have said only that I am sure, and prove to be mistaken, I am not liable to be rounded on by others in the same way as when I have said 'I know'. . . . We all *feel* the very great difference between saying even 'I'm absolutely sure' and saying 'I know': it is like the difference between saying even 'I firmly and irrevocably intend' and 'I promise'.[14]

The point here is that 'I know' has a special performative function. It is used not to describe a special state of mind, but to give my statement a backing or guarantee, to give you a permit to rely upon what I say, to stake my reputation on it, etc. None of this is achieved by saying 'I believe', or even 'I am quite sure'. When you ask me if I know whether the ice is thick enough, you are not interested in an autobiographical report on the contents of my mind. You want to know if you can rely upon the ice holding you up. But if you say 'I am certain, in my heart of hearts, that there is a God', you are not implying that you can prove God's existence, or have some special credentials, as Abraham might have had, for asserting His existence – not in the way you would if you stated that you *knew* there was a God. Austin describes the view that 'I know' is a description of a state of mind as the 'descriptive fallacy' – or an example of it. Just the same fallacy would be involved in treating 'I promise' as a description of what you are feeling. Put in the more technical language of section 1, he is saying that the illocutionary act typically performed by 'I know' is quite different from the illocutionary act typically performed by 'I believe', 'I feel sure', etc. It will follow, too, that claims to knowledge are liable to various infelicities that claims to belief are not. Thus I can believe something even if I am in no position to verify it; but it would be 'unhappy' to say 'I know' unless I can back up my claim in some way.

We still have the problem that if I know I cannot be mistaken – and this might seem to break the analogy with promising. For I can still be said to have promised to do X even if I fail to do it. But this shows that we must interpret 'If I know, I cannot be mistaken' correctly.

'When you know you can't be wrong' is perfectly good sense. You are prohibited from saying 'I know it is so, but I may be wrong', just as you are prohibited from saying 'I promise I will, but I may fail'. If you are aware you may be mistaken, you ought not to say you know, just as, if you are aware you may break your word, you have no business to promise. But of course, being aware that you may be mistaken doesn't merely mean being aware that you are a fallible human being: it means that you have some concrete reason to suppose that you may be mistaken in this case. Just as 'but I may fail' does not mean merely 'but I am a weak human being' . . . it means that there is some concrete reason for me to suppose that I shall break my word. It is naturally *always* possible ('humanly' possible) that I may be mistaken or may break my word, but that by itself is no bar against using the expressions 'I know' and 'I promise' as we do in fact use them.[15]

The point is this: given the performative function of 'I know', it must be wrong to say 'I know that P, but I may be mistaken about it'. For that would be to offer a guarantee with one breath, and take it away with the next. In the light of this, we can see what is wrong with the two views about knowledge mentioned earlier. The view that knowledge is a self-guaranteeing state of mind which entails the facts believed is wrong, since it misconceives the sense in which knowing entails the truth of what is known. The only sense in which it is true that knowing entails this is that it is self-defeating to *say* 'I know, but I may be mistaken'. (It is equally self-defeating to say '*He* knows that P, but he may be mistaken', since in saying 'He knows' I guarantee, and support, and give my backing to, what he claims.) The sceptics' view – that, since there is always the possibility of being mistaken, then I cannot know anything – is false, since it assumes that mere logical or 'human' possibility of error is sufficient to rule out knowledge. But, in fact, one is entitled to say 'I know' provided one has no special, concrete reason for supposing that a mistake is being made. Bare logical, or 'human' possibility of error no more removes the right to say 'I know' than the bare possibility of my failing to arrive at dinner removes the right to say 'I promise to come to dinner'. 'I know, but I may be mistaken' is only peculiar where 'I may be mistaken' means 'I have some reason to suppose that I am mistaken'.

The lesson to be drawn from this discussion is as follows: if, instead of asking 'What is knowledge?', we ask 'What is a man doing when he says "I know"?', we dissolve some of the old problems concerning knowledge and belief. We see that there is a distinction between the two, not because different states of mind are involved, but because the speech acts performed with the associated words are quite different. We see, too, that knowledge is never mistaken, not because it is such a beautifully self-guaranteeing state of mind, but because the speech acts performed by 'I know' and 'He knows' would be highly infelicitous if one added 'but I (he) may be wrong', where this suggests there is some special reason for doubt. Without claiming that Austin's account is beyond dispute, or complete, it must be admitted that his approach in terms of speech acts throws new light on an old problem.

B: REALITY

The question of what is real versus what is apparent is one of the oldest in philosophy. Most eminent philosophers have had a crack at answering it, and have produced any number of definitions of 'real'. It will be useful to glance at some of these. Bertrand Russell once defined a real thing as one which 'persists at times when it is not perceived'.[16] A. J. Ayer, trying to analyse what makes something a real rather than apparent property of a thing, defined the real properties as those which have the 'greatest value as sources of prediction'.[17] Thus the real shape of an object will be the shape it appears from moderately close-to, and not as it appears from very far-off or very, very close-to, since the first appearance puts us in the best position to predict what other appearances the object has from other angles and distances. Another favourite definition has been this: the real properties of a thing are those as observed by the normal perceiver in normal conditions. So, for example, we say that red is the real colour of the Russian flag because it looks red to the normal person under standard conditions, *eg* good daylight.

It is characteristic of philosophers who have suggested definitions like the above to assume that there is a single test for deciding when a thing or property is real. According to Austin, though, this assumption is quite unwarranted. If we look at the variety of things we call 'real', and the variety of reasons we have for calling them 'real', we shall see that no overall definition of, or single test for, reality could be given. It is easy, for example, to produce counter-examples against each of the definitions mentioned in the last paragraph. First, as against Russell's definition, we can point out that clay ducks are not real ducks; yet they certainly exist unperceived. Further, pains only exist when 'perceived', *ie* felt, yet we can speak of real pains as opposed to mere aches and twinges. Second, as against Ayer's definition, Austin makes the following point,

> If someone who isn't in the habit of drinking wine says of the glass I give him that it's sour, I might protest, 'It isn't really sour' – meaning thereby, not that the notion that it's sour will provide a poor basis for prediction, but that, if he savours it a bit more sympathetically, he'll realize that it just isn't *like* things that are sour, that his first reaction though understandable perhaps, was inappropriate.[18]

Finally, as against the definition in terms of how things appear to the normal observer, one can point out that when I say 'That isn't the real colour of her hair', I may mean no more than 'Her hair is dyed', and I

am saying nothing about how the hair would look to the average perceiver in reasonable light.

These examples show that the uses of 'real' in ordinary language are
too many, and too various to be captured by a single, short definition.
Austin goes on to explain why this is so. There are several reasons we have
for calling things 'real', and these reasons are very different from one
another. One reason for calling a thing real is to rule out the possibility
that it is of a certain sort. In calling a duck real, for example, I am ruling
out its being a clay duck. When I say the colour of her hair is real, I am
ruling out its being dyed. 'Real cream', 'real diamond', 'real taste', etc,
will serve to rule out various things that the cream, diamond, taste, etc,
are *not*. Among the possibilities that can be ruled out by calling a thing
real are that the thing is artificial, synthetic, mock, illusory, fake, hallu-
cinatory, or fictional. Quite what is being ruled out will depend upon the
speaker's intentions, and upon what sort of thing is being talked about.
It is because 'real' can exclude so many different possibilities that is one
of the major reasons for there being no single test for what is real. As
Austin puts it:

> This, of course, is why the attempt to find a characteristic common to
> all things that are or could be called 'real' is doomed to failure; the
> function of 'real' is not to contribute positively to the characterization
> of anything, but to exclude possible ways of being *not* real – and these
> ways are both numerous for particular kinds of things, and liable to
> be quite different for things of different kinds.[19]

A distinct type of function that 'real' plays arises in the following way:
often we come across new things which are pretty similar to, but not
quite like, things for which we already have names. It would be un-
economical for us to devise a new name for each new thing. What we
often do is to employ a number of auxiliary expressions in conjunction
with our old names to accommodate talk of the new things. Thus we might
not refuse to call an unusual insect a 'butterfly'; we might instead say
that, although a butterfly, it's not a *real* butterfly. The world of butterflies contains normal, paradigmatic butterflies, the real ones; and some
which are unusual, deviant, and not paradigmatic. Austin calls this use
of 'real' its use as an adjuster-word. The following passage exhibits a
good case of 'real' being used in this way:

> Suppose I ring up my employer asking for the morning off. When
> asked what for, I say I want to go to the dentist. 'Well', he says, 'you're
> the first man I've ever met who has *wanted* to go to the dentist.'
> Wearily I tell him that of course I don't *really want* to go to the dentist,
> who would? – but it is time for my annual check-up. *Really* to *want* to
> go to the dentist I should have to look forward to the visit with a

pleasurable anticipation which dentists have not yet succeeded in inculcating.[20]

Put in the language of the last section, we might say that often it would be infelicitous to apply a word 'X' without qualification, and infelicitous to refuse to apply it without qualification. So one thing we often do is to say 'Well, it's an X, if you like – but not quite a *real* one.'

No doubt 'real' has plenty of other functions. For example, there is its use in TV commercials, where the man says 'Mmm, this is *real* coffee (tobacco, beer, or soap).' Here 'real' seems to function simply as a term of praise. At any rate, it is clear that 'real' does have several functions. Or, as we may put it, 'real' can be used to perform a variety of different illocutionary acts – various acts of excluding or adjusting, for example. Like any other illocutions, ones performed with 'real' are liable to various infelicities. Particularly important is that an illocution performed with 'real' can only be happy if there are criteria for deciding whether something is real or not. There are such criteria in the case of real versus clay ducks, or real versus dyed hair. But not everything can sensibly be called real or unreal. There are no criteria for deciding whether an after-image is real or not, for example. What on earth could count, after all, as an unreal after-image? It is not so much false as senseless to speak of real (or unreal) after-images. 'I just had a real after-image' produces the same uneasiness as 'I promise to forget my own name', or 'I hereby appoint you God'. In these cases the required conditions for the felicitous functioning of 'real', 'promise', and 'appoint' in illocutions do not hold.

It has been suggested that this study of the various speech acts which can be performed with 'real' is largely irrelevant to the traditional epistemological debate concerning the nature of reality.[21] For, it is said, philosophers have been using 'real' in a special, technical sense, so that ordinary uses of it are immaterial. We should have to admit that some of the uses of 'real' discussed by Austin could be safely ignored by philosophers engaged in that old debate. However, it is not the case that all of Austin's considerations are irrelevant. First, even if older philosophers were using 'real' in a special, technical sense, many of them seem to have been unaware of this, and to have felt that they were analysing the normal concept of real. Anyway, one cannot decide that they were using the word in a special, technical sense unless one has decided what the ordinary senses are. Second, even if philosophers can safely ignore some uses of 'real', I think it is clear that some of them have gone astray by not analysing properly some ordinary uses that definitely are relevant. Let me give one example. Philosophers have often asked 'What is the real shape of a thing?', and they have come up with various answers. For example, the real shape is that as it appears to the normal perceiver under standard conditions, or the shape which offers maximum predictive value for judging how the thing will look in other circumstances. Such analyses do not sound too bad when we deal with nice, simple, stable objects like coins. Why do we say the real shape of the coin is round rather than elliptical? Perhaps suggestions like those given can provide the answer. But suppose we turn to a more complex object, like a cat. Austin says,

> What is the real shape of a cat? Does its real shape change whenever it moves? If not, in what posture *is* its real shape on display? Furthermore, is its real shape such as to be fairly smooth-outlined, or must it be finely enough serrated to take account of each hair? It is pretty obvious that there is *no* answer to these questions – no rules according to which, no procedure by which, answers are to be determined.[22]

The point is that, once we understand how 'real shape' functions, we see that some things cannot be said to have a real shape. So that definitions of 'real shape' which make everything have a real shape are not defining any normal sense of the expression. And what other senses are at issue here?[23] Once again we see, then, that by examining the types of speech acts in which 'real' occurs, we are better able to find our way around the traditional questions about the nature of reality.

3 Meaning and speech acts

At the end of Chapter 2, I concluded that the view that meaning is use was, as it stood, too vague to be assessed. We left the slogan 'Meaning is use' as a promissory note to be cashed once a more developed theory of use was brought forward. It is arguable that we now have such a developed theory. And I want to examine, and defend, the claim that meaning can be understood in terms of illocutionary acts, the performance of which is one of the major uses to which expressions can be put.

There are two good, *prima facie*, reasons for supposing that it will be the illocutionary use of expressions that is most relevant to explaining meaning. Meaning is a matter of convention. Expressions have meaning, and mean what they do, in virtue of rules and conventions governing them. Quite how convention generates meaning is another matter – but that it does so in some way is beyond dispute. Now when we discussed illocutions and perlocutions in section 1, we noted one important difference between them – that illocutions are *typically* rule- and convention-governed, whereas just about any sentence can be used to produce just about any perlocutionary effect, quite irrespective of convention (see *pp* 193–5). Because of the typically convention-governed nature of illocutionary acts, it is natural to look in this direction to cast light upon meaning, itself a convention-governed phenomenon. Second, there is clearly an important connection between meaning and intending. This is heralded by the fact that we speak of people meaning things by their words, and the word 'meaning' can often be replaced by 'intending' here. The connection between meaning and intending seems to be of the following sort. The basic point of employing meaningful expressions is to communicate with others. Now for a person to communicate a message to another, it is typically required that he at least [1] intends to produce a certain effect in the hearer, and [2] intends that the hearer recognizes this intention.[24] For example, my telling you that Smith is a murderer is an act of communication in a way in which my leaving Smith's lighter at the scene of the crime for you to find is not. In both cases I intend a certain effect – that you should believe Smith to be the murderer – but only in the former case do I intend that you should recognize that this is my intention.[25] Now for a speaker to succeed in this double intention, [1] and [2], it will in general be necessary for him to use meaningful expressions. If he does not, he is unlikely to produce the required effect in the hearer, and even less likely to get the hearer to recognize his intention to produce that effect. So it seems that there are at least two ways in which meaning and intentions are tied up. First, we possess and employ meaningful expressions in order, primarily, to carry out our intentions to communicate. Second, we can only succeed in communicating by employing meaningful expressions which the hearer will recognize our intentions by.

It is equally clear that there is an intimate connection between intentions and illocutionary acts. Whereas I can produce perlocutionary effects quite accidentally, it is *typically* required that an illocution be one I intended in order to be the illocution it is (see *pp* 193–5 once more). I do not, for example, *object* to what you say unless that is what I intend to do. So we see that both meaning and illocutions are intimately connected with intentions and conventions. We might, on the basis of this, hope to analyse meaning in terms of illocutions, rather than other aspects of use which do not have the same intimacy with intentions and conventions.

Let me sketch how I think meaning can be explicated in terms of illocutions, and how this task can be defended against a couple of plausible objections. In the main, I shall follow the account provided by William Alston in a number of writings. According to him, to say that one sentence means the same as another sentence is to say that both have the same illocutionary act potential. Both, that is, are capable of being used to perform one and the same set of illocutionary acts. What about expressions, like single words, which are not sentences? Let 'X' and 'Y' be such expressions. According to Alston 'X' and 'Y' mean the same if and only if they can be substituted for one another in a wide range of sentences without altering the illocutionary act potentials of those sentences.[26]

Alston says 'a wide range of sentences', rather than 'all sentences', in order to exclude, presumably, the sorts of sentences I called 'recalcitrant' in section 2 of Chapter 7. For example, one should not expect the illocutionary act potential of the sentence '"bachelor" has eight letters' to be unchanged when 'unmarried man' replaces 'bachelor' – but that is no argument against the synonymy of the expressions. So, assuming that we can exclude such irrelevant sentences along the lines suggested in Chapter 7, the suggestion is that two expressions mean the same provided that substitution of one for the other does not alter the range of illocutionary acts that can be performed with the sentences in which substitution takes place. This suggestion has to be tightened up in order to avoid some problems connected with ambiguity and homonymy, and Alston does this, so I shall not deal with them here.

The first objection that arises is this: it is completely circular to explain the meaning of a sentence in terms of illocutionary acts, since one would first have to know what the sentence means in order to know *which* illocutionary acts are being performed with it.[27] Suppose, for example, a person says 'Go and shut the door immediately'. I may be able to judge from his tone of voice, and the context, that a command is being issued. So to that extent I know what kind of illocutionary act is being performed. But to know which command is being issued – to know, that is, exactly which illocutionary act is being performed – I must surely first know what the sentence means. Indeed, what can one say about all the illocutionary acts performed by a sentence 'S' except that they are the acts which can be performed with 'S' – and this is hardly helpful unless one already knows what 'S' means.

Two points can be made about this objection.[28] The less important one is that it is simply untrue that *all* one could say about the illocutionary acts performed with a sentence is that they are the acts performed with that sentence. If I am asked what illocutions are typically performed with the sentence 'I promise to come to dinner', I can reply that they are acts which, given such conditions as [1] the sincerity of the speaker, [2] the belief of the speaker that he can control certain future events, and [3] the realization on the speaker's part that he is putting himself under obligation, etc, can be performed by uttering 'I promise to come to dinner'. In other words, while a full characterization of the act performed with a sentence may have to make reference to that sentence, we can still say a good deal about the conditions required for an utterance of that sentence to perform just that illocutionary act. Such information could clearly be valuable in getting a person to understand what is meant by the sentence.

The more important point to be made about the objection is that it is based upon a misunderstanding of what Alston is saying. The objector treats Alston as if the latter were claiming that the meaning of a sentence can be defined in terms of the illocutionary acts performed with it. But this is not what he says. Indeed, he specifically rejects this interpretation when he writes,

> Saying what the meaning of an expression is, is equivalent not to saying *what* its use (*ie* illocutionary potential) is, but rather to saying that it has the same use as another expression.[29]

Alston does not try to define expressions by specifying the illocutions performed with them, but in terms of other expressions. The insistence, though, is that it is possible to define one expression in terms of another because both have the same illocutionary act potential. The position is roughly this: a person will know how to use certain expressions and sentences, in that he can perform various illocutionary acts with them. Then he comes across an expression or sentence he does not understand. We illuminate him by pointing out that the expression or sentence in question has the same use as some other which he can already use. So the explanation of meaning does not take the form of spelling out the illocutionary acts to be performed with the expression, but of relating the expression to others which the person can already perform illocutionary acts with. Consequently the fact that it might be circular to try to explain the meaning of an expression by spelling out the illocutions performed with it is irrelevant to Alston's position.

The above objection does, though, bring an important point out into the open. There is a level at which we speak of 'grasping meanings' or 'recognizing an expression to be meaningful', which is prior to the level at which we actually specify meanings by definitions, paraphrases, or in terms of other expressions in some other ways. For, by Alston's account, I can only get you to understand 'S' by saying that it has the same illocutionary act potential as 'S′', if you already have some grasp of how to employ 'S′'. This prior sense of 'grasping meanings' is, according to Alston,

> The practical know-how sense of being prepared to use it [an expression or sentence, D.E.C.] to perform certain illocutionary acts and not others, and of being able to recognize misuses.[30]

At this level one does not have to be able to specify or give meanings in order to be credited with having a grasp of meanings – just as one can be credited with knowing how to ride a bicycle, though one cannot spell out how one does it. If, then, I use an expression to perform a range of illocutionary acts that it is properly capable of performing, to that extent I know its meaning in the 'know-how' sense. This is no empty claim – as were the claims in Chapter 2 that to grasp a meaning is to behave in a certain way, or have appropriate images. These claims were empty since no criteria could be found for deciding what counted as relevant behaviour or images. It would be empty, too, to claim that one grasps meanings when one is able to use words correctly, unless we can go on and decide which types of use are relevant. But we have now done this; it is use in performing illocutionary acts that is relevant. So, for example, a person's ability to use 'Good evening' to terrify people is no evidence for saying he understands the meaning of the expression. But his ability to use it as a form of greeting or farewell is – since these are illocutions.

Before considering a possible objection to all of this, it is worth relating what has been said here about meaning with what was said about synonymy in Chapter 7. The account of synonymy in this present section is, in fact, simply wider than the earlier account. Previously we said that two terms were synonymous if and only if they were interchangeable without altering truth values in all non-recalcitrant sentences. We are now saying that synonymous terms must not only be interchangeable in all true/false sentences – *ie* ones which perform constative illocutions – but also in other sentences with different illocutionary forces. Provided illocutionary force is not altered – whether it be in constative utterances or others – by interchanging terms, then these mean the same. This broadening of the test is important. For there are several expressions which, arguably, do not typically appear in true/false sentences at all, but in sentences used for different purposes from stating facts. For example, it may be that sentences of the form 'This is good' are not, strictly speaking, true or false – though this is controversial. But if so, then were we to confine ourselves to testing for synonymy by the interchangeability *salva veritate* test, we should be debarring ourselves from testing for the synonymy of these sorts of words like 'good'. Thus, we should ask whether 'This is good' and 'I commend this' have the same illocutionary force, rather than whether they necessarily have the same truth value, which is perhaps an illegitimate question.

Before we close the account of meaning, I want to consider the most common objection that is levelled against the view that meaning can be explicated in terms of illocutions. It is simply this: one can often, if not always, distinguish between what a sentence means, and what illocutionary act is performed with it. *Ipso facto*, meaning and illocutionary force cannot be the same.[31] For example, it is surely sensible, and may be true, to say each of the following: [1] I know what his sentence 'Pass the salt' means – but I do not know what illocutionary act he was performing; *eg* whether he was requesting, commanding, beseeching, etc. [2] I know what illocutionary act he was performing, from the tone of his voice and his subsequent behaviour; but I don't know what his sentence meant, since it was in Hebrew.

If we can say such things, how can meaning and illocutionary force be the same in any way; they are too obviously distinguishable.

Let us consider a problem that is in some ways analogous to this, before any hasty acceptance of the above objection. Consider the relation between a man's motive and his behaviour. I can certainly say both:

[1] He was ambitious, but he did not apply for the chairmanship.
[2] He did apply for the chairmanship, but he was not ambitious.

So certainly we can distinguish between a man's being ambitious and his behaving in a certain way in a certain instance. But would we want to conclude that ambition is one thing and behaviour such as applying for a chairmanship quite another? I think not. In calling a person ambitious one is, in part, saying that he is likely to behave in certain ways, in certain circumstances. The concept of ambition, it appears, is to be (partly at least) explained in terms of the disposition to behave in various ways. If so, the distinction between a man's ambition and his applying for a particular job is not the difference between one sort of thing and another sort of thing, but, put crudely, between the whole and the part. More precisely, applying for a particular position is one out of a range of activities that jointly go to make up, or explicate the concept of ambition. So ambition stands to a particular act of ambition as a whole range of typical activities stands to one out of that range.[32]

Similar considerations apply, I believe, to the distinction between the meaning of an expression and the illocutionary act performed with it on some occasion. One can of course distinguish between the two, and it would be a fallacy, one that is often committed, to conflate them. But it does not follow that meaning and illocutionary force are quite distinct aspects of an expression – any more than it followed that a man's ambition and his range of behaviour were two quite distinct phenomena. It may be that the distinction between the meaning of a sentence and a particular illocutionary act performed with it is the distinction between a whole range of acts that can typically be performed with it, and just one out of that range. To grasp what an expression means is to know what range of acts can be performed with it; not to know that it can be used to perform just this or that act. It is not required, either, that I should know, on every occasion of an expression's use, what particular act is being performed with it. It is this, and this alone, that makes it possible to say 'I know what "Pass the salt" means, but I do not know what illocutionary act he was performing'. So we can admit that 'What is the meaning of "S"?' and 'What illocutionary act is "S" being used to perform?' are distinct questions. But it in no way follows that the answer to the first does not require reference to illocutionary acts. All that follows is that reference need not be made to just that illocutionary act which is being performed with it on this occasion. In a similar way, the fact that a man can be known to be ambitious without its being known if he is going to apply for the chairmanship only forces us to distinguish between a range of typical activities and one out of this range – not between these activities and something else, ambition. I conclude, then, that this objection to the attempt to explicate meaning in terms of illocutions fails.

I would not pretend that the account of meaning sketched in this section has been precise enough to exclude all sorts of queries and objections being raised. At the very least, we would have to tighten up the criteria for what counts as an illocution as opposed to a perlocution. And we should have to examine in more detail what constitutes sameness of illocutionary force. However, the theory sketched does seem to have more chance of success than the other theories of meaning discussed – and more, I believe, than theories I have not discussed.

Notes

1   See L. Wittgenstein, *Philosophical Investigations.* 3rd edn. Macmillan, 1969. *circa* section 244.
2   J. Passmore, *A Hundred Years of Philosophy.* Penguin Books, 1968. *p* 450.
3   J. L. Austin, *How To Do Things With Words.* Oxford University Press, 1963. *p* 5. This book is based on lectures Austin gave at Harvard in 1955.
4   'Performative/Constative', in *Philosophy and Ordinary Language,* ed C. Caton. University of Illinois Press, 1963. *p* 23.
5   *ibid.*
6   *ibid, p* 24.
7   *How To Do Things With Words.* Oxford University Press, 1963. *p* 94.
8   *ibid, p* 101.
9   *ibid, p* 118.
10 For this point, see P. F. Strawson, 'Intention and convention in speech acts', *Philosophical Review, 73,* 1964, 439–60. Reprinted in *Symposium on J. L. Austin,* ed K. Fann. Routledge & Kegan Paul, 1969.
11 *How To Do Things With Words.* Oxford University Press, 1963. *p* 133.
12 *ibid, p* 147.
13 Descartes, for example, argued that one could not doubt a truth of which one had a 'clear and distinct idea'.
14 'Other minds', in his *Philosophical Papers.* Oxford University Press, 1962. *pp* 6–7. Originally published in *Proceedings of the Aristotelian Society (Supplementary Volume), 20,* 1946, 148–87.
15 *ibid, p* 66.
16 *Mysticism and Logic.* Unwin, 1917.
17 *The Foundations of Empirical Knowledge.* Macmillan, 1940.
18 *Sense and Sensibilia.* Oxford University Press, 1962. *p* 83.
19 *ibid, p* 70.
20 J. C. Gosling, *Pleasure and Desire.* Oxford University Press, 1969. *pp* 18–19. (Italicization of 'really' mine.) The author, incidentally, is not necessarily subscribing to the point made in the quoted passage.
21 For example, J. Bennett, 'Real', *Mind, 75,* 1966, 501–15. Reprinted in *Symposium on J. L. Austin,* ed K. Fann. Routledge & Kegan Paul, 1969.

22 *Sense and Sensibilia.* Oxford University Press, 1962. *p* 67.
23 'The wile of the metaphysician consists in asking "is it a real table?" . . . and not specifying . . . what may be wrong with it, so that I feel at a loss "how to prove" it *is* a real one'. J. L. Austin, *Philosophical Papers.* Oxford University Press, 1962. *p* 55.
24 See H. P. Grice, 'Meaning', *Philosophical Review, 66,* 1957, 377–88.
25 In fact a full act of communication will involve more intentions than the two I mentioned. See H. P. Grice, 'Utterer's meaning and intention', *Philosophical Review, 78,* 1969, 147–77.
26 *Philosophy of Language.* Prentice-Hall, 1964. *pp* 36–7.
27 See, for example, D. Holdcroft, 'Meaning and illocutionary acts', *Ratio, 6,* 1964, 128–43. Reprinted in *The Theory of Meaning,* ed G. Parkinson. Oxford University Press, 1968.
28 For a fuller account of what follows, see my 'Meaning and illocutions', *American Philosophical Quarterly, 9,* 1972, 69–78.
29 'Meaning and use', in *The Theory of Meaning,* ed G. Parkinson. Oxford University Press, 1968. *p* 159. Originally published in *Philosophical Quarterly, 13,* 1963, 107–24.
30 *Philosophy of Language.* Prentice-Hall, 1964. *p* 39.
31 See J. Searle, *Speech Acts.* Cambridge University Press, 1969. He says any attempt to equate meaning and illocution is to commit the 'speech act fallacy'. J. L. Austin, too, by regarding meaning as an aspect of locutionary acts, would appear to agree.
32 It is interesting to relate what I am saying here to what Wittgenstein says concerning the connection between *knowing how to go on* and actually going on in some case. See his *Philosophical Investigations.* 3rd edn. Macmillan, 1969. *Circa* section 151.

Bibliography

Since this book covers many topics, and several approaches to these topics, anything like a complete bibliography would be too inordinately long to include here. Instead, I suggest what seem to me the most useful books and articles to consult in connection with each chapter. I begin, though, with a short list of books of a fairly comprehensive nature, which may usefully be consulted in connection with all or most of the chapters.

General

ALSTON, W. *Philosophy of Language*. Prentice-Hall, 1964.
AYER, A. J. *Language, Truth, and Logic*. 2nd edn. Dover Books.
(English publisher, 2nd edn. Gollancz, 1946.)
BLACK, M. *The Labyrinth of Language*. Mentor Books, 1968.
BROWN, R. *Words and Things*. Free Press, 1958.
KATZ, J. J. *The Philosophy of Language*. Harper & Row, 1966.
LYONS, J. *Introduction to Theoretical Linguistics*. Cambridge University Press, 1968.
PASSMORE, J. *A Hundred Years of Philosophy*. Pelican Books, 1968.
QUINE, W. V. *Word and Object*. M.I.T. Press, 1960.
SEARLE, J. R. *Speech Acts*. Cambridge University Press, 1969.
WITTGENSTEIN, L. *Philosophical Investigations*. 3rd edn. Macmillan, 1969.

Chapter 2

AUSTIN, J. L. 'The meaning of a word', in his *Philosophical Papers*. Oxford University Press, 1962.
BLACK, M. *Language and Philosophy*. Cornell University Press, 1949.
BROWN, R. 'Meaning and rules of use', *Mind*, 71, 1962, 494–511.
CHRISTENSEN, N. *On the Nature of Meanings*. Munskgaard, 1965.
COHEN, L. J. *The Diversity of Meaning*. Methuen, 1962.

FINDLAY, J. 'Use, usage, and meaning', *Proceedings of the Aristotelian Society (Supplementary Volume)*, *35*, 1961, 229–42. Reprinted in *The Theory of Meaning*, ed G. Parkinson. Oxford University Press, 1968.

FODOR, J. and KATZ, J. J. Introduction to *The Structure of Language*, ed J. Fodor and J. J. Katz. Prentice-Hall, 1964.

FRIES, C. 'Meaning and linguistic analysis', *Language*, *30*, 1954, 57–68. Reprinted in *Theory of Meaning*, ed A. and K. Lehrer. Prentice-Hall, 1970.

GRICE, H. P. 'Meaning', *Philosophical Review*, *66*, 1957, 377–88. Reprinted in *Philosophical Logic*, ed P. F. Strawson. Oxford University Press, 1967.

HARRISON, B. 'Meaning and mental images', *Proceedings of the Aristotelian Society*, *63*, 1962–63, 237–50.

LOCKE, J. *An Essay Concerning Human Understanding*. Everyman Books, 1962. Book III.

MORRIS, C. *Signs, Language, and Behavior*. Prentice-Hall, 1946.

OGDEN, C. K. and RICHARDS, I. A. *The Meaning of Meaning*. Routledge & Kegan Paul, 1930.

QUINE, W. V. 'Meaning in linguistics', in his *From a Logical Point of View*. 2nd edn. Harper & Row, 1961.

RUSSELL, B. *An Inquiry into Meaning and Truth*. Pelican Books, 1965.

RYLE, G. 'The theory of meaning', in *British Philosophy in the Mid-Century*, ed C. Mace. Allen & Unwin, 1957.
 'Use, usage, and meaning', *Proceedings of the Aristotelian Society (Supplementary Volume)*, *35*, 1961, 223–29. Reprinted in *The Theory of Meaning*, ed G. Parkinson. Oxford University Press, 1968.

SCHAFF, A. *Introduction to Semantics*. Pergamon, 1964.

ULLMANN, S. *Semantics*. Blackwell, 1962.

WITTGENSTEIN, L. *The Blue and Brown Books*. Blackwell, 1964.

ZIFF, P. *Semantic Analysis*. Cornell University Press, 1967.

Chapter 3

BERLIN, I. 'Verification', *Proceedings of the Aristotelian Society*, *39*, 1938–39, 225–48. Reprinted in *The Theory of Meaning*, ed G. Parkinson. Oxford University Press, 1968.

CARNAP, R. *Introduction to Semantics*. Harvard University Press, 1959.

COOPER, D. E. 'Polar opposites', *Methodology and Science*, *1*, 1969, 1–12.

EVANS, J. 'On meaning and verification', *Mind*, *62*, 1953, 1–19.

FIRTH, J. *The Tongues of Men*. Watts, 1937.

FLEW, A. 'Philosophy and Language', in *Essays in Conceptual Analysis*, ed A. Flew. Macmillan, 1963.

FRANKENA, W. '"Cognitive" and "Non-cognitive"', in *Language, Thought, and Culture*, ed P. Henle. Michigan University Press, 1958.

GELLNER, E. *Words and Things*. Gollancz, 1963.

GRANT, C. 'Polar concepts and metaphysical arguments', *Proceedings of the Aristotelian Society*, *56*, 1955–56, 83–108.

HALL, R. 'Excluders', *Analysis, 20,* 1959, 1–7. Reprinted in *Philosophy and Ordinary Language,* ed C. Caton. Illinois University Press, 1963.

MALCOLM, N. 'Philosophy and ordinary language', *Philosophical Review, 60,* 1951, 329–40.

PASSMORE, J. *Philosophical Reasoning.* Duckworth, 1961. Chapters 5–6.

QUINE, W. V. 'Two dogmas of empiricism', in his *From a Logical Point of View.* 2nd edn. Harper & Row, 1961.

SCHLICK, M. 'Meaning and verification', *Philosophical Review, 45,* 1936, 339–69. Reprinted in *Theory of Meaning,* ed A. and K. Lehrer. Prentice-Hall, 1970.

STEVENSON, C. L. *Ethics and Language.* Yale University Press, 1960. *Facts and Values.* Yale University Press, 1963.

URMSON, J. O. *The Emotive Theory of Ethics.* Hutchinson, 1968.

WAISMANN, F. 'Verifiability', *Proceedings of the Aristotelian Society (Supplementary Volume), 19,* 1945, 119–50. Reprinted in *The Theory of Meaning,* ed G. Parkinson. Oxford University Press, 1968.

WATKINS, J. 'Farewell to the PCA', *Analysis, 18,* 1957, 25–33.

WHITE, A. 'A note on meaning and verification', *Mind, 63,* 66–69.

Chapter 4

AYER, A. J. 'Names and descriptions', in his *The Concept of a Person.* Macmillan, 1963.

COOPER, D. E. 'Searle on intentions and reference', *Analysis, 32,* 1972, 159–63.

DONNELLAN, K. 'Reference and definite descriptions', *Philosophical Review, 75,* 1966, 281–304. Reprinted in *Semantics: An Interdisciplinary Reader,* ed D. Steinberg and L. Jakobovits. Cambridge University Press, 1971.

FREGE, G. *Philosophical Writings,* trans M. Black and P. Geach. Blackwell, 1966.

GEACH, P. 'Russell's theory of descriptions', *Analysis, 10,* 1950. Reprinted in *Philosophy and Analysis,* ed M. MacDonald. Blackwell, 1954. *Reference and Generality.* Cornell University Press, 1962.

LOAR, B. 'Reference and propositional attitudes', *Philosophical Review, 81,* 1972, 43–62.

LINSKY, L. *Referring.* Routledge & Kegan Paul, 1967. 'Reference, essentialism, and modality', *Journal of Philosophy, 66,* 1969, 687–700. Reprinted in *Reference and Modality,* ed L. Linsky. Oxford University Press, 1971.

MEILAND, J. *Talking About Particulars.* Routledge & Kegan Paul, 1970.

MILL, J. S. *A System of Logic.* Longman, Green, Reader & Dyer, 1886. Book I.

PEARS, D. F. *Bertrand Russell and the British Tradition in Philosophy.* Fontana, 1967.

QUINE, W. V. *From a Logical Point of View.* 2nd edn. Harper & Row, 1961.

RUSSELL, B. *Logic and Knowledge*. Allen & Unwin, 1968. Especially
'On denoting' and 'The philosophy of Logical Atomism'.

SEARLE, J. R. 'Proper names', *Mind*, *67*, 1958, 166–73. Reprinted in
Philosophy and Ordinary Language, ed C. Caton. Illinois University
Press, 1963.

STRAWSON, P. F. 'On referring', *Mind*, *59*, 1950, 320–44. Reprinted in
Essays in Conceptual Analysis, ed A. Flew. Macmillan, 1963.
Individuals. Methuen, 1961.
'Singular terms and predication', *Journal of Philosophy*, *58*, 1961,
393–412. Reprinted in *Philosophical Logic*, ed P. F. Strawson.
Oxford University Press, 1967.

URMSON, J. O. *Philosophical Analysis*. Oxford University Press, 1956.

WITTGENSTEIN, L. *Tractatus Logico-Philosophicus*. Routledge & Kegan
Paul, 1961.

Chapter 5

BLACK, M. 'Some problems with "Whorfianism"', in *Language and
Philosophy*, ed S. Hook. New York University Press, 1969.

BOAS, F. *Race, Language, and Culture*. Macmillan, 1940.

CAPELL, A. *Studies in Socio-Linguistics*. Mouton, 1966.

CASSIRER, E. *The Philosophy of Symbolic Forms*. Michigan University
Press, 1958. Vol I.

GREENBERG, J. 'Concerning inferences from linguistic to non-linguistic
data', in *Psycholinguistics*, ed S. Saporta. Holt, Rinehart, &
Winston, 1961.

HOCKETT, C. 'Chinese versus English: an exploration of the Whorfian
theses', in *Language in Culture*, ed H. Hoijer. Chicago University
Press, 1959.

HOIJER, H. 'The Sapir–Whorf hypothesis', in *Language in Culture*,
ed H. Hoijer. Chicago University Press, 1959.
'Cultural implications of some Navaho linguistic categories', in
Language in Culture and Society, ed D. Hymes. Harper & Row, 1964.

HOLLIS, M. 'Reason and ritual', *Philosophy*, *43*, 1968, 231–48.

LEACH, E. *Lévi-Strauss*. Fontana/Collins, 1970.

LÉVI-STRAUSS, C. *Structural Anthropology*, trans C. Jacobsen and
B. Schoepf. Basic Books, 1963.

LÉVY-BRUHL, L. *La Mentalité Primitive*. Oxford University Press, 1931.

LOUNSBURY, F. 'Language and culture', in *Language and Philosophy*,
ed S. Hook. New York University Press, 1969.

SAPIR, E. *Language*. Harcourt & Brace, 1921.

WHORF, B. L. *Language, Thought, and Reality*. M.I.T. Press, 1969.

WINCH, P. *The Idea of a Social Science*. Routledge & Kegan Paul,
1963.
'Understanding a primitive society', *American Philosophical
Quarterly*, *1*, 1964, 307–24.

Chapter 6

ARBINI, R. 'Comments on linguistic competence and language acquisition', *Synthèse*, *19*, 1968–9, 410–24.

BROWN, D. G. 'Knowing how and knowing that', in *Ryle*, ed O. Wood and G. Pitcher. Macmillan, 1970.

BROWN, R. and BELLUGI, U. 'Three processes in the child's acquisition of syntax', in *New Directions in the Study of Language*, ed E. Lenneberg. M.I.T. Press, 1966.

CHOMSKY, N. *Syntactic Structures*. Mouton, 1957.
Aspects of the Theory of Syntax, M.I.T. Press, 1965.
Language and Mind. Harcourt, Brace, & World, 1968.
'Recent contributions to the theory of innate ideas', *Synthèse*, *17*, 1967, 2–11.

COOPER, D. E. 'Innateness: old and new', *Philosophical Review*, *81*, 1972, 465–83.

FILLMORE, C. 'The case for case', in *Universals in Linguistic Theory*, ed E. Bach and R. Harms. Holt, Rinehart, & Winston, 1968.

FODOR, J. 'How to learn to talk: some simple ways', in *The Genesis of Language*, ed F. Smith and G. Miller, M.I.T. Press, 1966.

GOODMAN, N. 'The epistemological argument', *Synthèse*, *17*, 1967, 23–8.

HARMAN, G. 'Psychological aspects of the theory of syntax', *Journal of Philosophy*, *65*, 1967, 75–87.

HOCKETT, C. *The State of the Art*. Mouton, 1967.

LAKOFF, G. 'On Generative Semantics', in *Semantics: An Interdisciplinary Reader*, ed D. Steinberg and L. Jakobovits. Cambridge University Press, 1971.

LEES, R. 'Review of *Syntactic Structures*', *Language*, *33*, 1957, 375–407.

LENNEBERG, E. *Biological Foundations of Language*. Wiley, 1967.

LYONS, J. *Chomsky*. Fontana/Collins, 1970.

MCCAWLEY, J. D. 'The role of semantics in a grammar', in *Universals in Linguistic Theory*, ed E. Bach and R. Harms. Holt, Rinehart, & Winston, 1968.

MCNEILL, D. *The Acquisition of Syntax*. Harper & Row, 1970.

NAGEL, T. 'Linguistics and epistemology', in *Language and Philosophy*, ed S. Hook. New York University Press, 1969.

PUTNAM, H. 'The Innateness Hypothesis and explanatory models in linguistics', *Synthèse*, *17*, 1967, 12–22.

STICH, S. 'What every speaker knows', *Philosophical Review*, *80*, 1971, 476–96.

STRAWSON, P. F. 'Grammar and philosophy', *Proceedings of the Aristotelian Society*, *70*, 1969–70, 1–20.

Chapter 7

AUNE, B. 'Is there an analytic *a priori*?', *Journal of Philosophy*, *60*, 1963, 281–90.

AUSTIN, J. L. 'Truth', *Proceedings of the Aristotelian Society*
(*Supplementary Volume*), *24*, 1950, 111–28. Reprinted in *Truth*,
ed G. Pitcher. Prentice-Hall, 1964.

CARNAP, R. *Meaning and Necessity*. Chicago University Press, 1947.

CARTWRIGHT, R. 'Propositions', in *Analytical Philosophy*, ed R. Butler.
Blackwell, 1966. 1st Series.

COOPER, D. E. 'Synonymy', *Ratio*, 1973, forthcoming.

GOODMAN, N. 'On likeness of meaning', *Analysis, 10*, 1949, 1–7.
'On some differences about meaning', *Analysis, 13*, 1953, 90–6.
(Both articles are reprinted in *Philosophy and Analysis*, ed M.
MacDonald. Blackwell, 1954.)

GRICE, H. P. and STRAWSON, P. F. 'In defense of a dogma',
Philosophical Review, 65, 1956, 141–58. Reprinted in *Necessary Truth*,
ed L. Sumner and J. Woods. Random House, 1969.

KANT, I. *Critique of Pure Reason*, trans N. Kemp-Smith. Macmillan,
1964. Introduction.

KNEALE, W. and M. *The Development of Logic*. Oxford University Press,
1962. Chapter X.

LEMMON, E. 'Sentences, statements, and propositions', in *British
Analytical Philosophy*, ed B. Williams and A. Montefiore.
Routledge & Kegan Paul, 1966.

MATES, B. 'Synonymity', in *Semantics and the Philosophy of Language*,
ed L. Linsky. Illinois University Press, 1952.

PAP, A. *Semantics and Necessary Truth*. Yale University Press, 1966.

PITCHER, G. Introduction to *Truth*, ed G. Pitcher. Prentice-Hall, 1964.

PUTNAM, H. 'The Analytic and the Synthetic', *Minnesota Studies in
the Philosophy of Science*. University of Minnesota Press, 1962. Vol 3.

QUINE, W. V. 'Two dogmas of empiricism', in his *From a Logical Point
of View*. 2nd edn. Harper & Row, 1961.
'Necessary truth', in his *Ways of Paradox*. Random House, 1966.

QUINTON, A. 'The *A Priori* and the analytic', *Proceedings of the
Aristotelian Society, 64*, 1963–4, 31–54. Reprinted in *Philosophical
Logic*, ed P. F. Strawson. Oxford University Press, 1967.

RYLE, G. 'Are there propositions?', *Proceedings of the Aristotelian
Society, 30*, 1929–30, 91–126.

STRAWSON, P. F. 'Truth', *Proceedings of the Aristotelian Society*
(*Supplementary Volume*), *24*, 1950, 129–56. Reprinted in *Truth*,
ed G. Pitcher. Prentice-Hall, 1964.

TARSKI, A. 'The semantic conception of truth', in *Semantics and the
Philosophy of Language*, ed L. Linsky. Illinois University Press, 1952.

WOOZLEY, A. *Theory of Knowledge*. Hutchinson, 1949.

Chapter 8

ALSTON, W. 'Meaning and use', *Philosophical Quarterly, 13*, 1963,
107–24. Reprinted in *The Theory of Meaning*, ed G. Parkinson.
Oxford University Press, 1968.
'Linguistic acts', *American Philosophical Quarterly, 1*, 1964, 138–46.

AUSTIN, J. L. *How To Do Things With Words*. Oxford University Press, 1963.
'Performative/Constative', in *Philosophy and Ordinary Language*, ed C. Caton. Illinois University Press, 1963.

COHEN, L. J. 'Do illocutionary forces exist?' *Philosophical Quarterly*, *14*, 1964, 118–37. Reprinted in *Symposium on J. L. Austin*, ed K. Fann. Routledge & Kegan Paul, 1969.

COOPER, D. E. 'Meaning and illocutions', *American Philosophical Quarterly*, *9*, 1972, 69–78.

FURBERG, M. 'Meaning and illocutionary force', in *Symposium on J. L. Austin*, ed K. Fann. Routledge & Kegan Paul, 1969.

GRICE, H. P. 'Utterer's meaning and intention', *Philosophical Review*, *78*, 1969, 147–77.

HARE, R. M. *The Language of Morals*. Oxford University Press, 1952.
'Meaning and speech acts', *Philosophical Review*, *79*, 1970, 3–24.

HARMAN, G. 'Three levels of meaning', *Journal of Philosophy*, *65*, 1968, 590–602.

HOLDCROFT, D. 'Meaning and illocutionary acts', *Ratio*, *6*, 1964, 128–43. Reprinted in *The Theory of Meaning*, ed G. Parkinson. Oxford University Press, 1968.

SEARLE, J. R. 'Meaning and speech acts', *Philosophical Review*, *71*, 1962, 423–32.
'Assertions and aberrations', in *British Analytical Philosophy*, ed B. Williams and A. Montefiore. Routledge & Kegan Paul. 1966. Reprinted in *Symposium on J. L. Austin*, ed K. Fann. Routledge & Kegan Paul, 1969.

STRAWSON, P. F. 'Intention and convention in speech acts', *Philosophical Review*, *73*, 1964, 439–60. Reprinted in *Symposium on J. L. Austin*, ed K. Fann. Routledge & Kegan Paul, 1969.

URMSON, J. O., HAMPSHIRE, S. and QUINE, W. V. 'A Symposium on Austin's method' in *Symposium on J. L. Austin*, ed K. Fann. Routledge & Kegan Paul, 1969.

ZIFF, P. 'On H. P. Grice's account of meaning', *Analysis*, *28*, 1967, 1–8.

Index